Understanding T

Understanding Teen Eating Disorders introduces readers to common teen eating disorder scenarios, their warning signs, and treatment options. Each chapter examines a teen or tween and brings the factors, whether they be environmental, genetic, co-existing conditions, etc. that contribute to his or her eating disorder, to life, while seamlessly integrating the latest research in gene inheritance, brain chemistry, and eating disorders in accessible, reader-friendly language. Each chapter provides treatment options, including outpatient, group therapy, and in-patient programs, for both the young person and the family. Each also ends with a Q&A section that reflects the concerns a parent, loved one, or treatment professional may have.

Cris E. Haltom is a Certified Eating Disorders Specialist who has treated eating disorders in her private practice in Ithaca, NY, for over 30 years. She has presented eating disorder training workshops at national and local conferences. She is past Education and Prevention Liaison of the Western New York Comprehensive Care Centers for Eating Disorders and she authored *A Stranger at the Table: Dealing with Your Child's Eating Disorder* (2004, Ronjon Publishing). She published research on her co-authored eating disorder education program, the *Parent Partner Program* TM. In addition to her clinical psychology practice, she is a Lecturer at Ithaca College in the Department of Psychology.

Cathie Simpson lives and works in Ithaca, NY, where she is a psychotherapist and editor. Her interests are diverse. She coauthored the book *American Dresses 1780–1900* with Elsie Frost McMurry (2001, Cornell University) and published the book *Remembering Infancy: Adult Memories of the First Months of Life* (2014, Scholars' Press). Once a month, she facilitates the local pet-loss group.

Mary Tantillo is a fellow of the Academy for Eating Disorders, Professor of Clinical Nursing at the University of Rochester School of Nursing, and Clinical Professor in the Department of Psychiatry at the University of Rochester School of Medicine and Dentistry. She has directed the Western NY Comprehensive Care Center for Eating Disorders since 2005 and founded The Healing Connection Inc. in 2010. Dr. Tantillo has treated eating disorders across all levels of care for over 30 years. She has presented and published research and clinical work on a relational/motivational approach to eating disorder treatment with a special focus on the use of Multifamily Therapy Group.

Understanding Teen Eating Disorders

Warning Signs, Treatment Options, and Stories of Courage

Cris E. Haltom, Cathie Simpson, and Mary Tantillo

NEW YORK AND LONDON

First published 2018
by Routledge
711 Third Avenue, New York, NY 10017

and by Routledge
2 Park Square, Milton Park, Abingdon, Oxon OX14 4RN

Routledge is an imprint of the Taylor & Francis Group, an informa business

© 2018 Taylor & Francis

The right of Cris E. Haltom, Cathie Simpson, and Mary Tantillo to be identified as the authors of this work has been asserted by them in accordance with sections 77 and 78 of the Copyright, Designs and Patents Act 1988.

All rights reserved. No part of this book may be reprinted or reproduced or utilised in any form or by any electronic, mechanical, or other means, now known or hereafter invented, including photocopying and recording, or in any information storage or retrieval system, without permission in writing from the publishers.

Trademark notice: Product or corporate names may be trademarks or registered trademarks, and are used only for identification and explanation without intent to infringe.

Library of Congress Cataloging in Publication Data
A catalog record has been requested for this book

ISBN: 978-1-138-06882-7 (hbk)
ISBN: 978-1-138-06883-4 (pbk)
ISBN: 978-1-315-15760-3 (ebk)

Typeset in Galliard
by Taylor & Francis Books

Contents

	Acknowledgments	vi
	Introduction	vii
1	Julie: She Could Run Like the Wind	1
2	Claire: Trouble Adjusting to College	28
3	Nick: Learning to Connect	50
4	Anna: Resistance to Recovery	71
5	May: Boyfriend Abuse	95
6	Emma: The Secret Eater	122
7	Maeve: Like Mother, Like Daughter	146
8	Preventing Eating Disorders	170
	Index	184

Acknowledgments

The authors wish to thank their brave patients and families who chose to pursue eating disorder treatment. Because of their willingness to pursue recovery we have learned from them in order to share with others.

Cris Haltom wishes to acknowledge the patience and consistent support of her family, especially her husband, Maurice, and friends, especially Scott Steelman, as she constructed the stories included in this book.

Introduction

Eating disorders are relatively common among tweens and teens. Estimates of lifetime prevalence rates for adolescents are 0.3%, 0.9%, and 1.6% for anorexia, bulimia, and binge eating disorders (Swanson, Crow, Le Grange, Swendsen, & Merikangas, 2011). Rates have remained roughly the same over the past few decades despite advances in empirically supported prevention and early intervention treatment methods. Eating disorders represent a serious threat to adolescent mental and physical health. They are frequently co-morbid with other psychiatric disorders including anxiety, mood disorders, and suicidality. Further, eating disorders are often enduring and difficult to treat, especially without early intervention. As such, they remain a public health concern, are costly, and have a negative impact on quality of life.

Although many teens with eating disorders seek treatment, few seek it specifically for eating or weight-related problems (Swanson et al., 2011). Women and those with anorexia and bulimia are more likely to seek it than men and those with binge eating disorder (Forrest, Smith, & Swanson, 2017). Even so, with only 20% seeking treatment overall (Forrest et al., 2017), unmet treatment needs remain prevalent among teens with eating disorders. It is hoped this book will encourage and enrich the expertise of those seeking to support and/or treat tweens and teens with eating disorders.

We present case studies to help illustrate the wide array of biopsychosocial contexts that can surround the onset of tween and teen eating disorders. Our seven cases are rich with a variety of interpersonal and family dynamics, heritability factors, life-stage variables, personality factors, motivational factors, medical issues, psychiatric comorbidities, and sociocultural influences. After developing each child's unique eating-disorder history, our stories turn to best practices in child and adolescent eating-disorder assessment, diagnosis, and treatment. Although case histories, characteristics, and symptom presentations vary greatly both in this book and in real life, we believe our cases represent experiences and approaches consistent with adolescent eating-disorder literature and our own clinical experiences.

Twelve-year-old Julie was a budding star on her cross-country team. Well accustomed to driving herself toward lofty goals, whether it was about her grades or her running, we see a young woman who has unusual tenacity and ambition. She found the eating disorder gave her a steely numbness to pressures from her coach. Leading up to the eating disorder, Julie had every intention to better herself through healthier eating and exercise. Then she descended into anorexia nervosa. At first her parents saw her efforts toward health as harmless enough, if not all that helpful. Then they realized how compulsive and extreme Julie had become in her self-imposed pursuit of perfection about her eating and her body. The family pediatrician gave a diagnosis of Anorexia Nervosa, Restricting type (*DSM*-5; American Psychiatric Association, 2013) and empirically supported, best-practice Family Based Treatment (Lock & LeGrange, 2015) was recommended. The family began an ultimately successful but exhausting course of outpatient treatment that was interrupted by medical instability and a one-month inpatient hospitalization in an eating-disorders program. The reader drops chronologically into various points in Julie's care. Probable neurological changes related to the illness are examined, as well as evolving changes in Julie's and her parents' thoughts, beliefs, attitudes, and emotions. Julie's movement in and out of hospital care demonstrates the importance of viewing eating-disorder treatment as a continuum of care in which treatment effectiveness is continually reassessed and adjusted to ensure optimal treatment outcomes.

Eighteen-year-old Claire was a public high school graduate going off to college to live away from home for the first time. A good student, Claire had aspirations for maintaining high grades while expanding her social life to new heights. She never had a boyfriend in high school and her first romantic relationship blossomed at college. Claire quickly became overwhelmed with the demands of studying, hanging out with her best friend and her boyfriend, partying, and maintaining a polished, attractive appearance. She became depressed, anxious, abused alcohol, and descended into a cycle of bulimic binge-eating-and-purge behavior. When she presented at her college's counseling center, her complicated psychological picture challenged staff to provide her with not only a treatment team for eating and mood disorders but also with brief harm-reduction treatment for alcohol abuse. She was diagnosed with Bulimia Nervosa, Major Depressive Disorder, and Alcohol Use Disorder (*DSM*-5; American Psychiatric Association, 2013). With a focus on mental health treatment, her psychotherapist used brief assessment tools, Motivational Interviewing (Miller & Rollnick, 1991), and ultimately chose Interpersonal Psychotherapy (IPT-BN; Whight et al., 2011) to treat depression and bulimia. Claire's case represents the complexity of diagnoses often seen in students who present at CAPS (Counseling and Psychological Services) in colleges across the country.

Sixteen-year-old Nick was a high school student who had always been a sensitive eater. Likely he struggled with ARFID (Avoidant Restrictive Food Intake Disorder; *DSM*-5; American Psychiatric Association, 2013) as a child. His eating issues evolved in adolescence into Anorexia Nervosa: Binge-Eating/Purge Type (*DSM*-5; American Psychiatric Association, 2013). A year before, at his annual physical, his eating-disorder diagnosis was missed by his pediatrician. It wasn't long, however, until discovery by a friend boxed Nick into a corner and obliged him to reveal his eating problems. An excellent student,

Nick was outgoing and well liked at school. He was known by many and helpful in a very personal way to a depressed friend, Jarrad. Subjected to the demands of a tyrannical eating disorder, Nick carefully hid and even lied about his eating-disorder behaviors. However, he eventually confided in Jarrad. Out of concern, Jarrad told other friends about the eating disorder and the group confronted Nick in an online group chat. Angry with his friends for ganging up on him, Nick was ultimately forced into telling his parents vis-à-vis a school guidance counselor. This unleashed a succession of outpatient assessments and interventions. Along the way, Nick admitted to self-induced vomiting to his outpatient psychologist. Once again, Nick was mandated to expose another eating disorder behavior that had previously been both cloaked and protected. This new revelation ultimately led to a higher level of professional care – a partial hospital program for eating disorders. An integral part of this was participation in Multi-Family Group Therapy (MFGT; Tantillo, 2006; Tantillo & Sanftner, 2010; Tantillo, Sanftner, & Hauenstein, 2013). Once he and his parents were actively involved in MFGT, real progress began. At first, seeing himself and the world around him through the distorted lens of the illness, Nick failed to notice the wall of disconnection the eating disorder had built around him. As he began to trust both members and leaders of the MFGT group, he began to find intra- and interpersonal connections and build mutuality with others, including his parents. Unable to continue feeding on his isolation, the eating disorder was thwarted and faded into the background.

Fifteen-year-old Anna's story starts out recounting her trip to the hospital after she became dizzy and passed out at school, bumping her head. In the emergency room, she admitted to laxative abuse and was found to have dangerous medical signs of dietary restriction and purge behavior. She was kept overnight for observation before being released to her parents. She was mortified to be diagnosed with an eating disorder. Kelly and Justin, Anna's mother and father, were left with a recommendation for residential treatment, but were loathe to send Anna so far away from home. They opted for Family Based Treatment (FBT), an outpatient treatment they received locally. They embarked on a journey of perseverance and determination against an eating disorder that seemed like taking on a rattlesnake. Sometimes causing them to doubt themselves, Anna was so overtaken by the illness that she fought her parents as persistently as they fought the eating disorder.

Anna was caught in a world of perfectionism about her body. She restricted her food intake and became increasingly desperate as she turned to secretly using laxatives, along with restricting. She was diagnosed with Anorexia Nervosa: Binge Eating/Purging Type (*DSM*-5; American Psychiatric Association, 2013). At first happy not to be "sent away" to residential treatment, Anna soon found the first phase of outpatient FBT unhappily challenging. Emboldened by the eating disorder, she struggled against her parents taking charge of her nourishment and monitoring her use of purge and exercise behavior. Ultimately, she became exhausted and started to eat more, gaining insight as she moved into remission.

Fourteen-year-old May was a high school student in her first romantic relationship. Unfortunately, her boyfriend Jarold was controlling and abusive. As she clung to her dating partner, her parents were beside themselves with worry. They watched their daughter's increasing isolation and deteriorating physical and mental health.

A review of cross-national research indicates that psychological/emotional abuse, the predominant kind of abuse May experienced at the hands of Jarold, is the most common kind of teen-dating violence (Leen et al., 2013). Among dating adolescents, rates of psychological abuse vary from 17–88% (Leen et al, 2013) and rates of physical and sexual abuse in the previous 12 months are estimated at 20.9% for girls and 10.4% for boys (Vagi, Olsen, Basile, & Vivolo-Kantor, 2015).

To cope with her struggles, May turned to binge eating and compensatory vomiting, and almost turned to self-cutting behavior. Eventually, she was diagnosed with Major Depressive Disorder and Bulimia Nervosa, Moderate (*DSM*-5; American Psychiatric Association, 2013). The eating disorder served many functions: comfort, numbing negative affects, distraction, self-punishment, and displacement of blame onto herself, rather than her abuser. Her distress around her relationship and conflict with her increasingly worried parents took a toll on May. Although frightened to reveal her secrets, she eventually did and ended up in a mix of professional treatments. She reluctantly entered parent-involved, group Dialectical Behavior Therapy (DBT; Linehan, 2015), skills training and cognitive behavior therapy adapted for adolescents with bulimia (CBT-A; Lock, 2005), and nutrition consultation and psychiatric care for medication treatment.

Born into a genetically determined, larger-than-average body, 16-year-old Emma struggled with a Binge Eating Disorder (*DSM*-5; American Psychiatric Association, 2013). Stricken with body dissatisfaction, Emma wanted to diet to lose weight. However, her efforts to restrict early in the day were followed by binge eating later in the day. As Emma made desperate attempts to manage her body size, she sank deeper into a cycle of daytime restriction and nighttime overeating. The disorder deepened when Emma found emotional solace in binge eating.

Meanwhile Emma's parents were worried about her exposure to weight bias and social stigma against her larger body size. They were not wrong. Emma experienced weight bullying in school and on the school bus. She did her best to cope with thin idealization among her peers and, in doing so, became increasingly secretive about binge eating. The importance of going underground was reinforced when Emma got well-meaning messages at home that her eating habits and body size were problematic. Her self-esteem plummeted as she found herself caught in a vicious cycle of binge eating and restricting. Although her weight remained stable, her eating became increasingly disordered. Ultimately, with the help of her pediatrician, Emma engaged in specialty-trained Cognitive Behavior Therapy-Enhanced (CBT-E; Fairburn, Cooper and Shafran, 2003; Fairburn, 2008) for eating disorders. She worked her way to healthful eating while sorting through a multitude of distorted and negative self-appraisals that had previously held her back.

Eleven year-old Maeve had loving parents who divorced when she was five. Her parents were amicable with each other, but chose to live at opposite ends of the US. After the divorce, Maeve and her mother, Ellen, moved from the West Coast to the East, where Maeve attended an urban private school. Ellen had a 20-year history of restrictive eating after partial recovery from untreated anorexia nervosa in college. As Maeve grew, Ellen projected her fears of weight gain onto Maeve and Maeve's eating behavior. Unfortunately, both Maeve and Ellen were prone to perfectionism and anxiety. This made them both vulnerable to dietary restraint and a perfectionist pursuit of the thin ideal. For Maeve, sociocultural influences (e.g., peer influence to be thin) interacted with an inherited risk for restrictive eating.

Ellen prided herself on healthy eating and careful vigilance over her daughter's dietary needs. However, she was surprised to discover Maeve had developed a restrictive eating disorder. Maeve did not meet full criteria for anorexia and was diagnosed with Other Specified Feeding or Eating Disorder (*DSM*-5; American Psychiatric Association, 2013). She was treated for disordered eating using Family Based Treatment (Lock & LeGrange, 2015) to normalize her eating. To support this, Ellen also engaged in individual Cognitive Behavior Therapy (CBT; Fairburn, 2008) to work on her own disordered eating. She discovered she could not depend on her skewed perceptions about eating, body image, and body size to guide her with Maeve. Positively motivated to identify and correct distortions, Ellen engaged in her own recovery and, in doing so, provided the best possible support for her daughter's recovery.

We end the book with a chapter on eating disorder prevention, with the hope that the recognition of risk factors will help parents and healthcare providers intervene to obviate illness, or identify illness and intervene to minimize its effects. We include a review of effective prevention strategies that target multiple eating-disorder risks and maintaining factors. Practical tips for preventing or altering known risk factors are offered.

We believe this book can be used as a learning tool for both healthcare practitioners and family members (e.g., parents and carers of tweens and teens with eating disorders). We draw from current and evolving eating-disorder research to provide knowledge useful to carers and healthcare professionals. We make the case that the best treatment is provided by specialty-trained practitioners who have educated themselves about how to best assess, diagnose, and treat eating disorders. Since carers are a critical part of the treatment, they too need to understand the specialty-care needs of their loved ones and, in doing so, can also offer support based on best practices. This book will provide carers and healthcare providers an understanding of the development, nature, and treatment of eating disorders. In doing so, healthcare providers and carers can work collaboratively to provide support to tweens and teens and foster hope for recovery.

References

American Psychiatric Association. (2013). *Diagnostic and statistical manual of mental disorders* (5th ed.). Arlington, VA: Author.

Fairburn, C. G. (2008). *Cognitive behavior therapy and eating disorders.* New York, NY: Guilford.

Fairburn, C. G., Cooper, Z., & Shafran, R. (2003). Cognitive behavior therapy for eating disorders: A "transdiagnostic" theory and treatment. *Behavior Research and Therapy*, 41:5, 509–28.

Forrest, L. N., Smith, A. R., & Swanson, S. A. (2017). Characteristics of seeking treatment among US adolescents with eating disorders. *International Journal of Eating Disorders*, 50(7), 826–833.

Klerman, G. L., & Weissman, M. M. (1993). *New applications of interpersonal psychotherapy.* Washington, DC: American Psychiatric Press.

Leen, E., Sorbring, E., Mawer, M., Holdsworth, E., Helsing, B., & Bowen, E. (2013). Prevalence, dynamic risk factors and the efficacy of primary interventions for adolescent dating violence: An international review. *Aggression and Violent Behavior*, 18(1), 159–174.

Linehan, M. (2015) *DBT skills training manual* (2nd). New York, NY: Guilford Press.

Lock, J. (2005) Adjusting cognitive behavior therapy for adolescents with bulimia nervosa: Results of case series. *American Journal of Psychotherapy*, 59(3), 267–281.

Lock, J., & LeGrange, D. (2015). *Treatment manual for anorexia nervosa: A family-based approach* (2nd). New York, NY: Guilford.

Miller, W. R., & Rollnick, S. (1991). *Motivational interviewing: Preparing people for change.* New York, NY: Guilford Press.

Murphy, R., Straebler, S.Basden, S., Cooper, Z., & Fairburn, C. G. (2012). Interpersonal psychotherapy for eating disorders. *Clinical Psychology & Psychotherapy*, 19, 150–158.

Swanson, S. A., Crow, S. J., Le Grange, D., Swendsen, J., & Merikangas, K. R. (2011). Prevalence and correlates of eating disorders in adolescents: Results from the national comorbidity survey replication adolescent supplement. *Archives of General Psychiatry*, 68(7), 714–723.

Tantillo, M. (2006). A relational approach to eating disorders multifamily therapy group: Moving from difference and disconnection to mutual connection. *Families, Systems, & Health*, 24, 82–102.

Tantillo, M., & Sanftner, J. L. (2010). Mutuality and motivation: Connecting with patients and families for change in the treatment of eating disorders. In M. Maine, D. Bunnell, & B. McGilley (Eds.), *Treatment of eating disorders: Bridging the gap between research and practice* (pp. 319–334). London, UK: Elsevier.

Tantillo, M., Sanftner, J., & Hauenstein, E. (2013). Restoring connection in the face of disconnection: An integrative approach to understanding and treating anorexia nervosa. *Advances in Eating Disorders: Theory, Research and Practice*, 1(1), 21–38.

Vagi, K. J., Olsen, E. O. M., Basile, K. C., & Vivolo-Kantor, A. M. (2015). Teen dating violence (physical and sexual) among US high school students: Findings from the 2013 National Youth Risk Behavior Survey. *JAMA Pediatrics*, 169(5), 474–482.

Whight, D. J., Meadows, L., McGrain, L. A., Langham, C. L., Baggott, J. N., & Arcelus, J. A. (2011). *IPT-BN (m): Interpersonal psychotherapy for bulimic spectrum disorders: Treatment guide.* Milwaukee, WI: Troubador Press.

1 Julie

She Could Run Like the Wind

Twelve-year-old Julie never much liked emotions. They got in the way. She left cross country practice at her middle school that Thursday night with a distinct sense of disgust toward her friend Amelia's breakdown an hour before. Coach had railed at his runners for "getting soft" during their Spring break. He singled out Amelia for being late to practice, reminding her that this was "no time to lose time." Perfectionist Julie wouldn't dream of being late for practice, but if she was, she would expect Coach to say something. If he didn't, it meant she wasn't important enough. Amelia was visibly shaken by Coach's insult, fighting back tears. Julie knew it. She liked Amelia a lot. She felt bad for her. She wanted to hug her or do something to help her friend, but not during practice. It just wasn't what winners did. When Julie stepped on the track, she was all about winning. She told herself, "Tears get you nowhere and weakness won't help the team." She noticed that some kids got really emotional about sports. They were the ones who seemed liked "losers" to her. Julie looked at every practice as a chance to measure herself against her own potential. Although painful at moments like these, Julie's first time on a competitive team was turning out to suit her ambitious nature well.

Julie had an unusual talent for running. She ran as soon as she learned to walk. Her parents encouraged her because they were also runners. They ran for exercise and good health. Julie's father, James, entered a triathlon every year and ran and trained daily before leaving for work. By the time Julie was in fifth grade, she was running with her father in the morning before school, and he was giving her tips on how to pace herself. By the time she was in seventh grade, she was old enough to enter modified sports competitions in middle school. Her times for all running events were exceptional. Long-legged and experienced, Julie's endurance and capacity for speed were undeniable and drew attention, first from her physical education teacher and then from her middle-school track coach.

Julie was deeply satisfied to be asked to run on the middle-school cross country team. The thought of running competitively was familiar, because she ran with her father when he prepared for his triathlons. It sounded like fun. She knew she would be good at any track event. Relays, 100 meter, 200 meter, and longer runs did not intimidate her. She welcomed the challenge. So far, running had been fun both as a family activity and a chance to excel at something with her friends. She found she enjoyed the camaraderie of other runners.

As expected, Julie's parents were thrilled with her invitation to join the middle-school track team. James and her mother, Kate, had determined years ago that they would not railroad their children into any sport, activity, or lesson. They wanted their children to explore many options for sports, art, music, or reading and were determined to follow their children's leads. Julie was the oldest child in her family – she had two younger brothers. When Julie chose to participate in track at school, Kate and James were relieved she had chosen something so easy for them to support. Running was not only a regular family activity, but they recognized that Julie truly enjoyed it. She would be doing something she found rewarding.

Julie had always been an agreeable, bright, and untroubled kid. She laughed often and seemed generally happy. She did her chores around the house without too much reminding, didn't grumble about school, got along with her friends, and rarely seemed to have trouble with anything. People liked her. She seemed to like people, but she was also content by herself, especially when she was running. She set high standards for herself, and her parents were proud of her. She never lacked for ambition. She was self-driven and perfectionistic. Yet she was humble and sensitive and rarely let on to her peers that she expected so much of herself. She handled disappointment as much as possible by turning it inward, not wanting to cause her parents or another child to feel her pain or share her burden. Running got her through her difficult times – it seemed to make everything okay.

When Julie ran with her father, she tried not to show him when she was winded or tired. Her thought was, "I can do this! If I push past the pain, it will get easier." After a certain number of miles, something seemed to just click, and there was nothing she couldn't do. Sometimes Julie's lack of vulnerability worried her parents, because she would brush off disappointments and hurts with an, "I'm fine," or "It'll be okay." One time when running with Julie, her father said, "Are you sure you're okay? You're red in the face, and I think you need to get your breath. We can stop for a minute. Take a drink of water." For Julie, this was an opening to prove herself. She said, "You know how it is, Dad. No pain, no gain." Julie's Dad replied, "Yeah – you're right, but being reasonable's important, too. You don't want to push yourself too hard."

At the same time Julie was tough on herself, she was sensitive to slights and valued her friendships deeply. Among her peers, Julie was often the child to whom her friends turned when in distress. A good listener, Julie appreciated her friends' struggles with their brothers, sisters, parents, and love interests. Julie had no particular desire to date, or get involved with boys. She was too busy with track practice, school, and music lessons to even consider the complexities of romance. She was content to sit on the outside of her friends' dilemmas and support them the best she could. Monday morning always brought a new round of concerns about whatever might have happened to her friends over the weekend – overnights, trips to the movies, and the latest intrigue with the who-likes-who stories were usually communicated hour-by-hour in friend-to-friend texting.

Julie enjoyed her social life, but shied away from conflicted situations. She had a much harder time leaning on others than she had with them leaning on her. One time she felt left out when her friends met at the Mall on a Saturday. She felt sad and rejected when she saw the posts on Instagram. However, rather than sharing her hurt feelings, she said nothing afterwards. In fact, she acted like nothing had happened when she saw her friends at school on Monday. She didn't want to burden anyone with her troubled feelings, or cause a conflict. None of Julie's friends seemed to notice the imbalance, where Julie was being leaned on more than she was leaning on others. It sort of flowed along from year to year as Julie ran her troubles away. Her best friends simply knew her to be quietly and compassionately there for them. Mostly. They saw a tenacious, single-minded Julie when they were in a competitive-sports situation. At those times, even in gym class, she was tough and focused.

Julie secretly admired the older track athletes in her school. She watched them practice and run. Further along the age spectrum, the eighth graders barely noticed her, but she noticed them, especially the ones who had the fastest times on the field. She began to think about their body shapes and sizes and how their physical characteristics related to their running ability. She noticed that the best runners tended to be thin. She began to associate thin with faster running times. As a perfectionist, she began to set a new internal standard for herself about body size: thin was faster.

Unfortunately for Julie, there's a problem with applying perfection to the body, which is that the body has its own intelligence and genetic balance. When the will tries to control the body, the two become at odds and trouble begins. It is no surprise that perfectionism can contribute to eating disorders (Bardone-Cone, Sturm, Lawson, Robinson, & Smith, 2010; Halmi et al., 2012; Lampard, Byrne, McLean, & Fursland, 2011; Stice, 2002). It is a common core feature of anorexia nervosa and bulimia (Bardone-Cone et al., 2007), and, as mentioned, Julie was a perfectionist.

Julie began to associate thin with how and what runners ate for lunch. Her strange habit of examining and connecting school lunches and snacks on the field with body size and speed began to generate new eating rules for her. Fast runners brought their lunch and didn't buy from the school cafeteria. Fast runners ate fruit and a sandwich. Fast runners sometimes ate even less for lunch and complained that their lunches weren't healthy. For example, a fast runner Julie had her eye on sometimes gave away the bag of chips from her packed lunch. Fast runners seemed to have no body fat. They were lean and lithe. "This type of body," thought Julie, "came through hard practice and healthy eating. This, no doubt," thought Julie, "increased their running speed." With these thoughts, Julie was heading into a compulsive relationship with running and a restrictive relationship with food.

Eating-disorder research has shown that those with restrictive anorexia are people who experience exaggerated or excessive inhibitory control on a neurobiological level. For some, this might be rewarding (Kaye, Wierenga, Bailer, Simmons, & Bischoff-Grethe, 2013). Anorexia has also been associated with neurobiological insensitivity to reward (Kaye et al., 2013) and poor awareness of internal emotional states (Heinzel et al., 2010). Together, these biological brain changes function to blunt affect and create a sense of emotional control for those with anorexia.

Take young athletes like Julie for example. Typically, they are boys and girls with exceptional talent who are often under intense pressure to perform at their peak. Their talents and accomplishments may have them working with coaches and directors who are at a higher level of expertise than those coaching or directing most junior or senior high school students. Elite, talented young people working with high-level coaches, music directors, and teachers often receive blunt corrective criticism and harsh direction. Their performance is viewed through a magnifying glass of excellence. The stakes are high – for winning or losing, getting good reviews, achieving better times in competitions, and receiving better scores on performances. There are often long hours of practice and weekend travel to shows, meets, and other competitive, or high-level affairs.

Julie was sensitive to her coach's criticism and harshness because she was a perfectionist and because she was starting to starve herself. Why would starvation lead to increased sensitivity to criticism? Perhaps related to alterations in brain functioning, those, like Julie, who have symptoms of anorexia nervosa are more attuned to negative and threatening signals toward them, while at the same time they are relatively unresponsive to positive feedback (Treasure & Schmidt, 2013). Yet the brain states that result from malnutrition and food restriction may not only be associated with increased sensitivity to punishing feedback. Paradoxically, they may also provide a way to cope with anxiety resulting from perceived threats and harsh criticism from coaches or teachers.

For example, the striatum structure of the brain releases dopamine in response to eating palatable food. Normally this would be experienced as pleasant. But those with anorexia nervosa experience the same dopamine release in response to food as anxiety-producing and unpleasant (Avena & Bocarsly, 2012). Perhaps due to brain dysfunction before or after the onset of anorexia, food avoidance associated with anorexia nervosa is a way to reduce anxiety. As Kaye, Bailer, Klabunde, and Brown (2010) note, "People at risk for AN [anorexia nervosa] find that restricting food intake makes them feel less anxious, and so they enter a vicious cycle where eating exaggerates anxiety and food refusal reduces it" (p. 6). The eating disorder thus functions to numb and distract from uncomfortable feelings. This may assist a young person to temporarily feel strong, invulnerable, and able to withstand psychological pressures. Unfortunately, it was exactly this "advantage" of restrictive eating and resulting weight loss that appealed to Julie.

Twelve-year-old girls, like Julie, can have incredible focus and persistence once they have found a purpose. Julie had found a new set of ideals: a thin, lithe body; healthy eating; and hard practice. Julie began to examine her body in the mirror for signs of her thin, muscular ideal. It seemed there were a few bulges that didn't look like the fast runners she observed with such minutia. With this in mind, she set about to increase her running speed and decrease her bulges. She wanted any non-muscular protrusions, lumps, or bumps to vanish. She imagined how nice it would be to cut them off with a very sharp knife.

Once Julie complained to her mother about her thighs and buttocks. Predictably, Kate was dismayed that Julie would criticize her body. As would be expected, Kate said, "You are fine just the way you are. You have a beautiful body. And you started your period this year – that means you are going through puberty. It's completely normal to grow and get curves like the grown-up you've always wanted to be." Julie retorted, "This is not growing up! Other girls look skinny. I don't." She seemed angry with her mother for what seemed to Kate to be reassuring information. Kate was frustrated by Julie's self-criticism. Julie realized her mother was not going to be sympathetic to any body dissatisfaction she might be having. "Mothers," she thought, "always think their daughters are great, no matter what." Julie smiled at her mom and realized she would not be an ally in getting rid of ugly bulges.

Julie began to systematically turn down desserts at home. Sugar was now unhealthy. If her parents said something to her about this, they were met with, "I'm full," "I am trying to eat healthy food," "I already had a cookie at school," "I don't want too much sweet stuff," or "Can't we have something healthier like fruit for dessert?" Kate also noticed Julie wiping butter off her vegetables at dinner. She used her napkin to quickly dab at any butter drippings. They noticed she ate one roll or piece of bread and no more. It seemed harmless enough to Kate and James. As a family, they had often talked about the need to eat a healthier diet. They complained about too many snacks around the house and the need to eat more vegetables and lean meat, like chicken. How could they complain about Julie's focused and disciplined attempts to eat in a healthier manner? "She's probably right after all," thought Kate. "We should switch to olive oil instead of butter and cut back on sweets."

Julie's family running activities made the whole family aware of their bodies. Kate was a morning runner, and she knew her body's limits. She knew that, because she hadn't eaten since the night before, she needed some energy-packed food before running. She often ate a small bagel, or buttered toast and peanut butter, to give her a boost plus a little staying power. Kate began to worry that Julie, who skipped breakfast and packed a very small lunch, would not have enough stamina to run. At this point, Julie was running every day after school. Although Kate initially agreed with Julie that sweets and fatty foods might be unhealthy, it occurred to her that Julie might not be getting enough fuel for her practices. What Kate didn't know was that by supporting Julie's lists of "unhealthy" foods (e.g., sweets), she was inadvertently supporting a growing eating disorder and the "all or nothing" thinking that accompanies it.

Julie was soon her track coach's favorite new runner. Young as she was, she was something like a running prodigy. Coach could see great potential in Julie, wanted her to practice hard, and could see she put pressure on herself to win.

She knew how to make her moves and find her place almost instinctively. It would be tempting to take a strict line with her, because he wanted her to be successful.

Julie noticed Coach paying more attention to her. That made her both excited and anxious. It was one thing to run for herself. It was another to run for someone else. This was Julie's first real coaching experience. The intensity of being watched both intimidated her and hooked her into longing for more of such attention. This was different from running with her parents, or having her father give her tips. It made her want to improve. There was a heady air of competition that Julie had not experienced before. She tried to imagine what it would feel like the day of her first meet. She wanted her times to keep dropping.

The girls she had watched in the cafeteria were now watching her. Having Coach's attention brought some unwanted attention from them. Even though everyone on the team was friendly and welcoming, they were also keenly aware of each other's abilities and of who was being singled out by Coach. Her teammates began to resent her. On the one hand, the girls on the team competed with each other and were jealous of any one girl getting ahead – especially in Coach's eyes. On the other hand, everyone knew that teamwork would get the prize. Julie was less aware of her teammates' jealousy than of her new-found place in the limelight.

Julie's coach saw where she needed work. At first he was gentle with her, because she was new and very young. He didn't want to undermine her motivation with punishing remarks. However, as time went on, he stepped up his directives. Not only was Julie good, she was also able to take correction and criticism. In fact, she seemed to welcome them. This made it tougher for Coach to withhold short, firm commands. Censures were not far behind.

More pressure didn't seem to disturb Julie. It almost seemed like permission to turn up the heat. On the other hand, if Coach detected any negative remarks on the part of team members, he quickly corrected them. Even though he seemed to be avoiding some runners and attending to others, he expected his team to support each other, get along harmoniously, and work in unity.

Meanwhile, Julie continued to pursue "healthy eating." She turned vegetarian – something Kate and James would later learn can be a sign of an emerging eating disorder. Research shows individuals with an eating-disorder history were considerably more likely to be vegetarians during or before the eating disorder and to admit vegetarianism was related to the eating disorder (Bardone-Cone et al., 2012; Michalak, Zhang, & Jacobi, 2012). In addition to being vegetarian, Julie was more determined than ever to cut out desserts. She figured the lighter she was, the faster she could run. And, in fact, her running times were dropping. Julie set her mind to consistently shave seconds from her mile runs. Whatever she was doing was working.

Unfortunately, part of what Julie was doing was forming complex rules to guide her food intake. Sometimes known as *safety behaviors*, she developed those rules to protect the eating disorder. Julie only allowed herself to eat a small group of foods that she determined would maintain leanness. Butter and mayonnaise disappeared from her diet, as did white bread and any pastries. Sugar was forbidden. After all, sugar and other calorie-dense foods were known in the media to be unhealthy.

Kate was now watching Julie's eating behavior. Although Julie no longer criticized her body, she had become a picky eater. She virtually never took seconds of her previously favored foods, like mashed potatoes. Quite the opposite – she seemed to push the food around the plate, was slow to eat, and seemed to deliberate every bite. Food used to be a pleasure for Julie. Now eating seemed like a hardship. Julie looked thinner, although it was easy to believe any body changes were due to a difficult training schedule. Nevertheless, Kate knew from her own running experiences that enough fuel in the form of food, before, during, and after practice, was important to training and should prevent major weight loss.

Kate and James noticed Julie stayed up long hours doing homework and put considerable pressure on herself to keep up with her studies while she trained for cross country. She was barely interested in friends when they texted or called. Once Kate overheard her make excuses when her friend Kristen came over after practice and asked her to come to a sleepover. "My parents said I could have somebody over Friday night after practice. It's been a while since we hung out, and I really want to see you, okay? We can watch Netflix, just like we used to. Remember that scary movie we watched last time you came over? The only reason I could watch it at all was because you were there telling me it was really just fake." Even after this strong appeal from her friend, Julie turned her down. "I can't. I'm sorry. It just won't work. I have a test on Monday I need to study for." Kate didn't know then that isolation is a symptom of starvation and can be a warning sign of an eating disorder really taking hold (Keys, Brožek, Henschel, Mickelsen, & Taylor, 1950).

Kate did notice how crest-fallen Kristen looked when Julie said this and felt bad for her. She also recognized that this was not like the old Julie. Kristen in particular was a longtime friend. Kate almost stepped in to object, but she realized she couldn't make Julie want to go to Kristen's house. A test on Monday had never stopped her before. Even though she usually looked ahead and planned carefully for her schoolwork, Julie also valued her friends and used to look forward to connecting with them on weekends. Something was changing in Julie. Kate began to think participating in cross-country running and Julie's dedicated, enhanced training was bringing about some negative results. She rarely laughed anymore.

Along with Julie's isolation, Kate noticed her daughter was also developing stoicism. Julie seemed better able to weather her practices with a kind of dispassion. She began to react to harshness from Coach with a blasé attitude – like when Coach said to her "You can do better than that – your pace on that run was dismal!" Armed with a numbing eating disorder, Julie was quite able to withstand such comments in a way she hadn't been able to before. She had discovered that her emotions were more manageable the more she restricted her intake.

In fact, Julie had increasing difficulty identifying or expressing her emotions (alexithymia). Due to the numbing impact of starvation on her affect, her emotional experiences were blunted, and she had inhibited behavioral responses to emotion. Neuroimaging research suggests that, depending on their environment, undernourished people with anorexia experience reduced neural responses to external stimuli. Underactive limbic neural circuitry, leading to dysfunctional emotional processing, combined with an overactive executive function (inhibition) in those with anorexia may account for this (Lipsman, Woodside, & Lozano, 2015). After prolonged nutrient restriction and despite her former sensitivity to criticism, now when Coach corrected Julie, she was unperturbed. Related to this, Miyake et al. (2012) used functional magnetic resonance imaging (fMRI) to compare the brain responses of patients with anorexia and healthy women as they processed negative words concerning interpersonal relationships. Compared to healthy women's brains, they found lower neural activity in three areas of the brains (the amygdala, posterior cingulate cortex, and anterior cingulate cortex) of women with anorexia. This type of research helped to define the neural underpinnings of alexithymia in those with anorexia (see also Moriguchi & Komaki, 2013). As Julie discovered, the association between alexithymia and anorexia is well established (Courty, Godart, Lalanne, & Berthoz, 2015). Out of touch with or confused by her emotional cues, Julie also had a decreased ability to be empathic with either herself or others. This hurt her friendships and made her appear increasingly indifferent.

Coach was harsh with Julie at times largely because she was so talented. He believed her great potential, drive, and ability needed his keenest direction. He corrected her often and, while doing so, made painful comparisons to other runners. As was the case for Julie's coach, coaches who compare their runners unfavorably are sowing seeds of dissension on the team. Coach made comments like, "If you don't practice every day, you will get slow like Lila. She missed practice twice last week." These comments were well intentioned, but hurt Julie – even in her stoicism. At the same time, Coach's favoritism motivated her. Julie wanted to be able to "take the pressure." She worked hard to perfect her body, speed, and determination. Quite accidentally, she discovered she was more able to withstand pressure when she was hungry, or had not eaten for a long time. For a time, this worked to her benefit, because she was able to perform, almost robotically, even while under pressure during a race, or while fielding Coach's comments. Her lowered emotional responsiveness to negative feedback, or race-related pressures, was a welcome relief, even though it meant her hungry body was deprived of fuel.

The more she seemed to "eat healthy," the more Julie seemed to function like a well-oiled machine. Hand her a task, and she could cope. This was in contrast to her early days of practice when Coach first singled her out. Although outwardly she had seemed tough, inwardly she crumbled each time Coach delivered a criticism – in the past she had felt punished and inferior. She never wanted to appear weak or soft or weepy, so she had kept her feelings in and silently managed by becoming even harder on herself and more determined. Now it was easy to weather Coach's blunt directives and putdowns.

Julie's coach encouraged healthy eating related to running ability. He said things like, "It's best to avoid stuff like sugar, chips, and soda, because those junk foods aren't as nutrient rich as other foods that are healthier and will build a stronger body." Coach didn't realize that his words would be treated like gospel by Julie and others on her team. His comments were interpreted as directives for avoiding foods that would make his runners soft and fat. He did not realize that, for a vulnerable girl like Julie, increased body dissatisfaction would fuel disordered eating as an aid in achieving the idealized thin body (Bucchianeri & Neumark-Sztainer, 2014). As part of our culture, most young women are already body conscious, so giving a directive to sort foods into healthy and unhealthy categories and being told to avoid certain foods are taken as ways to avoid an unacceptable, larger-sized body. Further, unnecessary guilt is produced when foods labeled unhealthy are inevitably consumed – a pressure contraindicated for growing girls. In the end, Coach unwittingly reinforced Julie's disordered eating and unhealthy weight control practices.

Julie wasn't the only athlete to find herself in this predicament. Cross country is conventionally classified as a lean sport (versus a non-lean sport like wrestling). The culture in cross country is usually marked by a high degree of inter-team, performance-related awareness of the body's functional fitness. In 2006, Smith and Ogle explored the culture of one high school girls' cross country team. Of interest was whether or not interactions between coaches and athletes, and athletes themselves, contributed to athletes' body-related attitudes and behaviors. Their analysis of transcribed interviews and researcher field notes revealed an interesting sensitivity on the part of athletes to not want to appear too thin, or to appear to have an eating disorder. Rather, teammates, as well as coaches, placed a value on unity, harmony, and healthfulness.

In turn, in the Smith and Ogle study, these values framed individual experiences of the body and team interactions (Smith & Ogle, 2006). While all athletes in the study expressed relatively positive feelings about their bodies and none of them reported regularly dieting, evidence of body dissatisfaction and negative coach influence was evident. In all, three patterns of body-related coach-athlete interactions were identified: verbal interventions for the regulation of athlete attitudes and behaviors; deferential avoidance (avoiding discussions that might be hurtful or embarrassing); and condemnations and censures. Although Julie's coach tried to avoid potentially hurtful comments about his runners' bodies (deferential avoidance), he demonstrated condemnation and censure. He once made an off-hand comment that Julie absorbed like a sponge: "I don't really understand how Hannah runs so fast – she is so muscular, and smaller runners are usually the fastest."

Additionally, two patterns of body-related athlete-to-athlete interactions emerged in the Smith and Ogle (2006) study: fat talk and deferential avoidance. Among Julie's teammates, athlete-to-athlete interactions weren't always so harmonious. She noticed a fair amount of "fat talk" from some of the older runners in the locker room. Although the team culture was one of positive body talk, and Coach never talked about dieting as a means to improve times, a few of the older, more mature girls seemed to have a negative attitude about their bodies. One of her teammates said to another about Julie – within earshot of Julie – "Do you see how thin she is? – No wonder she beats us all. I feel disgusting when I stand next to her." Even though it was surprising and gratifying to be considered truly thin, the girl's negative self-talk was familiar to Julie. She, too, criticized her thighs and stomach, but it was odd to hear her revered teammates be so outwardly self-critical. She was used to this sort of self-berating, negative body talk going back years in school, but among athletes it seemed out of place. After all, they were exercising intensely. She knew most of the fastest runners were eating healthy food – she had studied their food behaviors from across the cafeteria. How could these girls with perfect physiques be so focused on "being fat" and self-hate their bodies?

It is well established that engaging in fat talk is contagious and associated with body dissatisfaction, dietary restraint, and a drive for thinness (Lin & Soby, 2017). Although Julie mostly overheard these conversations, rather than participating in them, they nonetheless influenced her. Because her teammates could see she was "all business" on the field, they usually didn't include her in their gossip sessions. She didn't seem to appreciate girl talk (which commonly includes fat talk), and they were right. They didn't realize how "checked out" Julie was from social interactions in general. But the team was close enough that Julie overheard their exchanges. Their fat talk definitely influenced her list of rules for better performance. She wanted to avoid fat food, a fat body, and a fat reputation. Unfortunately, Julie was setting herself up for inevitable internal conflict, because girls Julie's age should, as part of normal development, be adding fat to their bodies.

Coaches who put the benefit and development of their players first are generally not revered unless they also win. It is a rare parent who can recognize good coaching in a losing effort. We seem to expect kids to pick up positive character traits by osmosis. Condemnation by coaches leaves bad feelings that eat away at motivation. Excelling at sports requires emotional energy, which can be used up on negative feelings. Human energy can be created. It comes from emotions (Izard, 2013), and emotions are released by the ideas we generate in response to experience. We have an untapped reservoir of energy available to us if the right combination of ideas can evoke the emotions that will tap into the reservoir.

Fat talk reinforced Julie's own ideas about food and body size and gave her energy to maintain her strict avoidance of fat. Later, during her recovery, she spoke for many excellent athletes when she said, "I work incredibly hard on something when the motivation comes from *me*. When the goal is someone else's goal for me, I may work hard, but often only to the degree that I think is necessary to satisfy someone else, not to the point of achieving excellence." In recovery, she learned that it wasn't because of the fat talk in the locker room that she avoided certain foods – the idea was already hers, which is why she could work so hard to restrict her eating in the drive for perfection. The locker-room talk mainly served to reinforce her ideas and efforts.

To be fair, most athletic coaches of teens acknowledge that their influence on athletes is huge and can inadvertently contribute to unhealthy attitudes and behaviors. They understand comments about food, appearance, body shape and size, weight, and even exercise, as well as dismissive, censuring, or critical comments about performance need to be avoided or handled with considerable guardedness. The National Eating Disorder Association (NEDA, 2016) provides the *Coach & Athletic Trainer Toolkit* to assist coaches in avoiding some of the pitfalls Julie experienced with her coach. The National Collegiate Athletic Association (NCAA, n.d.) also distributes a free handbook, *Mind, Body and Sport: Understanding and Supporting Student-Athlete Mental Wellness,* that contains a section on eating disorders. Unfortunately, many coaches and athletic trainers receive little training on eating disorders. They may not recognize early warning signs and do not know what the athletes are doing outside of practices.

In Julie's situation, Coach had no idea that she used any spare moment she wasn't busy with homework to practice. She got up early each morning and, after a granola bar, ran three miles before school. Kate and James were concerned by this. They suggested she ran enough at practice after school and her rigorous morning training wasn't necessary. Julie ignored them. Finally, when Julie appeared thin and tired more days than not, Kate intervened. She didn't take "No" for an answer, but insisted on an appointment with their pediatrician, Dr. Kahn.

This checkup revealed that Julie had dropped significantly off the growth trajectory Dr. Kahn had marked out for her using her growth chart for both weight and body mass index (BMI). Julie's body was clearly depleted. She was running on empty and starting to do some real damage to her growing frame. "Although Julie has dropped time during cross country trials, those small improvements will not last," the pediatrician shared. Dr. Kahn ultimately diagnosed Julie with Anorexia Nervosa: Restricting type (American Psychiatric Association, 2013; *DSM*-5). This diagnosis is reserved for those whose weight loss, like Julie's, occurs mostly through "dieting, fasting, and/or excessive exercise" (p. 339). Julie had the following symptoms that satisfied the diagnosis of anorexia nervosa:

1 "Restriction of energy intake relative to requirements, leading to a significantly low body weight in the context of age, sex, developmental trajectory, and physical health" (p. 338). Julie: "I don't want to eat anything more for lunch but salad – I'm not hungry."
2 "Intense fear of gaining weight or of becoming fat … even though at a significantly low weight" (p. 338). Julie: "Mom – don't make me eat that cake – cake is fattening and unhealthy."
3 "Disturbance in the way in which one's body weight or shape is experienced, undue influence of body weight or shape on self-evaluation, or persistent

lack of recognition of the seriousness of the current low body weight" (p. 339). Julie: "I hate my butt – and my legs are huge! I feel so disgusting."

The fact that her pediatrician told her that she needed to leave cross country until her health was restored shocked Julie. He viewed the eating disorder like any other sports injury. Julie needed rest and nourishment – in other words, she needed to recover her health, which meant she had to quit the team. Julie was devastated. The season had started 2 months before, the team was doing really well, and now she would have to stop? It didn't make any sense to her. She complained bitterly. "After all the work I've done training, if I leave now, I will never be able to get back in such peak shape. I will lose everything I have built up. The other girls will go ahead without me. I have to work out, or I'll lose my best running times ever." Not only was Julie worried that her skills might fall behind but, like many athletes with eating disorders who need to take a break to heal, she was also concerned she might be stigmatized by her coach or teammates.

Until she could figure out a way to get back to her team, Julie needed to buy time. She told her mother she didn't want anybody at school to know there was something wrong. Unaccustomed to seeing herself as ill, she felt ashamed and embarrassed. She was sure that if Coach or her teammates found out, she would feel humiliated beyond words. She wanted this all kept secret, not realizing that recovery would not be easy, or quick.

Julie's fear of being discovered was well founded. Smith and Ogle (2006) found that sports teammates may gossip and be critical of each other's suspected eating disorders.

Julie's loud resistance to recovery was shocking to Kate and James. She had always been so agreeable and happy. Who was this stomping, stubborn tyrant? It was difficult for them to separate her from the illness. They worried about what their sons were feeling as they gave so much time to Julie's health issues. They were angry with Julie and scared for her at the same time. They had a family therapist now, Judy, which meant they had two members on their *treatment team* – her and Dr. Kahn, who had recommended they hire her. She reminded them that Julie's strong determination to succeed at sports in the past paralleled the determination she was using to fight their interventions to recover now. At 13, Julie didn't want to gain weight. She didn't care that she hadn't menstruated in 6 months. Infertility and bone-loss possibilities didn't matter to her. Foods with fat were anathema to maintaining her self-perceived, lean-body success. All Julie seemed to focus on was the horror of losing her athletic ability.

Upon recommendations from Judy and Dr. Kahn, Julie's parents began to meet Julie at school for lunch, since she regularly used her school lunchtime as an opportunity to not eat. Long ago, Julie had alienated her closest friends, those who dared to suggest she eat, by meeting their concern with stony silences, or glares. Still, she was accustomed to daily lunch with them and her teammates, even though they all worried silently about her poor eating. No one at her lunch table dared to mention her skimpy provisions. In order to make sure that she ate, Julie was now joining either her mother or her father in the car in the parking lot behind the school. She complained to Kate, "I'm missing lunch with my friends. And you're worried about me not socializing. Well – this is making it worse. What do I tell them? That I have to eat lunch with my mom? I can eat on my own!" The anorexia nervosa illness had Julie terrified of meals, so her parents' presence for lunch was both dreaded and embarrassing. Using principles from the Family Based Treatment (FBT) approach (Lock & Le Grange, 2015a, 2015b), Kate stopped running in the morning in order to try to feed Julie. She also didn't want to irritate Julie by so obviously running when Julie couldn't. Anything to help Julie recover. James pleaded with Julie to eat, sometimes threatening that she might have to go away to receive treatment if she didn't start feeding herself. When Kate and James refused to let Julie go to school until she had consumed breakfast, Julie would reluctantly eat. Kate and James felt empowered against the illness when this strategy worked. It didn't always. Consistent with FBT, Judy continued to assure them that they had successfully fed their daughter up to the time of the eating disorder, and they could continue to feed her now, even in the face of her resistance.

While Kate and James felt pressured by Julie's unrelenting anger and resistance, they also wanted to see an early weight increase, because they knew that to start with too low a caloric intake would risk cardiac problems. But it was complicated. They had really done their homework, so they knew refeeding was not as simple as it sounded. On the one hand, they were familiar with the common practice of starting a person's refeeding with low-nutrient intake and building up slowly to avoid what is known as *refeeding syndrome*. Refeeding syndrome is a rare metabolic disturbance that can result from restoring nutrition too quickly to a previously starved person. It can lead to respirocardiac failure (Fuentebella & Kerner, 2009). The approach of adding food slowly fit their temptation to follow Julie's lead to eat minimally, even though they knew to do so was to accommodate the demand of the eating disorder.

On the other hand, Kate and James knew that starting out with a too-low energy intake could negatively affect weight gain and thus exacerbate cardiac problems resulting from starvation (O'Connor & Nicholls, 2013). And they were acutely aware from their treatment team that nutrition (and thus weight) restoration at this juncture was the single most important goal for Julie's health (Attia, 2010). They felt pressured by strong evidence that early weight gain had the best prognosis for recovery (Le Grange, Accurso, Lock, Agras, & Bryson, 2014). To resolve their questions, they added a third person to their team, a professional nutrition counselor. She recommended Julie consume a minimum of 2500 kcal per day. Kate and James took this advice with the utmost seriousness. However, when they tried to convince Julie to eat this much, she responded with tantrums and swearing.

Despite small victories over the eating disorder, Kate and James were increasingly concerned about how much time they were losing from work.

They were exhausted and spent. They decided they needed a break to tend to their sons, their work, and their own health and began considering sending Julie for inpatient treatment. About two-thirds of adolescents with anorexia are successfully treated in inpatient care (Schlegl et al., 2015), so Kate and James were open to this alternative. While outpatient care was not failing – often a criterion for inpatient care – Kate and James were close to depleting their time and energy resources and risking becoming ill themselves.

Despite the fact that research doesn't show any particular long-term advantage of inpatient care for eating disorders over outpatient care (Meads, Gold, & Burls, 2001), Kate and James were sorely in need of a respite. And they were beginning to feel oppressed. As encouragement, Dr. Kahn told them something he had read related to adolescent eating disorders. "Patients often seem worse before they recover; these behaviors usually reduce in frequency as long as parents stay calm and consistent in their limit setting" (Katzman, Peebles, Sawyer, Lock, & Le Grange, 2013, p. 437). Dr. Kahn refused to get upset when Kate and James floundered. He had seen children like Julie before – angry at everyone who tried to intervene with the eating disorder, sulky, and bitter. He normalized versus "pathologized" what was happening with Julie and encouraged Kate and James' efforts to intervene even when Julie was giving them the silent treatment. Even when they felt defeated, he was there to help them blame the eating disorder and not themselves. Judy echoed Dr. Kahn's recommendations. Judy and Dr. Kahn operated well as a team, both supporting Kate and James in their home feeding of Julie. With their sons present, Judy reminded Kate, James, and Julie, "You didn't cause the eating disorder and while you may become discouraged and frustrated about your progress, you have many skills you bring to the table to help Julie eat normally again. Don't give up even in the face of her anger. It is the eating disorder, not Julie, pushing back on you. It wants Julie all to itself."

Julie's anger about leaving cross country the month before was particularly overwhelming to Kate and James. When Julie couldn't run cross country, she insisted on exercising to compensate and, in her mind, to keep up her strength and skills. The fact that the later endeavor was an illusion was unknown to Julie because the eating disorder had eclipsed her mind and removed any sense of logic related to her body's needs. Kate and James often felt overwhelmed by Julie's fury, her refusal to stop exercising, and her daily resistance to eating in a more balanced way. When they supervised her exercise and limited her to walking, they found Julie lying to them about secret workouts. Julie's teacher found her exercising in an empty bathroom at her school and called her parents.

No doubt exercising depleted Julie's resources so that she was having difficulty gaining weight commensurate with her recently increased food intake. Kate and James were unable to grasp how all of this could happen. "Who was this stranger?" Kate asked herself. Gone was the Julie who liked spending time with her parents, worked collaboratively with them, and faced a problem with them, together. This new Julie was angry, bitter, sullen, noncommunicative, and, most of all, resistant to any of the interventions they were advised to undertake in order to help her. Lock and Le Grange (2015b) advise parents that "their daughter's self-starvation and emaciated state is first and foremost a medical crisis that should be addressed without delay" (p. 88). They go on to encourage therapists to coach parents "to get their daughter to eat more than she ordinarily would" (p. 88).

Three weeks into starting Family Based Treatment with Judy, the final decision for a higher level of care was made for Kate and James when Julie's blood pressure and heart rate dropped to a level too low for medical safety. Under those circumstances, Dr. Kahn suggested Kate and James table their hopes for at-home care and allow themselves to rest and regroup during the time Julie would be hospitalized in a specialized eating-disorders program. He reminded Julie and her family that no one treatment fits all eating disorders, and treatment for eating disorders was best thought of as a continuum of care. He said, "Multidisciplinary care should be continuously assessed and adjusted, including stepping up (e.g., to inpatient care) or stepping down (e.g., to outpatient services) as needed." Julie was approximately 80% of her expected weight. Her malnourished state had caught up with her. Her medical safety was too compromised for her to remain at home. She would need to undergo aggressive nutrition restoration in the hospital in an effort to restabilize her health. Then maybe she could return to home care.

Meanwhile, Kate and James had been reading about eating disorders. Neither one had any known family or personal history of eating disorders, so they were on a steep learning curve. Because of their reading, they had no illusions about residential or hospital care bringing about a cure. They were hoping they would have more energy and a chance to better organize their resources to tackle the eating disorder when Julie came home. Whether or not she moved to a residential treatment center, stayed in a hospital, or moved to an intensive outpatient program, they already knew about the potential for a recurring cycle of relapse, inpatient care, and outpatient care (Katzman, Peebles, Sawyer, Lock, & Le Grange, 2013). They knew they needed to reinvigorate and stabilize themselves for a possible long-term battle. When hospitalization was recommended, they welcomed turning over the feeding process, even if temporarily, to a hospital staff. Anxious about Julie's perilous medical status, they looked forward to the break. Julie did not. She was mortified at the thought of being hospitalized.

For Julie, hospitalization meant all-out war. She felt like a failure, even though everyone told her she had an illness that neither she nor her parents had caused. In her life as an athlete, she had been programmed to win and to do so with a good deal of self-determination. The hospital was perceived as a loss – of her will; of her right to be thin, and therefore a fast runner; and of her right to choose her own steps to recovery. She was determined to win by not cooperating. All the way to the hospital, Julie refused to speak to her parents. James said to her at one point, "We know you think we're giving up on you and abandoning you. This is just as hard for us as it is for you. We want more than anything for you to get better. But now you're medically unsafe. We don't have a choice but to take you to the hospital. Even if we did have a choice, we want you to get the best and most aggressive help out there. We want you to be able to get back to your old life – back to school and back to running. The truth is, you're just too ill right now to do those things." Silence. Julie suspected her parents felt guilty. "They should," she thought. "I hate them," she told herself.

In fact, Julie spent the first 5 days in the hospital refusing to eat meals. When given the choice to eat meals or drink cans of nutrient supplements, she chose the supplements and did her best to leave some of the liquid in the cans. She was aware of a vague threat of a nasogastric tube and had already decided that would be the ultimate indignity. At the same time she imagined some relief at not having to chew or swallow food at all. Exercise in the hospital was forbidden in order to minimize energy expenditure. However, Julie exercised under the sheets at night whenever she could. She maintained a surly attitude. None of these resulted in her release. Her parents refused to take her home. She felt betrayed, alone, and trapped.

Finally, on the sixth day, Julie relented. She ate one meal along with her supplements. Typical of someone with an eating disorder, she was terrified and depressed about it (Frank & Kaye, 2012). In fact, as pointed out earlier, evidence suggests that avoiding eating relieves the anxiety brought on by the prospect of eating (Kaye, 2014). Julie was just as terrified of being kept in the hospital as she was of eating. At least if she were discharged – in her eyes, freed from prison – she could get back to restricting her food intake and resume some secret running.

In the hospital eating-disorders program, Julie received nutritional guidance, psychotherapy, weekly medical check-ups, and management. The hospital was nearby her family, and they remained involved in treatment. She reluctantly ate and gained weight. She experienced painful *gastroparesis*, which is a condition marked by delayed gastric emptying, a feeling of fullness after only a small amount food consumption, stomach cramping, and bloating. Gastroparesis is almost always associated with excessive weight loss and is commonly found in those with anorexia nervosa (Norris, Harrison, Isserlin, Robinson, Feder, & Sampson, 2016). It is weight restoration and sometimes medication that resolve this condition (Mascolo, Geer, Feuerstein, & Mehler, 2017).

Disgusted by her body, Julie was miserable most of the time she was in the hospital. She felt even worse whenever a new patient came in looking thin. "Lucky her," she would think. Her only hope was to be discharged. She said and did what she had to in order to trick those in charge into setting her free. She said she would maintain her eating gains and keep working toward full nutrition restoration. She kept to herself in the hospital, determined to follow her new, abridged plan.

The staff at the hospital were careful not to let Julie know her weight. Clinical judgment suggested that, as she increased nutrition, she would simply fixate on her weight and become more anxious if she began to compare current, increasing numbers on the scale to old numbers. She had been weighed at each session with Judy so this was an adjustment for her. Julie described herself as "grossed out" by eating and still preferred cans of supplement to normal food.

After the first week, once she relented in order to bring about her liberation, the hospital staff helped her desensitize to a number of the foods she had not allowed herself to eat. Although unintended, Julie found it easier and easier to take in sustenance. This was threatening to the eating disorder, and the eating-disorder voices in her head often told her "No!" to all but a few "safe" foods. Nonetheless, she pushed herself to eat, all the while concocting ways to lose weight once she was released. Still, the aim was for Julie *not to be* in the one-third of hospital-treated adolescents with anorexia nervosa who weight-restore but still suffer from other eating disorder symptomology (e.g., fear of weight gain; Schlegl et al., 2015).

Finally, when Julie was released from the hospital, she was happy to be heading back home. She was discharged after a month of intensive inpatient nutrition restoration with the understanding that she would maintain her new levels of energy intake, continue to gain weight, and resume menses. Although Julie agreed to these goals, she lied – she still secretly rejected them. She was partially recovered because of weight and nutrition restoration, but she was psychologically still struggling.

It is common for those with anorexia to resist treatment and even relapse after their early start at recovery in a hospital setting. Once in outpatient treatment, about 30% to 60% of those who have had anorexia for less than 3 years recover with family-based treatment (Stiles-Shields, Hoste, Doyle, & Le Grange, 2012). Since Julie was young and her parents remained determined, the prognosis remained hopeful. The outlook for those with prolonged illness, however, is poorer (Treasure & Russell, 2011). This is perhaps because treatment is undermined by brain changes related to starvation, such as poor motivation for positive outcomes and a strong fear response to anticipated recovery signs, like weight gain. It may be that treatment becomes more difficult once the illness is entrenched, or embedded. Kate and James were dedicated to this not being the case for Julie.

When their daughter came home, Kate and James were re-energized to help her. The more they understood her disorder, the more confident they felt in fighting it. They were determined to try to beat the odds at whatever the cost, or whatever continuum of care was required. Julie initially dropped a few pounds of weight post hospital discharge. Nonetheless, Kate and James, now fully aware and fortified by meeting with other parents of hospitalized patients with eating disorders, worked on meal support for all of Julie's meals. Reinvigorated, their intention was to do that for a minimum of 3 months, or until she was stable, ready to begin weaning from their support, and able to resume autonomous eating.

As it turned out, it took another 6 months of outpatient treatment for Julie's internal stubbornness to fully relent to the external pressures around her to recover. She thought about holding out until she was a legal adult at age 18. At that point, she could effectively resist parent-sanctioned treatment.

However, that was a long way off, and she was tired of fighting. She began to take an anxiety-reducing and antidepressant medication (fluoxetine) to lower her stress response to eating, exercise inhibition, and body-size concerns. At first she resisted the idea of medication, thinking it would cause weight gain or, worse yet, take away her anxious edge. After all, she relied on her negativity, anxiety, and pessimism about "being healthy" to give her inspiration to remain ill. However, in her exhaustion and desire to recoup a normal life, she relented.

Julie didn't know it at the time, but she was lucky. She was fortunate to have a mother and father who saw what was happening to their daughter, partly because they were runners and knew how to train correctly, and partly because they paid attention and weren't afraid to be wrong in taking her to the doctor. As a result, Julie's world had crashed around her. She had devoted so much time to her sports practice and so much energy to eating "correctly," that to be interrupted in her pursuit had been devastating. Nevertheless, Kate and James probably saved her life, although it felt like anything but that to Julie. Her running career was put on hold for over a year while her body healed and Julie learned new ways to feed herself "healthily." When she graduated to ninth grade, it was very difficult to encounter the other runners in the hallways. She had to continually remind herself that running was actually secondary to being a healthy person. Rather than dedicating herself to running, Julie's incredible focus and persistence found a new purpose: healing her body for strength. But it took some time for her to come around to such an acceptance.

Schmidt and Treasure (2006) developed the cognitive-interpersonal maintenance model for anorexia nervosa. An important part of their model is the interpersonal interactions between parent caregivers and their loved ones with an eating disorder. Conventional wisdom posits that caregivers' responses to eating disorders can be helpful or unhelpful. In the case of unhelpful-caregiver behaviors, it is usually the case that caregivers can inadvertently behave in ways that perpetuate rather than diminish symptoms. In collaboration with Schmidt and Treasure, Hibbs et al. (2015) uncovered several dimensions of caregiver skills that were clinically related to phenomena known to either undermine or enhance treatment of those with anorexia. We now know that caregivers' intensely expressed emotions, such as outward hostility or overt disappointment, are related to poorer recovery outcomes (Kyriacou, Treasure, & Schmidt, 2008).

The same is the case for behaviors that accommodate and enable an eating disorder (e.g., parents giving their children with an eating disorder low-calorie or diet foods to avoid conflict; Zabala, Macdonald, & Treasure, 2009). At first, James had succumbed to hostility against Julie when he was frustrated by her lack of progress. When the family therapist observed this, instead of criticizing James, Judy took a stance that the eating disorder loved James' hostility – in fact, fed on it. She pointed out, "James, you couldn't be expected to know that. You didn't know you were supporting the illness when you got angry at Julie for not eating. It's okay. Going forward, you can thwart the eating disorder with your patience and persistence." Caregivers who have the ability to pan back and see the bigger picture, engage in positive self-care, hold back criticism, show acceptance and empathy, and handle frustration fare better in supporting their children with eating disorders.

Kate and James' learning curve for how to best provide a healing environment for their child included some changes that made them more effective. First, they realized they were not managing their anxiety levels. Despite their pediatrician's and therapist's best efforts to help them build confidence, they had been so overwhelmed by their distress, it rendered them less effective. They realized they needed to calm down. Julie's admission to the hospital helped. When she was discharged, they realized they had a back-up plan if she relapsed. Julie could be re-admitted if she became medically unstable. Kate was most frightened of a medical complication, so this particular reassurance was important to her.

Among signs of unbridled parent distress was Kate's tendency to get pulled into repetitive arguments with Julie about what to eat, how much to eat, and weight. Judy and the staff at the hospital helped Kate realize, as with James' initial hostility, that the eating disorder thrived on her argumentativeness and that she would never win an argument with the eating disorder. She learned to externalize the eating disorder and, moving forward, she remained calmer in the face of its wily ways. It took Kate gaining insight into Julie's illness to come to terms with what she hadn't understood: Julie was generally a logical and reasonable person on any subject, but when it came to food, eating, exercise, size, and weight, she wasn't rational.

Kate also came to realize that when Julie said, "I can't eat that … I feel sick when I eat that," she was telling her the truth. Gastroparesis was truly uncomfortable for 3 to 4 months. Further, Kate understood Julie may have been having the closest brush with brain-based delusional thinking she would ever experience. Her mind was telling her she was fat. Her brain was registering panic in the face of food. Her stomach felt full when she was still starving. She had stomachaches when she ate, which led her to not eat. When she looked in the mirror, she saw grotesque deposits of fat on her body, because her brain distorted what she saw. She could not alter this perception for many reasons. All of these things were Julie's truths as she experienced them.

So with understanding and compassion, Kate and James moved forward, finally grasping the seriousness and depth of the illness. Kate had to learn to resist the urge to get drawn into arguments about the very topics Julie was obsessed with. Things like her weight, her issues with the erroneous thinking of her treatment professionals, her perception of the grossness of her body size, her arguments about the unhealthiness of challenging meals, and her staunch stand about the importance of keeping the illness a secret (which was related to Julie's shame). Kate had to learn to be calm with Julie even when she was speaking nonsense, or resisting what Kate and James knew was best for her. To draw upon Treasure's (Treasure & Alexander, 2013) animal metaphors for different carer styles, Kate and James needed to switch from occasional rhinoceros behavior (attempts to influence Julie to recover by arguing and confronting) to more dolphin-like behavior (nudging Julie to safety while recognizing she was clinging to the eating disorder like it was a "life preserver"; p. 106).

Kate and James learned to take better care of themselves. They had been so preoccupied with Julie's well-being that they had neglected their own needs to sleep, eat, and socialize in healthy ways. Once Kate said to James, "I can't leave the house. I'm afraid she'll exercise or start throwing up. What if her brothers start teasing her? She can't take it." Just like Julie, they stopped seeing friends so they could stay home and monitor their daughter. The eating disorder created many disconnections between family members and isolated them from others. It had them all "in the frying pan," suffering together. They needed to learn that they could trust Julie to deal with day-to-day stresses, rather than trying to protect her from anything they thought might trigger a symptom.

If Julie did relapse, they learned to calmly intervene without getting over-protective or angry. Slowly, as Julie's heath improved, Kate and James learned to trust she could draw on tools she had learned in treatment. Kate and James made a point to have a date night each weekend, leaving Julie and her brothers home with a babysitter. At 14, Julie resented a babysitter. However, her parents explained this freed her up for her own activities and left the caretaking responsibilities for her younger brothers to the older babysitter. Maybe she could babysit next year, if she wanted.

No longer perched outside the bathroom door to make sure Julie wasn't vomiting (which she wasn't) or exercising, Kate got to bed at reasonable hours. Kate and James also set a boundary for Julie about keeping the eating disorder a secret. They didn't want to enable her misguided shame. They wanted to underscore that Julie's illness was not a choice or caused by them or something she did. They told their closest friends and relatives about it, because they needed support.

Julie was able to return to running despite her catastrophic predictions otherwise. To build up to a full cross country practice, she slowly increased her body-building exercise so it matched what she was able to support with adequate nutritional intake. For example, she no longer avoided carbohydrates, because she learned from a nutritionist that carbohydrates are necessary for building muscle – something she valued as she improved her sports performance.

Gradual exposure to lost old foods, introduction to new foods, improvements in brain functioning, constant exposure to a healthier body, and a growing weariness with the struggle against the eating-disorder voices that judged her every morsel of food, slowly brought Julie to a place where she could see the eating disorder as something outside of herself. She was no longer one with it, no longer completely immersed and unable to see beyond it. Julie thoroughly understood the saying, "You can't see the forest for the trees." Outside the eating disorder, sometimes just for few hours, not yet for whole days, she saw the illness for what it was – a slave driver, a task master, a reflection of her most voracious self.

As a girl who never much liked emotions, part of the final stage of Julie's healing included recognizing them when they occurred. Labeling them was hard. Shades of emotional meaning and intensity came to her, although at first they were unfamiliar. Kate and James helped. Part of their learning curve was honestly expressing their feelings about the eating disorder and owning the feelings as their own. For example, James said, "I've been very angry at this illness. I know it's not you but the illness talking when you scream at us about your body size. I see this illness as an unwelcome visitor in our home. It took you over and scared us all. I'm still scared you won't get well, and I'm angry this illness took you so far away from us." By expressing his feelings about the eating disorder openly, James set an example for Julie. He told Julie, "Feelings won't kill you. They aren't bad. They're just feelings. They serve a function. They're reactions, not actions. They just are. No need to hate them or suppress them. They come and they go. Sometimes they're hard to handle. But they won't kill you."

These were hard lessons for Julie, who a while back had been disgusted by Amelia's emotions at cross country practice. As she discovered feelings were not a sign of weakness, Julie stopped trying to hate her emotions and judge them so harshly. Her mindfulness work with her therapist allowed her to observe and describe her emotions without negatively judging them or herself. If Coach was harsh, she acknowledged it made her feel inferior and sad. If Coach praised her, she let herself feel encouraged about her developing skills. If her teammates were jealous, she felt rejected. If someone like Amelia was upset during practice, she empathized with her sadness and comforted her openly. Hard as it was for a 14-year-old with the overwhelming capacity for intense emotions that comes with puberty, Julie learned to manage her emotions. One step at a time.

Question

As a parent how can I tell when my daughter's sports practice has turned into compulsive exercise and put her at risk for an eating disorder?

Answer

It is true that high levels of compulsive exercise have been identified as a risk factor for eating disorders. Compulsive exercise is implicated in the etiology, development, and maintenance of eating disorders (Meyer, Taranis, Goodwin, & Haycraft, 2011). Teen girls and boys who engage in compulsive exercise have been shown to have higher levels of eating-disorder behaviors (Levallius, Collin, & Birgegård, 2017). A recent study found about 44% of adolescents with eating disorders engage in compulsive exercise, especially those with bulimia nervosa and partial syndrome eating disorders (Levallius et al., 2017). The most common reasons for engaging in compulsive exercise for adolescent athletes include a mythical belief, like Julie, that a leaner body subjected to intense practice will improve sports performance. It is important to point out that while compulsive exercise is a common problem with eating disorders it is not restricted to them. Also, unless exercise dependence has been stably present for a long period of time it may not be considered compulsive.

What is compulsive exercise? Perhaps the most well-known measure of it is the Compulsive Exercise Test (Taranis, Touyz, & Meyer, 2011), which has been useful for examining exercise in adolescents (Goodwin, Haycraft, Taranis, & Meyer, 2011). Key features of compulsive exercise measured in this test include:

1. Rule-driven exercise that is followed rigidly
2. Guilt if exercise is not engaged in
3. Using exercise to control weight
4. Lack of exercise enjoyment (e.g., exercise becomes a mandatory chore)
5. Over-dependence on exercise to control mood and anxiety (e.g., feeling depressed if an exercise routine is not engaged in).

If you suspect that your child is compulsively exercising, it may be a serious problem. Compulsive exercise could be part of the Female Athlete Triad (Nazem & Ackerman, 2012), a syndrome named by the American College of Sports Medicine in 1993. Seen in female athletes, it involves interrelated disordered eating, menstrual irregularity, and low bone mass (De Souza et al., 2014). Each of these can be exacerbated by dependence on over-training and an unwillingness to increase training gradually at the beginning of the season. Stress or full bone fractures, menstrual irregularity, and/or failure to increase fuel intake commensurate with increased exercise are signs of the Female Athlete Triad. If you suspect disordered eating behaviors along with signs of over-training, it is time for a specialty-trained eating disorder evaluation by a pediatrician, family physician, nutrition counselor, or mental health professional.

The co-occurrence of compulsive exercise with an eating disorder is associated with the more severe eating disorders. Therefore, exercise may be temporarily restricted by treatment professionals once someone has been diagnosed. While exercise has many positive benefits and may, under supervised conditions, improve health in those with eating disorders (Ng, Ng & Wong, 2013), it is usually recommended to curtail driven and compulsive exercise.

The trend is for young people to decrease their exercise participation as they progress into their teens. Therefore, healthy and recovered adolescents should be encouraged to participate in middle and high school sports. Moderate, balanced sports participation based on having fun and focused on how the body can function, instead of on how it appears, can protect young people from body dissatisfaction and eating disorders.

Question

My son was withdrawn from sports participation by his pediatrician and treatment team because he was diagnosed with bulimia nervosa. Since his laboratory tests and medical evaluation indicated he is stable, why is this important?

Answer

Laboratory tests and biological indicators may demonstrate stable health, however, as long as eating-disorder behaviors such as binge eating and self-induced vomiting continue, serious health risks remain. Individuals with bulimia nervosa are especially at increased risk for cardiovascular problems (e.g., hypotension, tachycardia, and heart arrhythmia) that can be life threatening. Ninety percent of purge behaviors in bulimia nervosa are self-induced vomiting and stimulant laxative abuse (Westmoreland, Krantz, & Mehler, 2016). These can lead to electrolyte (e.g., potassium) abnormalities that, in turn, can result in serious cardiovascular risk and death. Blood tests should not be used as a sole basis for determining health, because they provide data only on the amount of extracellular electrolytes. Dangerously low levels of electrolytes inside cells can also lead to death. An athlete may be withdrawn from sports participation if there is purge behavior at a sufficient frequency to suggest a health risk.

In addition, with bulimia nervosa, excessive exercise is often used to compensate for caloric intake during binge eating. If a treatment team suspects excessive or driven exercise, sports participation may be curtailed in order to interrupt the athlete's use of exercise to manage weight.

A person with an eating disorder may be embarrassed or afraid to tell her or his coach or instructor they cannot participate in sports because of an eating disorder. Treatment team members and parents may be in the best position to inform coaches and instructors about the nature of the eating-disorder illness and to present professional treatment recommendations. Coaches and sports instructors can help in the following ways:

1. Be supportive, positive, and encouraging to athletes in recovery.
2. Be willing to adopt treatment-team recommendations about when, where, and how much an athlete will be allowed to participate in sports. Develop a care plan naming those who will be points of contact for the athletic association, the family, and the professional treatment team. The care plan should include communication with the athlete about setting realistic goals upon return to her or his sport.
3. Respect the privacy of an athlete in treatment making sure to abide by appropriate confidentiality regulations (e.g., not sharing an athlete's private information with other coaches or teammates).
4. Identify how an athletic organization can best support an athlete upon her or his return from a time of sports absence. Be willing to learn enough about eating disorders to demonstrate empathy and informed communication with ill or previously ill athletes and their carers.
5. Finally, be able to detect and communicate signs of relapse.

Question

I have noticed my daughter is increasingly anxious around sports practices and competitions. I suspect she and her coach are not getting along and this is affecting her mental health and her eating difficulties. Can problems with a coach contribute to eating disorders?

Answer

Shanmugam, Jowett, and Meyer (2014) examined a number of factors that contribute to disordered-eating behaviors in college athletes. They noted the impact of coach-athlete, parent-coach, and teammate-athlete conflict on eating psychopathology over a 6-month period. As it turned out, it was an athlete's perceived interpersonal conflict with a coach that was the only significant predictor of eating psychopathology.

Like Julie, as adolescents progress into specialized sports participation during middle and high school years, they increasingly depend on coaches for personal guidance and instruction. This can leave young athletes vulnerable to the risk for eating disorders associated with coach-athlete conflict. Shanmugam and colleagues (2014) summarized the potential impact of coach-athlete conflict:

> Therefore, given the prominent role that the coach plays in an athlete's life (i.e., in terms of athletic and personal development), athletes may engage in unhealthy eating behaviors in an attempt to cope with the conflict experienced in the relationship, as well as to gain an immediate sense of "control," which is perceived to be lacking in their interactions with their coach (Shanmugam et al, 2014, p. 474).

Athletes experiencing interpersonal conflict with their coaches may be struggling to remain loyal to their coach and their team while simultaneously using eating-disorder symptoms to cope with (numb) tension and negative emotions. For example, they may use an eating disorder to disconnect from internal discomfort created by conflict with an authoritative, critical, and/or intimidating coach. It is important for coaches and parents to recognize signs of strain and disordered eating and tactfully approach athletes displaying those signs. In the case of coach-athlete strife, parents may need to step in to either advocate for their child, or support withdrawal from a toxic sport environment.

References

American Psychiatric Association. (2013). *Diagnostic and statistical manual of mental disorders* (5th ed.). Washington, DC: Author.

Attia, E. (2010). Anorexia nervosa: Current status and future directions. *Annual Review of Medicine*, 61(1), 425–435.

Avena, N. M., & Bocarsly, M. E. (2012). Dysregulation of brain reward systems in eating disorders: Neurochemical information from animal models of binge eating, bulimia nervosa, and anorexia nervosa. *Neuropharmacology*, 63(1), 87–96.

Bardone-Cone, A., Fitzsimmons-Craft, E., Harney, M., Maldonado, C., Lawson, M., Smith, R., & Robinson, D. (2012). The inter-relationships between vegetarianism and eating disorders among females. *Journal of the Academy of Nutrition and Dietetics*, 112(8), 1247–1252.

Bardone-Cone, A. M., Sturm, K., Lawson, M. A., Robinson, D. P., & Smith, R. (2010). Perfectionism across stages of recovery from eating disorders. *International Journal of Eating Disorders*, 43(2), 139–148.

Bardone-Cone, A. M., Wonderlich, S. A., Frost, R. O., Buli, C. M., Mitchell, J. E., Uppala, S., & Simonich, H. (2007). Perfectionism and eating disorders: Current status and future directions. *Clinical Psychology Review*, 27(3), 384–405.

Bucchianeri, M., & Neumark-Sztainer, D. (2014). Body dissatisfaction: An overlooked public health concern. *Journal of Public Mental Health*, 13(2), 64–69.

Courty, A., Godart, N., Lalanne, C., & Berthoz, S. (2015). Alexithymia, a compounding factor for eating and social avoidance symptoms in anorexia nervosa. *Comprehensive Psychiatry*, 56, 217–228.

De Souza, M. J., Nattiv, A., Joy, E., Misra, M., Williams, N. I., Mallinson, R, J., … Matheson, G. (2014). 2014 Female athlete triad coalition consensus statement on treatment and return to play of the female athlete triad: 1st International Conference held in San Francisco, California, May 2012 and 2nd International Conference held in Indianapolis, Indiana, May 2013. *British Journal of Sports Medicine*, 48(4), 289–302.

Frank, G., & Kaye, W. (2012). Current status of functional imaging in eating disorders. *International Journal of Eating Disorders*, 45(6), 723–736.

Fuentebella, J., & Kerner, J. A. (2009). Refeeding syndrome. *Pediatric Clinics of North America*, 56(5), 1201–1210.

Goodwin, H., Haycraft, E., Taranis, L., & Meyer, C. (2011). Psychometric evaluation of the compulsive exercise test (CET) in an adolescent population: Links with eating psychopathology. *European Eating Disorders Review*, 19(3), 269–279.

Halmi, K. A., Bellace, D., Berthod, S., Ghosh, S., Berrettini, W., Brandt, H. A., … Strober, M. (2012). An examination of early childhood perfectionism across anorexia nervosa subtypes. *International Journal of Eating Disorders*, 45(6), 800–807.

Heinzel, A., Schäfer, R., Müller, H. W., Schieffer, A., Ingenhag, A., Northoff, G., … Hautzel, H. (2010). Differential modulation of valence and arousal in high-alexithymic and low-alexithymic individuals. *Neuroreport*, 21(15), 998–1002.

Hibbs, R., Rhind, C., Salerno, L., Gianluca, L. C., Goddard, E., Schmidt, U., … Treasure, J. (2015). Development and validation of a scale to measure caregiver skills in eating disorders. *International Journal of Eating Disorders*, 48(3), 290–297.

Izard, C. E. (2013). *Human emotions*. Berlin, Germany: Springer Science.

Katzman, D. K., Peebles, R., Sawyer, S., Lock, J., & Le Grange, D. (2013). The role of the pediatrician in Family-Based Treatment for adolescent eating disorders: Opportunities and challenges. *Journal of Adolescent Health*, 53(4), 433–440.

Kaye, W. H. (2014, May 06). Eating disorders: Understanding anorexia nervosa. *Neurology Times*. Retrieved from www.neurology_times_-_eating_disorders_understanding_ anorexia_nervosa_-_2014-05-28.pdf

Kaye, W. H., Bailer, U., Klabunde, M., & Brown, H. (2010). Is anorexia nervosa an eating disorder? How neurobiology can help us understand the puzzling eating symptoms of anorexia nervosa. Retrieved from https://popularmythology.files.wordpress.com/2015/01/kaye2010neurobiologyofan.pdf

Kaye, W. H., Wierenga, C. E., Bailer, U. R., Simmons, A. N., & Bischoff-Grethe, A. (2013). Nothing tastes as good as skinny feels: The neurobiology of anorexia nervosa. *Trends in Neurosciences*, 36(2), 110–120.

Keys, A., Brožek, J., Henschel, A., Mickelsen, O., & Taylor, H. L. (1950). *The biology of human starvation* (Vols. 1–2). Minneapolis: University of Minnesota Press.

Kyriacou, O., Treasure, J., & Schmidt, U. (2008). Expressed emotion in eating disorders assessed via self-report: An examination of factors associated with expressed emotion in carers of people with anorexia nervosa in comparison to control families. *International Journal of Eating Disorders*, 41(1), 37–46.

Lampard, A. M., Byrne, S. M., McLean, N., & Fursland, A. (2011). Avoidance of affect in the eating disorders. *Eating Behaviors*, 12(1), 90–93.

Le Grange, D., Accurso, E., Lock, J., Agras, S., & Bryson, S. W. (2014). Early weight gain predicts outcome in two treatments for adolescent anorexia nervosa. *International Journal of Eating Disorders*, 47(2), 124–129.

Levallius, J., Collin, C., & Birgegård, A. (2017). Now you see it, now you don't: compulsive exercise in adolescents with an eating disorder. *Journal of Eating Disorders*, 5(1), 9.

Lin, L., & Soby, M. (2017). Is listening to fat talk the same as participating in fat talk? *Eating disorders*, 25(2), 165–172.

Lipsman, N., Woodside, D. B., & Lozano, A. M. (2015). Neurocircuitry of limbic dysfunction in anorexia nervosa. *Cortex*, 62, 109–118.

Lock, J., & Le Grange, D. (2015a). *Help your teenager beat an eating disorder* (2nd ed.). New York, NY: Guilford.

Lock, J., & Le Grange, D. (2015b). *Treatment manual for anorexia nervosa: A family-based approach* (2nd ed.). New York, NY: Guilford.

Mascolo, M., Geer, B., Feuerstein, J., & Mehler, P. S. (2017). Gastrointestinal comorbidities which complicate the treatment of anorexia nervosa. *Eating Disorders*, 25(2), 122–133.

Meads, C., Gold, L., & Burls, A. (2001). How effective is outpatient care compared to inpatient care for the treatment of anorexia nervosa? A systematic review. *European Eating Disorders Review*, 9(4), 229–241.

Meyer, C., Taranis, L., Goodwin, H., & Haycraft, E. (2011). Compulsive exercise and eating disorders. *European Eating Disorders Review*, 19(3), 174–189.

Michalak, J., Zhang, X. C., & Jacobi, F. (2012). Vegetarian diet and mental disorders: Results from a representative community survey. *International Journal of Behavioral Nutrition and Physical Activity*, 9(1), 67.

Miyake, Y., Okamoto, Y., Onoda, K., Shirao, N., Okamoto, Y., & Yamawaki, S. (2012). Brain activation during the perception of stressful word stimuli concerning interpersonal relationships in anorexia nervosa patients with high degrees of alexithymia in an fMRI paradigm. *Psychiatry Research: Neuroimaging*, 201(2), 113–119.

Moriguchi, Y., & Komaki, G. (2013). Neuroimaging studies of alexithymia: Physical, affective, and social perspectives. *BioPsychoSocial Medicine*, 7(1), 8–19.

Nazem, T. G., & Ackerman, K. E. (2012). The female athlete triad. *Sports Health*, 4 (4), 302–311.

NCAA. (n.d.). Mind, body and sport: Understanding and supporting student-athlete mental wellness. Retrieved from www.ncaapublications.com/p-4375-mind-body-and-sport-understanding-and-supporting-student-athlete-mental-wellness.aspx?CategoryID=0&SectionID=0&ManufacturerID=0&DistributorID=0&GenreID=0&VectorID=0&

NEDA. (2016). Coach & athletic trainer toolkit. Retrieved from www.nationaleatingdisorders.org/coach-trainer

Ng, L. W. C., Ng, D. P., & Wong, W. P. (2013). Is supervised exercise training safe in patients with anorexia nervosa? A meta-analysis. *Physiotherapy*, 99(1), 1–11.

Norris, M. L., Harrison, M. E., Isserlin, L., Robinson, A., Feder, S., & Sampson, M. (2016). Gastrointestinal complications associated with anorexia nervosa: A systematic review. *International Journal of Eating Disorders*, 49(3), 216–237.

O'Connor, G., & Nicholls, D. (2013). Refeeding hypophosphatemia in adolescents with anorexia nervosa: A systematic review. *Nutrition in Clinical Practice*, 28(3), 358–364.

Schlegl, S., Diedrich, A., Neumayr, C., Fumi, M., Naab, S., & Voderholzer, U. (2015). Inpatient treatment for adolescents with anorexia nervosa: Clinical significance and predictors of treatment outcome. *European Eating Disorders Review*, 24(3), 214–222.

Schmidt, U., & Treasure, J. (2006). Anorexia nervosa: Valued and visible. A cognitive-interpersonal maintenance model and its implications for research and practice. *British Journal of Clinical Psychology*, 45(3), 343–366.

Shanmugam, V., Jowett, S., & Meyer, C. (2014), Interpersonal difficulties as a risk factor for athletes' eating psychopathology. *Scandinavian Journal of Medicine and Science in Sports*, 24(2), 469–476.

Smith, P. M., & Ogle, J. P. (2006). Interactions among high school cross-country runners and coaches: Creating a cultural context for athletes' embodied experiences. *Family and Consumer Sciences Research Journal*, 34(3), 276–307.

Stice, E. (2002). Risk and maintenance factors for eating pathology: A meta-analytic view. *Psychological Bulletin*, 128(5), 825–848.

Stiles-Shields, C., Hoste, R., Doyle, P. M., & Le Grange, D. (2012). A review of family-based treatment for adolescents with eating disorders. *Reviews on Recent Clinical Trials*, 7, 133–140.

Taranis, L., Touyz, S., & Meyer, C. (2011). Disordered eating and exercise: Development and preliminary validation of the Compulsive Exercise Test (CET). *European Eating Disorders Review*, 19(3), 256–268.

Treasure, J., & Alexander, J. (2013). *Anorexia nervosa: A recovery guide for sufferers, families and friends*. Abington-on-Thames, UK: Routledge.

Treasure, J., & Russell, G. (2011). The case for early intervention in anorexia nervosa: Theoretical exploration of maintaining factors. *British Journal of Psychiatry*, 199(1), 5–7.

Treasure, J., & Schmidt, U. (2013). The cognitive-interpersonal maintenance model of anorexia nervosa revisited: A summary of the evidence for cognitive, socio-emotional and interpersonal predisposing and perpetuating factors. *Journal of Eating Disorders*. Retrieved from www.jeatdisord.com/content/1/1/13

Westmoreland, P., Krantz, M. J., & Mehler, P. S. (2016). Medical complications of anorexia nervosa and bulimia. *The American Journal of Medicine*, 129(1), 30–37.

Zabala, M., Macdonald, P., & Treasure, J. (2009). Appraisal of caregiving burden, expressed emotion and psychological distress in families of people with eating disorders: A systematic review. *European Eating Disorders Review*, 17(5), 338–349.

2 Claire

Trouble Adjusting to College

Claire had barely slept. She was finally here – she and her parents had arrived yesterday evening. She had dreamed of going away for school for years. "I'm here! I'm here! This is really happening!" she thought. At this moment, all the struggles to make college-application deadlines seemed far behind. Her parents were going to drop her off at campus this morning and drive away. She would finally be an adult, with the last word on what she did and when she did it.

As her mother, Sarah, lingered in Claire's new dorm room savoring the minutes they had left together, Claire could see her becoming sad. "Mom, it's okay. I'll be fine." "I know you will, honey. Your father and I are so proud of you. We love you so much." "I love you too, Mom," Claire responded. Sarah stared out the window as she stalled, putting off the moment when she and Tom, Claire's dad, would have to leave. Tom pulled on Sarah's arm to get her moving. "Sarah – I think it's time to go." Sarah teared up as she kissed Claire good-bye one more time. "Make sure you and Ky [Claire's roommate] get enough sleep. Are you sure your meal plan is figured out? I see there's a snack bar right downstairs. And the exercise room off the lobby looks great. It's a good thing your first class isn't until 10:00 – you have quite a walk to the main campus." "Sarah," Tom said. "I think it's time for moms here to leave – to our car actually." Claire cast her father a grateful look. Sarah felt Tom's determination and headed out the door, taking one last look over her shoulder – a mental picture of her daughter to be filed away until Thanksgiving vacation. "Take care, honey!" "Bye Mom!"

Claire felt a little bad about leaving her younger brother Jimmy back home alone with her strict parents. But her guilt was short-lived. She was happy to start her life away from home, on her own, meeting new people, taking the bus into New York City on weekends when she wanted, and generally being the one in charge of her life. There was no more getting permission to be out at night. No more need to let her parents know where she was. Like lots of freshman going to college for the first time, Claire had been a public-school kid. The longest she had spent away from home were the two times she stayed at a sleep-away summer camp and the two class trips she took to Europe for Spanish class.

When Claire and Ky were told by their college that they would be sharing a dorm room, they connected on Facebook and Instagram. They spent all summer getting to know each other. Their room decorations had been jointly chosen. They discovered they were both late-to-rise, late-to-sleep, nocturnal types. They anticipated long nights spent getting to know each other even more in person.

Ky's parents had left them with an apartment-sized refrigerator and plenty of snacks, but despite a room full of goodies, awesome matching comforters, and unlimited access to Netflix, both Claire and Ky quickly began finding reasons to leave their room, especially at night. The allure of 24/7 social possibilities was seductive. Arrangements were often made spontaneously by text. Ky often signaled Claire during the day with "wiu" (What is up?) so they could make plans for later in the day. For the first time, the only boundaries in Claire's life were self-imposed. A test of her maturity, it often came down to how she could balance her time across a myriad of important or interesting choices. Every day she felt pulled in at least a few different directions. It was true she and Ky hit it off well. Together they explored the possibilities.

"Ky – can you text Jacob about tonight? I promised him we would hang out." Ky was pulling out her phone as fast as Claire, who was lying on her bed across the room, was speaking. Her thumbs flew over the keys as she texted Jacob. Ky was friends with Jacob first; they had known each other in high school. Ky and Claire planned to study for a while, then hang out with Jacob, Mark, and Ethan. Only 2 weeks into the start of classes and Claire was beginning to have a crush on Jacob.

Jacob and she had briefly "hooked up" at a party at Jacob's suite the previous weekend. Afterwards they hung out in Jacob's room talking. It got so late that Ky found her and wanted to go home. As Claire left Jacob to go with Ky that night, she hoped Jacob's memory of her would extend past a few Saturday night beers, the brief excitement of dancing, and a decent DJ. When she left, Jacob said, "Let's hang out this week – maybe Wednesday." A lot better than "See you," Claire thought to herself. She took this good-bye-I-want-to-see-you-again as a positive sign Jacob wanted to continue their relationship. To say she was eager to spend more time with Jacob was an understatement. She was barely able to keep her mind on her freshman writing course assignment due on Monday. "I am crushing so bad on Jacob," she told Ky.

On Wednesday, Claire checked her phone repeatedly for a word from Jacob. After what seemed too long a time, Jacob finally texted her and Ky to come to his suite after dinner. Claire was fairly certain she and Jacob would hook up again. She had learned in high school that getting too attached too soon was a big mistake, so she made up her mind she wouldn't appear too eager – she would make sure not to spend too much time with Jacob in the future if things went well.

Claire spent at least an hour trying on different outfits before going off with Ky that night. Her long blonde hair was pulled back in a stylish ponytail. Her makeup was freshly reapplied for the occasion – maybe a little more lipstick than usual. She had her best jeans on, expensive and, according to Ky, "slimming." Ky lent her a new top that looked great. She was self-conscious about her body. She had her mother's wide hips and often thought she was too fat.

But she had the same hips she'd had since she was 14 or 15 – a gift of puberty, she told herself. She wished for a different body, but that was not an option. So she did her best to wear jeans that pulled her stomach in and tops that accentuated the contrast between her full breasts and her small waist.

Things went well. Claire was beyond excited. Jacob kept his attention focused on Claire as the minutes flew by. They not only made out, but Jacob asked her questions about her family and her hometown. Before she knew it, it was 2 am, she had a 10 am class, her essay wasn't quite done, and she had more late night studying to do. Ky had gone home without her, encouraged by Claire to leave her behind.

Claire was falling for Jacob. In urban dictionary vernacular, she was "catching feelings." Her new relationship was time consuming. Meanwhile Ky was finding her own love interests. Their almost-nightly forays out of their dorm were perfectly coordinated, exhilarating, and in many ways the picture of a charmed first semester at college. Nonetheless, Claire began to face the reality of having too little time for studying. She suggested she and Ky study together a few nights during the week. In their dorm there was a lounge area with modern Ikea-style furniture – quiet, with easy access to a late-night café. But Ky was less than interested. She didn't seem to have the same issues with her homework and grades. "How does she do it?" Claire wondered. "Where is she squeezing in time to study?"

It wasn't long before the lure of 7-nights-a-week social possibilities were taking their toll on Claire's grades. She was having too much fun to stop – yet the end of her first semester was drawing to a close, and she was sporting C's in most of her classes. "This sucks," she complained bitterly to herself. This was a far cry from her high school High Honor roll status. Claire wanted good grades. Her self-esteem had always depended on them.

College was harder than high school – more reading, intimidating professors, and exams that required lots of studying. And it was almost too easy to tune out during class. In her only class with Ky, Claire once found herself whispering to Ky, "Look at this – amazing!" She showed her an awesome pair of Jimmy Choo shoes on sale for 70% off. The sale was on one of four websites open on her iPad screen during their biology lecture. Ky was as excited as Claire. "Yeah – that is awesome – get them!" Since PayPal was an option and her size was available, she happily hit the BUY button for a shopping victory. She felt a certain amount of satisfaction for scoring a great pair of shoes.

Claire and her parents had set up a bank account in Claire's new location, and Claire connected it to PayPal for easy shopping. As she spent on things like new shoes, she started to realize she needed to pace herself. Monthly deposits by her mother dried up faster than she expected. Ky, on the other hand, didn't seem to worry about spending. She seemed to have it all. It was like there was superfluous money waiting to be drained from some endless stream that flowed into her credit-card account. Claire felt intimidated by Ky's spending power.

And Ky was beautiful; she had long black hair and olive skin. A Filipino mother and Anglo father gave her a magic mix of exotic genes. She moved with grace as if on a stage when she smiled and greeted people she knew. She was lithe and ethereal, yet grounded – a strange mix of charm, grace, and mystery combined with an easy accessibility to others. People clearly noticed her when she walked into a room.

Claire was considered a beauty in her own right with her long, straight hair and sharp but small nose. Her grandfather was Native American, which probably accounted for her high cheekbones. For 4 years now, her naturally dark-brown hair had been carefully concealed by bleaching. It had been so long since Claire had dark hair, she wouldn't have recognized herself in the mirror if she suddenly had it again. When she first dared to lighten her hair, her mother had objected, suggesting to Claire she was quite beautiful as she was, so "Why would you want to change?"

Claire and Ky made a striking pair moving around campus. Instagram pictures of the two of them were popular with friends. "Yo," Jacob's roommate said to him upon finding Ky and Claire's picture on Instagram, "You're dating this babe?" Claire enjoyed her popularity even though it too often seemed to her she basked in Ky's light. Claire knew all of it was based way too much on her looks, "but why not enjoy it while I can?" Claire thought to herself. Still there was a little voice inside her that nagged. "Life on a stage or an imagined stage – a stage that was ubiquitously present in her imagination – was so, well, fake," thought Claire. She told herself she would take a rest from her ongoing "performance" as the popular, attractive girl when she went home at Thanksgiving. Until then, she disconnected from the shyer person she was inside and reinvented herself as a campus queen. Happy to be happy, or at least to look happy, Claire moved through her days with apparent ease.

Before long, Thanksgiving break arrived and Claire's C's were still C's. She was in a rut. Out too late and sleep deprived, she planned to catch up with her studies over the break. She didn't let on to her family she didn't have it "all under control." She told herself, "I've got time to do some last minute work." She wouldn't be distracted like she was on campus. But instead of catching up with her assignments, she caught up with high school friends. The lure of late nights over break telling college stories with old friends was too irresistible.

Back at school, Claire was determined to extract some willpower from deep within herself for a last minute push to face finals and maybe make a few B's where the C's had been. Between time with Jacob, going out with Ky, and finding last minute study refuge in the undergraduate library with her cell phone on airplane mode, Claire was getting in study time, but a new anxiety was germinating. She was so far behind, it was too late to read all the material she had missed. The best she could do was skim over PowerPoint slides posted for her classes and hope for the best.

She did catch up on sleep when she was home, but it wasn't long before her now old habit of 4 to 5 hours of sleep per night set in. Exhausted, she drank coffee and sometimes stayed up late studying after seeing Jacob. She dragged herself to class in the morning – once falling asleep during a lecture. Ky happened to be with her and elbowed Claire awake as they sat an embarrassing three rows from the front of the lecture hall. Claire seemed to be slipping, thought Ky. She also noticed Claire was not always up for going out like she had been.

Food became Claire's friend when she studied. She wanted to eat herself into a happier state when she was tired. Plus she was missing out on the fun when she was at the campus library. She suffered anxiety from what is known as FOMO – "fear of missing out" – generated by Snapchat pictures of Ky and other friends enjoying themselves while Claire tried to study. That's where food came in. For a few minutes while studying, she could sink comfortably into a plate of hot French fries from the café. It temporarily made her forget what she was missing.

Occasional social separation from Ky prompted a new anxiety – she had been so enamored with Ky and Jacob and her small group of new friends, she failed to recognize the limited circle she moved in. Sometimes she missed meeting Ky for meals because she was squeezing in study time. Then, alone for meals for the first time, she walked into the cafeteria nearest her dorm, looked around for somebody she knew, and realized everyone was a stranger. "I don't really know anybody here," she thought. A new feeling of increasing regret about the way she had isolated herself with Ky and Jacob was settling in. Never having been depressed, Claire was starting to descend into periods of gray moods. Quite used to masking her feelings from others, she told Ky she was tired. She still tried to act like she was having fun and in control of her life. That was by now a well-honed performance – except for those rare moments, like when she fell asleep in class.

Since maintaining her looks was important, Claire began to find ways to hide her increasing love of comfort food and what she was sure was her increasing stomach size. She was not one to vomit – vomiting after snacking was completely out as an option. The idea disgusted Claire, bordering on *emetaphobia* (a phobia of vomit and vomiting). Plus, she didn't want to be the stereotypical desperate girl "puking her guts out" in secret. Exercise was an option, but when? The easiest solution seemed to be laxatives and diuretics. She was increasingly on the Internet in the library reading blogs and postings about how to manage weight while at college. She readily understood the myth of the *Freshman 15* – gaining 15 pounds the first year of college.

At college, food was available all the time – there was round-the-clock snack food, pizza delivery options, and warm cookies fresh out of the late-night café oven. Skipping meals when not with Ky, to make up for late-night snack eating, was another doable course of action, Claire reasoned. Lots of girls online wrote about their success wrangling their bodies back into control with the strategic use of skimping and skipping meals combined with creative methods of "getting rid of it" – like using diuretics and laxatives. Claire was surely desperate enough to try some of these options even if it meant she would soon be juggling more balls in the air.

In New York City with Ky one weekend, Claire snuck into a Duane Reade drugstore and purchased both diuretics and laxatives. "I might as well do this right," she told herself. As it turned out, Ducolax® was not her friend. Too much and she not only successfully "got rid of it" with diarrhea, but she was also left with intense stomach cramping and dizziness from the resulting dehydration. Aware enough to read up on electrolyte imbalance that could be caused by excess fluid loss, Claire quickly gave up the idea of diuretics and resorted to a milder stimulant laxative so she could sleep at night without being awakened with cramps and the need to find a toilet. Claire settled into a harmful routine of behavior typical of bulimia nervosa. She was happy she found a way to offset nighttime eating for the time being. What Claire didn't realize about laxative use was that, after eating and taking laxatives, laxatives sped up evacuation of her large intestine after most of her nutrient intake was absorbed by her small intestine. Most of what she "got rid of" was water, not nutrients. Nonetheless Claire liked the feeling of a flatter stomach achieved by emptying her large intestine. She told herself that when she caught up with her work at school, she would knock off the laxatives. She was beginning to be disgusted with herself.

Some of the risks of laxative abuse like Claire's are dehydration, hypotension, tachycardia, dizziness, syncope, and, over time, irritation and ulceration of the colon mucosa, pancreatitis, fecal incontinence, steatorrhea (fat in the feces), and kidney damage (Roerig, Steffen, Mitchell & Zunker, 2010). Claire was not aware of the long-term consequences of laxative abuse. Nor might she have cared. Other than avoiding the irritation of painful cramps and feelings of dizziness, Claire was much more motivated by a flat stomach than by avoiding illness resulting from laxative abuse.

How aware was Claire that she was daily sinking herself deeper into an eating disorder? She was, and she wasn't. She knew exactly what she was doing and was deeply ashamed. At the same time, she didn't fully recognize how much trouble she was in physically or psychologically. She had been exposed to eating-disorder education as early as eighth grade, and it did not make a difference (Haltom, Kaiser, & Osgood, 2016). At the same time that she was succumbing to an eating disorder, Claire was patching together desperate attempts to cope with time demands, social demands, and a shortage of internal resources. She lacked the tools she needed to cope more constructively – to just say "No," prioritize, and organize her time. Sometimes she would remember a few rules of healthful eating and promise herself she would eat normally when her life was less chaotic.

All the while, Claire's secret life of weight management – which she saw and experienced as a good way to master her physical appearance – was indeed a secret. And so was the deeper psychological significance of those efforts – secret even to herself. Meals became an internal battleground not shared with anyone – especially not Ky who was still beautiful, smart, and so on top of things Claire couldn't possibly admit a weakness like solo binge eating at night, or laxative use. And she certainly could not admit to herself the deeper significance and meanings related to her eating and purging behaviors (i.e., feeling flawed and not good enough).

At meals with Ky, or Jacob, or both, she ate perfectly normally. Just the right amount of salad at lunch – no croutons, some white-meat chicken, lots of vegetables, and oil and vinegar dressing. At dinner, a chicken breast or fish, a few French fries, salad, and a cookie or two if they were especially fresh and the right kind. For public eating, Claire adopted a motto, "Just the right amount – not too much, not too little." It all looked right, although the truth was, no one in her friend group even cared or noticed how Claire ate. Claire was projecting her fears about an ugly body onto others, so that she imagined others criticizing her body. And simultaneously and unknowingly, through her projection of an ugly body, she was also projecting her belief that it did not measure up to her peers. These projections perpetuated the disconnection from her genuine self and her body – the main aim of an eating disorder.

As she descended further into an eating disorder, Claire began to notice she assessed what everyone else was eating. She remembered what people ate and how much they ate of it. She began to be troubled if someone chose to eat less than she did. She would not want to eat more than what was acceptable. She didn't want to eat too little and appear to be picky like a girl with anorexia. She didn't want to eat too much and thereby appear to be gaining weight, or out of control with her eating. Food eaten was increasingly carefully crafted and mentally measured.

Now that Claire's brain was hijacked by a deepening eating disorder illness – Bulimia Nervosa with purging (*DSM*-5, American Psychiatric Association, 2013) – she increasingly lost control of her obsessions about weight, food calculations, and laxative use. She started to scare herself. The scale told her she was moving up and down the numbers – each day's weight check leading to new anxieties about success or failure with weight management. The numbers led to fluctuations in mood. Success was measured by relatively lower numbers (loss), and failure was indexed by higher-than-yesterday numbers.

Anxiety grew around facing food at each meal. Claire's concentration and attention on other life matters shared space in a brain already crowded with obsessions and calculations of what, when, and where to eat. Clinical depression (Major Depressive Episode, Moderate; *DSM*-5; American Psychiatric Association, 2013), marked by a sense of being overwhelmed, poor stress tolerance, a negative self-concept, irritability, and reduced ability to experience pleasure became an issue.

It was depression that got Claire into treatment. Here is how that happened. Claire wanted to perform better in school, so she approached her psychology professor for advice after class one day. They briefly checked in about her grade and discussed what she would need to do to bring it up. While they were talking, Claire indicated that her grades had fallen off because she wasn't sleeping well and she hadn't felt well. Her professor asked her a few other questions and then asked if she needed help coping with stress. The professor reflected, "It sounds like you're a bit overwhelmed, and it's catching up with you and making you not feel well. Have you thought about talking with someone at the counseling center?" Claire responded with, "Well no, but I guess it might help."

Claire mentioned the idea of counseling to Ky, who was already worried about Claire. She saw Claire staying up late at night trying to study after dates with Jacob, or just struggling with too much homework. She also noticed Claire wasn't eating much and seemed anxious about her weight. Claire made comments like, "Shit – I think the Freshman 15 are happening to me." Ky tried to reassure Claire by telling her she looked great and she wasn't fat. But none of that worked, and Claire kept bringing up the topic. Claire had started asking Ky how much she was exercising, with questions like, "How many Fitbit steps did you take today?" Ky wasn't sure why this mattered to Claire, but she sensed some kind of competition she wasn't comfortable with. "I don't know," Ky responded. Altogether, Ky was happy Claire might go for counseling. She tried to persuade her, "Yeah – I know you don't have time to go to the health clinic, but maybe they can give you medication or something to help you sleep. I wasn't supposed to say anything, but Jacob asked me if you were OK. I think you should go." Claire was embarrassed that Jacob had commented. She would go to counseling, but told Ky not to tell Jacob.

Claire worked up the courage to call CAPS. CAPS, or Counseling and Psychological Services, is a type of counseling center found on most college campuses. The truth was, Claire was exhausted. Otherwise she would have postponed reaching out for help a while longer, because that's what happens with most teens who are under the spell of an eating disorder – they have just enough energy to keep up appearances and maintain their hidden behaviors. Fortunately, Claire couldn't manage that any longer.

Claire's intake appointment at CAPS was embarrassing for her, but the direct questions the social worker asked were hard to skirt. A depression assessment using the Beck Depression Inventory-II (BDI-II; Beck, Steer, & Brown, 1996) revealed significant clinical depression without suicidal ideation. The counselor identified lots of pessimism, self-loathing, lethargy, and periods of feeling "wired and tired." Unfortunately, because she was filled with shame, Claire revealed nothing about her eating problems during her intake appointment. Besides, Claire believed that if she got more sleep and felt more on top of her life, she would stop her weird eating habits.

At a CAPS follow-up appointment, Claire's intake therapist, Todd, asked her about her sleeping and eating habits. Embedded in the questions were questions from the SCOFF (a screening tool for eating disorders; Morgan, Reid, & Lacey, 2000):[1] "Do you make yourself sick when you feel uncomfortably full?" Claire answered, "No – I hate vomiting." The therapist continued, "Do you worry that you've lost control over how much you eat?" "Well, sometimes," answered Claire. "Have you lost more than 14 pounds in the past 3 months?" "I'm not anorexic if that's what you mean." "Do you believe yourself to be fat when others say you're too thin?" "I think I could have a problem there," Claire admitted. "Would you say that food dominates your life?" Claire felt defensive, "I think a lot about food, but I'm not obsessed."

Todd was seasoned at working with college populations where the risk for eating disorders tends to be higher than in any other age group (reviewed in Hoek & van Hoeken, 2003; see also Eisenberg, Nicklett, Roeder, & Kirz, 2011). He asked Claire more questions like, "Can you tell me more about your eating habits." Claire was reluctant to answer because she, like many college students, was completely aware that a psychotherapist might be snooping around for an eating disorder, especially since she was a female college student. And Todd was aware she would likely be reluctant. Upon being questioned about her eating habits, Claire responded with a little flare of anger, "What do you mean? I definitely eat." Todd responded with, "Maybe we can start with you telling me what you eat in a typical day – walk me through your last day starting with the last time you ate." As Claire responded to Todd's concrete question, she revealed more about her eating patterns. Todd was building rapport with Claire, working hard not to judge her behavior so she would feel free to talk. And he recognized signs of possible eating-disordered behaviors – skipped meals, intermittent weight loss and weight gain, guilt about eating, and excessive worry about healthy eating. He said to her, "It sounds like you're tired, stressed, overwhelmed, and getting more preoccupied with eating and how your body looks."

Using techniques of Motivational Interviewing (Miller & Rollnick, 1991), Todd helped Claire identify some of her values and goals in college and, in doing so, tied in ways by which better nutrition might help her reach her objectives. Todd knew evidence-based treatments for disordered eating called for specialized training and usually involved a treatment team, including nutrition counseling and medical oversight, as well as mental health services. (Research has shown that a team approach to treating college eating disorders results in students staying in therapy longer and ending therapy in a planned manner; Mitchell, Klein, & Maduramente, 2015.) Todd contacted a colleague, Amina, at CAPS who not only specialized in eating-disorder treatment, but also could address Claire's clinical depression and increasing anxiety. Todd explained his treatment recommendation to Claire, and she was internally transferred to Amina.

Right away Claire recognized that Amina understood her eating issues by the questions she asked. "Do you experience anxiety when faced with food? Do you feel out of control of your eating? Do you eat secretively? Do you feel guilty after you eat? Do you find yourself comparing your body size to others'? What percent of your waking hours do you think about food, weight, and how you assess your body size and shape?" Claire responded, "Yes, yes, yes, yes, and yes" to the first five questions. With regard to waking hours spent obsessing, her answer was "about three-quarters of the time." Claire wasn't sure she could trust Amina, but Amina seemed to understand her internal landscape.

Amina explained she had gathered referral information from Todd. She repeated administration of the BDI-II (Beck et al., 1996), given to Claire by Todd 2 weeks earlier. Amina needed to know how Claire's depression level compared. Because results showed Claire was more depressed on the second test administration, Amina referred Claire to an on-campus psychiatrist for an antidepressant-medication evaluation.

There was something about discussing the eating disorder and her stress that helped Claire connect to her own internal pain – depressing, but important. She knew that what she was doing to keep her life balanced wasn't working, so she was ready to get help. Like so many people with eating disorders, Claire wanted freedom from obsessing about food, but, at the same time, she wanted to recover "only if I don't have to gain weight." Amina expected this dilemma initially. She knew she would have to help Claire gradually move away from her concern about weight and, instead, learn to focus on normal eating and the emotional underpinnings of the eating disorder. Claire was routed to an on-campus nutritionist, as well as a nurse practitioner, both of whom had specialized training in eating disorders and both of whom had already worked on a treatment team with Amina. All three treatment professionals began to collaborate in order to move Claire toward recovery.

At first, Claire was disarmed. She was overwhelmed with even more appointments. She reluctantly complied with a medical evaluation. She was a bit anemic, with slight electrolyte abnormalities from her use of laxatives. Claire found the feedback about the state of her body helpful. She tried to disregard her weight concerns and even opted for "blind weights" (being weighed during medical evaluations without being told the numbers) for a while in treatment. She did this so she could detach herself from the numbers-on-the-scale game that so often kept her anxious. With Amina's encouragement, Claire gave up her Fitbit for the same reason – the number of calories burned or steps taken had become too anxiety provoking in her obsessive pursuit of weight management. The numbers on the scale or Fitbit had become a measure of her self-worth. Then they became the barometer of her mood. The goal of therapy was to help reconnect her with her internal barometer – emotional and bodily states that signal her genuine needs and feelings.

As it turned out, Claire was working against the odds by seeking help with Todd, and then Amina and her treatment team. Research has shown that anywhere from 8% to 21% of college students struggle with eating disorders (Eisenberg, Nicklett, Roeder, & Kirz, 2011; Tavolacci et al., 2015). Yet Eisenberg et al. found that of the 13.5% of college women who screened positive for eating disorders in their sample, only 20% received previous-year mental-health treatment. Further, Tavolacci et al. found a significant relationship between the presence of eating disorders in female college students and depression, stress, alcohol abuse, and cyber-addiction. Those were trends that Amina had seen in many patients, including Claire.

In addition to having Bulimia Nervosa, being clinically depressed, stressed, tired, and overwhelmed, Claire also abused alcohol. Although she hadn't come to college with the intention to drink every day, that's how it was turning out as she went with the flow of what seemed fun in the moment. Over time, binge eating, purging, and alcohol helped quell her anxiety and regulate her mood. She and Ky frequently mixed their late-night socializing with multiple drinks, often combining beer and hard liquor. Claire didn't drink when not out with friends. But when she was out she binge drank – at least five drinks in an evening, many more on weekends. The thought of not drinking when out with friends was not even a possibility in either Claire's or Ky's minds. It was a given. Claire tried to drink less on nights she was going to study after coming home. She found it was too hard to work when she was still fuzzy from alcohol. She looked forward to weekends – which usually started on Thursdays – when she rationalized that she didn't have to think as much about studying.

Amina screened Claire for alcohol abuse with questions like, "How often do you drink in a typical week?" and "How many drinks do you consume in an average drinking event?" She used a shortened version of the College Alcohol Problem Scale – Revised (O'Hare, 1997; Maddock, Laforge, Rossi, & O'Hare, 2001), a commonly used screening tool for problem college drinking (Winters et al., 2011). Amina asked Claire how often, as a result of drinking alcohol in the past 3 months, she had unplanned sex ("three to five times"), failed to use protection when having sex ("one or two times"), felt bad about herself ("10 or more times"), and felt sad, blue, or depressed ("10 or more times") – and more. Claire hadn't really considered alcohol an issue. Clearly it was.

Claire fit the norm for heavy problem drinking found on many college campuses (Hingson & White, 2012). She also fit an observed pattern of the interrelationship between problem drinking and depression symptoms during the first year of college (Geisner, Mallett, & Kilmer, 2012). Amina knew she would need to move Claire toward harm reduction with alcohol consumption, so she paired brief alcohol reduction treatment with an eating disorder focus. She was aware that if drinking reduction could not be achieved quickly, drinking would both compromise the focus on depression and bulimia and mean Amina would need to adjunctively assign Claire to an outside alcohol and drug program for further evaluation and treatment.

The good news was Claire was not experiencing blackouts. She was motivated to feel better, so she was willing to try – not eliminating alcohol consumption – but reducing it. This was especially important because alcohol can increase symptoms of anxiety and depression. Further, Claire was recommended for anti-depressant medication, which is contraindicated with alcohol use. Alcohol combined with antidepressants can cause greater impairment of judgment and motor coordination than alcohol alone. In addition, substance abuse of any kind is an indicator of poor outcomes for most mental health treatment. Although not drinking was the preferred outcome, Amina knew stopping under-age, illegal drinking was not even on the table for Claire. Her friends drank. College kids often drink, even if there are negative consequences. Drunken selfies at parties, declaring oneself an "alchie," or being a beer pong champ are coveted trophies of a good night out. So Amina knew Claire would continue to drink, but Claire agreed to drink less. Amina worked with Claire over time to move closer to two drinks in a night when out with friends. She explained to Claire that her ability to control her drinking was a prerequisite for psychotherapy success.

Ultimately, Claire received the following diagnoses: Bulimia Nervosa, Moderate; Alcohol Use Disorder, Mild; and Major Depressive Disorder, Moderate, Recurrent (*DSM*-5; American Psychiatric Association, 2013). For individual therapy, Amina worked with Claire, as did Todd, using Motivational Interviewing (Miller & Rollnik, 1991). Since treatment of eating disorders is not a one-size-fits-all endeavor, treatment professionals like Amina often develop the skill to use multiple treatment tools, which is why she also utilized Interpersonal Psychotherapy (IPT; Cuijpers et al., 2011; Cuijpers et al., 2016; Klerman, Dimascio, Weissman, Prusoff, & Paykel, 1974; Klerman & Weisman, 1993; Mufson, 2004; Weissman, Markowitz, & Klerman, 2000). IPT is well suited to on-campus mental-health services, because it can be completed in 3 to 4 months – the general length of a semester. IPT is one of many evidence-based treatments for depression, anxiety, or bulimia, or some combination of these symptoms. It is a brief, attachment-focused psychotherapy that has been successfully applied to depression and eating disorders. It focuses on the interpersonal context(s) found to precipitate and maintain an individual's mental health disorders.

IPT centers on resolving interpersonal problems and achieves symptomatic recovery by following a structured and time-limited approach. In particular, research has shown IPT to be useful for preventing more severe, major depression in adolescents (Horowitz, Garber, Ciesla, Young, & Mufson, 2007). Most importantly, IPT has been shown to have significant effects on bulimia (Agras, Walsh, Fairburn, Wilson, & Kraemer, 2000; Fairburn, Jones, Peveler, Hope, & O'Connor, 1993; Murphy, Straebler, Basden, Cooper, & Fairburn, 2012). Although it is generally considered a second-choice therapy for those with eating disorders compared to Cognitive Behavior Therapy – Enhanced (e.g., it takes a bit longer than CBT to effect change; CBT-E; Fairburn et al., 2015), for Amina, IPT fit Claire's issues well.

When Claire began college, she had no previous history of an eating disorder, depression, or substance-abuse issues. She experienced a difficult transition to college. She had moved away from home, entered into her first significant romantic partnership, faced a challenging college curriculum, and begun a pattern of episodic alcohol abuse. After the onset of clinical depression, the symptoms of depression boomeranged back to interfere with Claire's interpersonal relationships. No longer energetic enough to keep up with Ky, she was anxious about her future. She felt pessimistic about herself, and her confidence in living up to being Jacob's partner was eroding. At one point Claire said to Ky, "I don't think I'm going to make it. I might have to go home. I think I'm going crazy or something." She was overwhelmed, tired, and far too obsessed about body image, food, and weight to think clearly.

Claire's movement into a full-blown eating disorder during the course of her freshman year was a reflection of her relatively poor adjustment to college. In 2016, Haltom and two associates (Kaiser & Osgood) examined the relationship between college-lifestyle variables and a drive for thinness, bulimia, and body dissatisfaction among 324 college students (male and female), as measured by the Eating Disorder Inventory-3 (EDI-3; Garner, 2004). Among freshmen, there was a significant *decrease* in bulimia scores between early in the first semester and later in the same semester (Haltom et al., 2016). By contrast, Claire's level of bulimic symptoms *increased* over the semester.

Nevertheless, Claire shared several lifestyle characteristics with Haltom et al.'s (2016) study participants. Claire was skipping meals on a regular basis and developed bulimia nervosa. Similarly, Haltom et al. found that the fewer meals eaten in a day during college, the more likely students were to struggle with a drive for thinness and body dissatisfaction. Claire regularly visited pages on Facebook, Instagram, and related websites that basically promoted eating disorders by glamorizing dieting, exercise, and a hyper-thin appearance. Haltom et al.'s data showed that for college females there was a significant positive relationship between (a) exposure to social media about eating disorders, eating, or weight-related topics, *and* (b) their drive for thinness, body dissatisfaction, and bulimia.

When Amina asked Claire whether she had looked at websites or social media sites that "talked about ways to be thin," Claire answered with a reluctant "Yes." Evidence shows that online exposure to pro-eating-disorder material decreases a sense of subjective well-being (Turja et al., 2017) and is associated with eating-disorder pathology (Peebles et al., 2012; Rodgers, Lowy, Halperin, & Franko, 2016). With this in mind, Amina actively discouraged Claire from this kind of online activity. For Claire, this meant stopping something she had only recently started – staring at *thinspirational* images of bony or thin women in order to fuel her desire to lose weight. In fact, Claire found the more she looked at these images, the more she wished for the day when she could post pictures of herself in a thinned-down state. No doubt her online thinspiration activity was hurtling her further into the world of eating disorders.

Haltom et al. (2016) found that for college females, there was a significant positive relationship between having conversations with people in the past month about weight, shape, or body size *and* their drive for thinness, body dissatisfaction, and bulimia. Consistent with these findings, Ky was beside herself with frustration when Claire repeatedly expressed worry about her weight and shape, sought reassurance about her body size, and wanted to compare their levels of exercise. Ky thought Claire was obsessed and she wanted no part of it. She was happy to talk to Claire about other topics. But conversations about other topics were becoming rare. Either Claire didn't want to talk much, or she wanted to fret about her body and her exhaustion. Interestingly, with regard to general socializing, Haltom et al. found the fewer hours spent interacting face-to-face with people, the more likely women were to have a negative body image, overeat, or emotionally eat. Similarly, as Claire's social connections with others dropped off and her preoccupation with eating and weight intensified, she drifted further into a pattern of binge-eating and purge behaviors.

Haltom et al. (2016) found for both college females and males there was no significant relationship between education about eating disorders during college *and* drive for thinness, body dissatisfaction, and bulimia. Even though Claire had learned about eating disorders in health class in high school and in her college psychology class there was a disconnection between what she knew about the negative consequences of eating disorders and her own issues with bulimia nervosa. She suffered shame and embarrassment about binge eating and her use of compensatory laxatives. She could quote chapter and verse about the negative consequences of eating disorders for others, but when it came to preventing her own progression into the same illness – an illness she had both studied and felt deep compassion for in others – she seemed unable to stop herself. The eating disorder thrived on her blaming and hating herself for having succumbed. The truth was she never asked for the eating disorder and she was not to blame.

With regard to Claire's psychotherapy treatment, IPT helped her identify and resolve targeted interpersonal problems, linking them to past and present relationships, as well as to current symptoms of depression and bulimia. In 2011, Whight et al. manualized the treatment (IPT-BN [m]), helping psychotherapists by giving them a standard progression of treatment-intervention steps to follow. Consistent with IPT, Amina first worked to establish a friendly, warm, and trusting relationship with Claire. She created an atmosphere of assurance and a therapy norm of collaboration about treatment goals (Lipsitz & Markowitz, 2013).

Following IPT-BN (m) protocol, Amina began with basic psychoeducation about bulimia nervosa and depression, clarifying and reflecting back to Claire her relatively recent history of depressed moods, binge eating, use of laxatives, and periodic restricting in efforts to manage weight. Along the way, Amina explained to Claire how common bulimia nervosa was among college students. Doing so helped normalize Claire's eating-disorder issues and dismantle her deep well of shame about bulimia.

For example, Amina said to Claire, "Many college students struggle with bulimia and anywhere from 10 to 20% struggle with some kind of eating disorder. Not everyone steps forward for treatment, so you are courageous to have done so." Claire responded with, "I just want to stop so I can get my life back. I'm wasting so much time on this thing. It sucks the air out of me." Amina empathized, "I understand. You sound frustrated. I hear that you are very motivated to stop obsessing. You want to wrestle precious time and energy back from the eating disorder so you can focus on friendships and study efficiently. I hear that you understand that if the eating disorder is allowed to hang on, it will be very difficult for you to reach your goals." Amina added principles of Motivational Interviewing (Miller & Rollnick, 1991) here to help resolve any ambivalence Claire might have about beating the bulimia.

Next Amina explained to Claire why she had decided to treat her problems using Interpersonal Psychotherapy adapted for bulimia spectrum disorders (Whight et al., 2011). She explained, "IPT allows us to focus on the relationship between troubled patterns in your interpersonal networks and out-of-control eating, using laxatives, and restricting meals." Claire agreed to keep a daily diary of binge eating and laxative-use to help her be accountable to herself and her treatment team and to help her find links between eating behaviors and interpersonal stressors. She also agreed, with the support of her nutritionist, to a structured eating plan of three meals a day plus three snacks roughly evenly spread throughout the day. Even if Claire had a difficult week between appointments, Amina made sure to remain hopeful, supportive, and focused on therapy goals.

In keeping with IPT-BN (Whight et al., 2011), Amina gathered information about Claire's family and their interaction patterns as she prepared to help Claire tie in the development of the eating disorder. Looking back into her history of interpersonal relationships, Claire recalled her mom worried about Claire's tendency to stick with one friend and not date. Sarah said things to Claire in the past like, "I really like Eve – why don't you make some other friends as well – maybe you lack self-confidence." Claire explained that while she felt like she might have failed her mother's expectations for her social life, she also thought her mother was right. She really did want more friends. She had always wanted to be popular and have a boyfriend like other girls, but somehow that didn't happen in high school. Reflecting on her relationship with her mom during her teen years, Claire revealed, "I used to be furious at my mother for criticizing me about something so sensitive for me – how many friends I had and how much time I spent with them. I hated it when Mom bothered me about that."

Throughout psychotherapy, prompted by Amina, Claire learned to describe patterns in her relationships with her parents, her brother, Ky, and a handful of other important people. Most importantly, she learned to describe related emotions and link the interpersonal patterns and emotions to her eating-disorder symptoms. For example, Amina asked Claire to recount a recent incident where she had binged and used laxatives. Claire told Amina about a few nights before when she had been drinking with Jacob. "I had a test the next day. I left Jacob's room that night and went to the library. On the way, I can't believe it but I ordered three large slices of pizza at the lunch truck." She laughed as she recounted sneaking the pizza slices into her backpack as she moved through the halls of the library until she found a far, private corner. She remembered, "When I was out of sight from anyone else in the library I ate the pizza so fast it was like I inhaled it! I was just trying to calm my nerves so I could study."

With Amina's prompting, Claire recognized how the plan for this particular binge had fomented long before her late-night trip to the library. She recalled earlier moments in the day when she restricted her lunch to make room for, if not enhance, the rewarding binge she planned for that night. Further, she disclosed she had taken laxatives both the night before and the night of the binge. Amina, moving Claire toward the interpersonal context in which bulimia occurred, asked about her relationships with the people she had been out with on the night of the binge. Remembering that she had been out with Jacob before going to the library she said, " I was worried, like most nights, that my need to study was getting in the way of my time with Jacob. And I wanted to spend time with Ky that night, too, but I couldn't. I am so behind with my papers and studying. The pizza made it better for a while anyway. But then I felt so guilty afterwards, all I could think about was taking laxatives to get rid of it. Then I had trouble concentrating on my work." As she talked with Amina, Claire recognized the complicated web of eating-disorder thoughts, anxieties, and behaviors that typically riddled her day and caused her to increasingly disconnect from her genuine feelings and needs and those she cared about.

Through the use of IPT, Amina helped Claire focus on aspects of her transition to college that lay at the core of her current eating-disorder issues. Claire felt pressured to expand her social horizons at college and to look good while doing it. So when Ky came along and they got along well, she jumped on the chance to start a new, more active social life. She pushed herself into new friendships without considering balance and taking adequate care of herself. For Claire, there were clear links between interpersonal events and the onset of depression and bulimia nervosa.

Starting college, Claire overwhelmed herself and lost control. She attempted to regain a semblance of order in her life using emotion-numbing, self-destructive, weight-management behaviors. In the process of psychotherapy with Amina and her treatment team she came to terms with the devastating impact of depression and bulimia on her life. Amina helped Claire give herself permission to temporarily adopt a "sick role," encouraging her to name the illnesses that she struggled with and give herself space and time to heal. Claire learned to set better boundaries with Jacob. She took charge of both her drinking and her time with him. She came to terms with her over-dependency on Ky and Jacob. She realized she needed to spread her dependencies across a wider range of people.

Claire built on her close connection with Ky. Instead of isolating and keeping shameful secrets, Claire trusted Ky enough to confide in her about her eating and body-image struggles. She took a risk that paid off. Ky stepped forward with increased investment in her friendship with Claire. Claire saw that Ky was naïve about eating disorders, so she taught Ky how to better support her recovery – for example, how to support her at meals and how to avoid those dreaded conversations about weight, body size, and shape.

Claire also learned that deep down she was grieving her loss of family connections vis-à-vis living away from home for the first time. She missed talking with her mom every day and she missed her little brother. Claire reached out to her mother for support. Not surprisingly, Sarah rushed to websites like F.E. A.S.T. (Families Empowered and Supporting Treatment of Eating Disorders; F.E.A.S.T., n.d.) and NEDA (National Eating Disorders Association; NEDA, 2016) in an effort to support her daughter. She entered into online exchanges with other parents who were similarly trying to support their older children in recovery. Frightened at first, Sarah wanted to lecture Claire and fix her daughter's issues. Instead she did a laudable job of supporting and encouraging her.

Claire's eating-disorder urges and behaviors were a way to cope with strong feelings in her troubled interpersonal relationships. Her alcohol abuse reflected her fear that she would be no fun if she did not binge drink. As Claire increased her ability to navigate and build her interpersonal network, she reduced her dependency on bulimic behaviors and alcohol. She began by weaning herself from laxative use. She was tempted to restrict how much food she ate to compensate for not using laxatives to control her weight, but she recognized this was a shell game in which she took a win – "got rid of the laxatives" – at the expense of a loss – "kept myself in the eating disorder by just finding another way to offset calories – by restricting." Claire gradually tackled laxative use, eating restrictions, and binge-eating behavior by focusing on normal eating. She adjusted to three balanced meals a day with afternoon and evening snacks.

During her treatment, Claire was afraid to eat normal food and give up eating-disorder behaviors because she was sure she would gain weight. The blowback from the eating disorder to not give up her enslavement to it was considerable. Eating disorders are possessive – they want to own their hosts. Facing down the storm of anxiety and anger from the eating disorder took repeated courage. Every meal Claire planned met with mixed reviews from within. She trudged on – sometimes two steps forward one step back. For example, she was afraid to eat breakfast alone in an empty dining hall – "No one eats breakfast at my school!" That fear was relieved when Ky offered to support her by joining her early in the morning in the dining hall. It was an act of caring Claire would always remember. Ky was a good friend. Claire's other fears were relieved with time and proof that life would be okay without the eating disorder.

Question

My daughter is eager to begin college. She had an eating disorder in high school and is struggling to maintain recovery. We are concerned about her starting college in a few months. Should we assume she will improve in college with a fresh start and more independence?

Answer

People sometimes believe that independence in college and a new start away from old stressors and old "people, places, and things" will improve an eating disorder. Unfortunately, this is not true. Eating disorders are illnesses that tend to linger even in a new environment, or with novel distractions. They require focused and sustained attention to remit. Success in recovery often depends on the nearby support of family, friends, and providers who are specialty-trained in eating disorders. Using new coping strategies to replace reliance on disordered eating takes motivation, dedication, time, and practice. Success with new coping strategies, including well-established healthy eating, needs to be firmly in place before venturing to college. Otherwise the stressors that come with the new environments at school will quickly overrun fragile, newly acquired coping skills. Under pressure, the tendency is to fall back on old eating-disorder patterns. Those in recovery need to be ready to effectively meet this challenge.

In college, 100% of meals and all exercise are unsupervised. A prospective college student needs a substantial period of autonomous eating and moderate exercise at home to demonstrate her or his ability to maintain healthy eating and body composition. Treatment professionals are in a good position to judge readiness for college based on assessment over time of nutrition maintenance, psychological readiness, and medical stability prior to college. If a college-age student is not able to achieve and sustain recovery, it may be best to delay college admission and continue treatment at home. Alternatively, gradual transition to college may occur by taking one or more courses, or attending a community college while living at home. Then, when the student demonstrates an ability to meet the rigors of college study, she or he may successfully transfer to residential college living.

When a student is ready for college, it is important for patients and their families to assess the availability of specialized follow-up treatment either in the new college community, or, preferably, at the college health-services facilities. Follow up with nutrition, mental health, and medical services is critical. Once begun, those services can decrease in frequency as recovery is achieved and solidified over time. It is essential to make college health services aware of a student's eating-disorder history before arrival. College health-service providers will need health and treatment records for effective follow-up. Furthermore, a signed consent giving parents and home treatment professionals access to college providers is important for continuity of care – both for successful transition to and from college and to address any health decline.

Question

I am starting college in the fall, and I am concerned about weight gain. My new school has great food available at all hours of the day. What can I do to avoid fabled freshman weight gain?

Answer

College represents a huge change in the old ways of eating. Foods and places and times for eating often vary from day to day, especially in the beginning, as new eating environments are explored. This is a time in life when being open to new experiences is exhilarating and challenging. Being obsessed about weight and size will hopefully not be a priority when so much else is available to investigate.

Keep in mind that weight may fluctuate related to changed living habits and experimenting with new foods. This is normal. Take small weight changes in stride. Eventually, more stable exercise and eating habits will take hold. Remain positive. Poor eating habits resulting from attempts to diet and compensate for guilt-ridden pleasure eating can lead to unhealthy weight fluctuations that are stubborn and difficult to correct. Avoid dietary restraints such as skimping and skipping meals, diets, and restriction from classes and types of food that carry a negative judgment ("junk food," "unhealthy food"). The old adage of three balanced meals a day with intermittent snacks carefully spread evenly across waking hours is a good guideline. This helps prevent binge eating and maintains energy throughout the day. Consuming a wide variety of foods in moderation at intervals throughout the day makes the most sense.

Question

Binge eating in college seems to be almost normal, just like binge alcohol consumption. What are some tips for avoiding or correcting binge eating in college?

Answer

Eating celebratory snacks in college is common (a) after a hard night's studying, (b) when taking a social break, (c) after a night of social activity, or (d) just because you are bored. No longer restricted to the family home's kitchen, students now have many sources for some of the tastiest snack foods. They are available at late-night restaurants, from food trucks, or by delivery. It is easy to allow food to be a reward, a comfort, or the central feature of a social gathering. College provides an environment in which disordered-eating behaviors, like binge eating, are normalized, if not encouraged.

Occasional pleasure eating and experimenting with enjoyable foods are not problems. However, approximately 7.8% of college students in the US struggle with a full-blown binge-eating disorder (Filipova & Stoffel, 2016). This compares with prevalence rates of 3.5% for women and 2% of men (Hudson, Hiripi, Pope, & Dessler, 2007) across all age groups. Similarly, Stice, Marti, and Rohde (2013) found that the highest risk period for developing Binge Eating Disorder (*DSM*-5; American Psychiatric Association, 2013) for females is ages 18 to 20. When binge eating becomes problematic, just like in the case of Claire, classroom productivity, daily activity, and health are all negatively affected (Filipova & Stoffel, 2016).

Several risk factors have been found to be related to binge eating in college. Students who engage in less physical activity and sleep fewer than 6 hours a night are at greater risk (Filipova & Stoffel, 2016). Staying socially connected, getting enough sleep every night, and engaging in a moderate amount of high intensity physical activity (over 75 minutes per week) will help lessen the chances of troublesome binge eating.

Ample evidence stresses the importance of learning emotional-regulation skills to manage binge eating. Years of research found a strong relationship between emotional dysregulation and binge-eating problems (Eichen, Chen, Boutelle, & McCloskey, 2017). Eating to cope with distress and intense emotions helps distract us from realities we don't want to face. The reward centers in our brains are stimulated by food and are thus afforded momentary, pleasurable escape. Even though this experience is often followed by pain and shame, the cycle of coping with food continues and can become habitual. The solution is to figure out what our needs are and to find effective ways other than eating to meet those needs. Joining a Dialectical Behavior Therapy skills training group (Wallace, Masson, Safer, & von Ranson, 2014) or learning cognitive behavior therapy skills for regulating emotions can help prevent and manage binge eating.

Note

1 SCOFF (the name comes from the questions)
- Do you make yourself **S**ick because you feel uncomfortably full?
- Do you worry that you have lost **C**ontrol over how much you eat?
- Have you recently lost more than **O**ne stone (14 lb.) in a 3-month period?
- Do you believe yourself to be **F**at when others say you are too thin?
- Would you say that **F**ood dominates your life?

References

Agras, W. S., Walsh, B. T., Fairburn, C. G., Wilson, G. T., & Kraemer, H. C. (2000). A multicenter comparison of cognitive-behavioral therapy and interpersonal psychotherapy for bulimia nervosa. *Archives of General Psychiatry*, 57(5), 459–466.

American Psychiatric Association. (2013). *Diagnostic and statistical manual* (5th ed.). Washington, DC: Author.

Beck, A. T., Steer, R. A., & Brown, G. K. (1996). *Manual for the Beck Depression Inventory-II*. San Antonio, TX: Psychological.

Cuijpers, P., Donker, T., Weissman, M. M., Ravitz, P., Ioana, A., & Cristea, I. A. (2016). Interpersonal psychotherapy for mental health problems: A comprehensive meta-analysis. *American Journal of Psychiatry*, 173(7), 680–687.

Cuijpers, P., Geraedts, A. S., van Oppen, P., Andersson, G., Markowitz, J. C., & van Straten, A. (2011). Interpersonal psychotherapy for depression: A meta-analysis. *American Journal of Psychiatry*, 168(6), 581–592.

Eichen, D. M., Chen, E., Boutelle, K. N., & McCloskey, M. S. (2017). Behavioral evidence of emotion dysregulation in binge eaters. *Appetite*, 111, 1–6.

Eisenberg, D., Nicklett, E. J., Roeder, K., & Kirz, N. E. (2011). Eating disorder symptoms among college students: Prevalence, persistence, correlates, and treatment-seeking. *Journal of American College Health*, 59(8), 700–707.

F.E.A.S.T. (n.d.) Families empowered and supporting treatment of eating disorders. Retrieved from www.feast-ed.org

Fairburn, C. G., Bailey-Straebler, S., Basden, S., Doll, H. A., Jones, R., Murphy, R., … Cooper, Z. (2015). A transdiagnostic comparison of enhanced cognitive behaviour therapy (CBT-E) and interpersonal psychotherapy in the treatment of eating disorders. *Behaviour Research and Therapy*, 70(1), 64–71.

Fairburn, C. G., Jones, R., Peveler, R. C., Hope, R. A., & O'Connor, M. (1993). Psychotherapy and bulimia nervosa: Longer-term effects of interpersonal psychotherapy, behavior therapy, and cognitive behavior therapy. *Archives of General Psychiatry*, 50(6), 419–428.

Filipova, A. A., & Stoffel, C. L. (2016). The prevalence of binge eating disorder and its relationship to work and classroom productivity and activity impairment. *Journal of American College Health*, 64(5), 349–361.

Garner, D. M. (2004). *Eating disorder inventory-3 (EDI-3). Professional manual.* Odessa, FL: Psychological Assessment Resources.

Geisner, I. M., Mallett, K., & Kilmer, J. R. (2012). An examination of depressive symptoms and drinking patterns in first year college students. *Issues in Mental Health Nursing*, 33(5), 280–287.

Haltom, C., Kaiser, E., & Osgood, L. (2016). Relationship between college lifestyle variables and drive for thinness, bulimia, and body dissatisfaction as measured by the Eating Disorder Inventory-3. Unpublished raw data.

Hingson, R. W., & White, A. M. (2012). Prevalence and consequences of college student alcohol use. In C. J. Correia, J. G. Murphy, & N. P. Barnett (Eds.), *College student alcohol abuse: A guide to assessment, intervention, and prevention.* Hoboken, NJ: Wiley.

Hoek, H. W., & van Hoeken, D. (2003). Review of the prevalence and incidence of eating disorders. *International Journal of Eating Disorders*, 34(4), 383–396.

Horowitz, J. L., Garber, J., Ciesla, J. A., Young, J. F., & Mufson, L. (2007). Prevention of depressive symptoms in adolescents: A randomized trial of cognitive-behavioral and interpersonal prevention programs. *Journal of Consulting and Clinical Psychology*, 75(5), 693–706.

Hudson, J. I., Hiripi, E., Pope, H. G., Jr., & Dessler, R. C. (2007). The prevalence and correlates of eating disorders in the national comorbidity survey replication. *Biological Psychiatry*, 61(3), 348–358.

Klerman, G. L., & Weissman, M. M. (1993). *New applications of interpersonal psychotherapy.* Washington, DC: American Psychiatric Press.

Klerman, G. L., Dimascio, A., Weissman, M., Prusoff, B., & Paykel, E. S. (1974). Treatment of depression by drugs and psychotherapy. *American Journal of Psychiatry*, 131(2), 186–191.

Lipsitz, J. D., & Markowitz, J. C. (2013). Mechanisms of change in Interpersonal Therapy (IPT). *Clinical Psychology Review*, 33(8), 1134–1147.

Maddock, J. E., Laforge, R. G., Rossi, J. S., & O'Hare, T. (2001). The College Alcohol Problems Scale. *Addictive Behaviors*, 26(3), 385–398.

Miller, W. R., & Rollnick, S. (1991). *Motivational interviewing: Preparing people for change.* New York, NY: Guilford Press.

Mitchell, S. L., Klein, J., & Maduramente, A. (2015). Assessing the impact of an eating disorders treatment team approach with college students. *Journal of Eating Disorders*, 23(1), 45–59.

Morgan, J. F., Reid, F., & Lacey, J. H. (2000). The SCOFF questionnaire: A new screening tool for eating disorders. *Western Journal of Medicine*, 17(3), 164–165.

Mufson, L. (2004). *Interpersonal psychotherapy for depressed adolescents* (2nd ed.). New York, NY: Guilford Press.

Murphy, R., Straebler, S., Basden, S., Cooper, Z., & Fairburn, C. G. (2012). Interpersonal psychotherapy for eating disorders. *Clinical Psychology & Psychotherapy*, 19, 150–158.

NEDA. (2016). National Eating Disorders Association. Retrieved from www.nationaleatingdisorders.org

O'Hare, T. (1997). Measuring problem drinking in first time offenders: Development and validation of the College Alcohol Problem Scale (CAPS). *Journal of Substance Abuse Treatment*, 14(4), 383–387.

Peebles, R., Wilson, J. L., Litt, I. F., Hardy, K. K., Lock, J. D., Mann, J. R., & Borzekowski, D. L. (2012). Disordered eating in a digital age: Eating behaviors, health, and quality of life in users of websites with pro-eating disorder content. *Journal of Medical Internet Research*, 14(5), e148.

Rodgers, R. F., Lowy, A. S., Halperin, D. M., & Franko, D. L. (2016). A meta-analysis examining the influence of pro-eating disorder websites on body image and eating pathology. *European Eating Disorders Review*, 24(1), 3–8.

Roerig, J. L., Steffen, K. J., Mitchell, J. E., & Zunker, C. (2010). Laxative abuse: Epidemiology, diagnosis, and management. *Drugs*, 70(12), 1487–1503.

Stice, E., Marti, C. N., & Rohde, P. (2013). Prevalence, incidence, impairment, and course of the proposed *DSM*-5 eating disorder diagnoses in an 8-year prospective community study of young women . *Journal of Abnormal Psychology*, 122(2), 445–457.

Tavolacci, M. P., Grigioni, S., Richard, L., Meyrignac, G., Dechelotte, P., & Ladner, J. (2015). Eating disorders and associated health risks among university students. *Journal of Nutrition Education and Behavior*, 47(5), 412–420.

Turja, T., Oksanen, A., Kaakinen, M., Sirola, A., Kaltiala-Heino, R. & Räsänen, P. (2017). Proeating disorder websites and subjective well-being: A four-country study on young people. *International Journal of Eating Disorders*, 50, 50–57.

Wallace, L. M., Masson, P. C., Safer, D. L., & von Ranson, K. M. (2014). Change in emotion regulation during the course of treatment predicts binge abstinence in guided self-help dialectical behavior therapy for binge eating disorder. *Journal of Eating Disorders*, 2(1), 35.

Weissman, M. M., Markowitz, J. C., & Klerman, G. (2000). *Comprehensive guide to interpersonal psychotherapy*. New York, NY: Basic Books.

Whight, D. J., Meadows, L., McGrain, L. A., Langham, C. L., Baggott, J. N., & Arcelus, J. A. (2011). *IPT-BN (m): Interpersonal psychotherapy for bulimic spectrum disorders: Treatment guide*. Milwaukee, WI: Troubador Press.

Winters, K. C., Toomey, T., Nelson, T. F., Erickson, D., Lenk, K., & Miazga, M. (2011). Screening for alcohol problems among 4-year colleges and universities. *Journal of American College Health*, 59(5), 350–357.

3 Nick

Learning to Connect

Joanne hoped multifamily group therapy (MFGT; Tantillo, 2006; Tantillo & Sanftner, 2010; Tantillo, Sanftner, & Hauenstein, 2013) near the huge city of Cleveland would be a place for patients with eating disorders and their families to share their experiences in an informal way – offering insight and mutual support. Joanne and her husband Tim were still reeling with fear and exasperation after they discovered half way through Nick's tenth-grade year in high school that he had anorexia nervosa. At this juncture for Joanne, group support with other families would be a welcome relief. Life with her son Nick was anxiety-provoking and stressful. She desperately wanted information and ideas about how to handle his condition but most of all she wanted relief. To make matters worse, Nick didn't want to talk about the eating disorder. He didn't want to eat more when he needed to. He didn't want to admit he had an issue.

Joanne and Tim were here at their first MFGT meeting as part of their son's partial hospital program for eating disorders. Over one year before, Joanne had reported to Nick's pediatrician that her already-too-thin son (6'2" tall and 122 pounds) complained about being dizzy and constipated. At that time, Nick weighed in at the pediatrician's office at a lower weight than his typical growth trajectory would have predicted. He had been born premature. Throughout his childhood, his body mass index (BMI) was never more than the 20th percentile, because he tended to be tall and thin. Joanne remembered how trying to find clothes that fit was always hard for such a tall thin kid. Now in his tenth-grade year, Nick had dropped from the 20th BMI percentile to below the 5th in the 8 months since his last pediatrician's visit. "The red flags were there signaling an eating disorder," Joanne later lamented. But the pediatrician didn't see them. She and Nick left the office with orders to increase salt (to address dizziness) and eat more fruit and vegetables to relieve constipation. Joanne carefully followed up with these recommendations. Not suspecting an eating disorder, there were no attempts to increase Nick's weight. Joanne noted that nothing got better.

After his pediatrician's medical evaluation for dizziness and constipation, Nick went further underground with his food restriction. The doctor's visit came too close to a discovery of the underlying eating disorder. Partly, Nick hid because he never wanted to let his parents down. Sensitive to their concerns, he recognized his mother was operating out of care for his health. On the other hand, Nick wondered why his mother was making such a fuss over his eating habits. "What was the big deal?" he thought to himself. He was in a conundrum. He needed to protect his parents from his weight-control secrets. He didn't want them to stop him. He had carefully concealed his under-eating. He intended to continue doing so. He was in a relational bind. Should he remain connected with the eating disorder and do its bidding, or should he honor his connection with his parents and be honest about what was going on? Because the illness would not allow him to connect with himself to identify what he really needed to do to preserve his health, he couldn't be honest with himself or his parents. Reflecting on this time in his life, Nick later said, "I didn't expose any outward signs of having an eating disorder for as long as possible. I hid the fact that I was not eating very well from my parents for months. I was very good at lying, and I used this to cover up what was going on. It was clear that my mood was extremely foul, but I don't think my family guessed from my mood alone."

Nick's parents tried to get him to eat more of the foods recommended by the pediatrician. To Nick, any outside attention on his food intake was ominous. Now feeling a little desperate to keep his secrets, Nick considered possible ways to further hide anorexic behaviors. "Disguise and conceal, even if it means lying," he said to himself. So Nick, a person with a high IQ, applied his considerable ingenuity and resourcefulness to concealing disordered eating behaviors. Unbeknownst to his parents, anorexia now controlled his mind like an alien invader. Normally an honest kid, Nick was habitually lying and conniving to cover up weight-management efforts. He continually worried about being stopped.

"I need to get more ideas from those websites," Nick reasoned to himself. By this time, Nick was well acquainted with pro-eating-disorder blogs, websites, chats, and social media postings. Like others seeking to prevent discovery by loved ones, he learned a lot from them that he put into practice (Rodgers, Lowy, Halperin, & Franko, 2016). For example, he broke his food up into pieces and then pushed the pieces around his plate. That made it look like he ate more than he did. He lied to his parents about eating lunch when they asked. He hid his food between his iPad case and his iPad. He threw away food he was supposed to eat. He was successful at concealing even when his parents were in the room. He knew he was deeply ensconced in restrictive eating, but he didn't want to be stopped. The pediatrician's visit was a call to battle for him.

Nick was losing large amounts of time and energy to the eating disorder, but he stubbornly held onto it until he did something unusual that led him to break through the barriers of his own deception – he eased up on his dogged protection of the eating disorder with a friend – he told his secret. That disclosure precipitated a chain of events ultimately turning Nick's life around and putting him on the track of health, although at first it seemed to make things worse.

Nick told his secret about the eating disorder during an interaction with his friend, Jarrad, who had problems with depression. Jarrad confided in Nick. In response, Nick spent many hours supporting Jarrad through dark times. Never did Nick tell anyone what Jarrad had confided in him. So in the intimacy and trust of their friendship, Nick told Jarrad his own secret: a restrictive eating disorder. To Nick's surprise, Jarrad had trouble with it. Jarrad decided he couldn't keep Nick's secret because he was worried about Nick's safety. He told mutual friends. Then those friends undertook trying to get Nick to eat. But that wasn't enough. Even with friends pushing, Nick was not getting better. So one day Nick's friends all gathered on a planned group messaging exchange on WhatsApp.com.

The group plan they came up with was to jointly confront Nick. Unsuspecting, Nick was invited to a group-messaging event. At the appointed time on WhatsApp.com, his friends told him they were going to tell the guidance counselor at school about his eating problems, because they were worried. Nick, taken by surprise, got very angry. He felt betrayed – especially by Jarrad, who never admitted he had "spilled the beans." Nick saw his friends as interfering. His mind, controlled by the eating disorder, roiled with rage. He lashed out and said regrettable things that ultimately caused a permanent rift with his friends.

The morning after the group confrontation, at 5:30 a.m., Nick embarked on his next move. He was determined he would get to the guidance counselor before his friends did. Distressed and embarrassed from the previous night's group messaging, he figured he would appear more trustworthy and self-responsible to the guidance counselor if he preempted his friends' report and confessed the eating disorder. Not that he wanted to confess, but under the circumstances the focus had to be on damage control. The eating disorder, now threatened, insisted on keeping Nick all to itself. Nick thought that if he could appear willing to get help for his problem, he would lessen the impact and negotiate outcomes in his favor. The eating disorder led him to "play everyone" so that he would not have to face the calamity of the school telling his parents. He believed that if he got to the guidance counselor first, he could negotiate the terms of his "help" and control the inclusion of his parents. For better or worse, his scheme worked. Nick brokered a deal with the guidance counselor. He got to tell his parents first, with the agreement that the guidance counselor would follow up to make sure Nick shared his secret. Not easy, but so far all was going according to plan.

As part of his effort to control the damage, Nick hated to, but told his parents. It was now 7 months after the pediatrician's visit for dizziness and constipation. Nick wanted it to look to his parents like he was going to get help and make improvements in his eating. He convinced them he would eat more. He figured that was the only way to maintain some control of the situation, and maybe get away with less supervision from his folks. That also worked. It was agreed Nick would be monitored weekly by his pediatrician until he could receive specialty-trained outpatient services for eating disorders. Meanwhile

Nick ate more to please his parents. What Nick's parents didn't know was that he had started vomiting regularly to compensate for his increased food intake. The eating disorder had raised the stakes. In fact, at the height of his purge behavior, Nick vomited four to five times a day. Once again, Nick concealed his efforts to get rid of as much food as he was putting in. The net result was a worsening of the eating disorder.

Joanne was now operating from a permeating fear for her son. She got up with it in the morning and went to bed with it at night. The high anxiety she felt in the face of the eating disorder left her intermittently immobilized. Historically she was a good problem-solver, but she could not figure out what to do for Nick. She felt she could not protect him from the eating disorder that prevented him from advocating and caring for himself. Knowing her son was struggling was painful enough, but feeling she could not reduce his suffering was excruciating. It exacted a great toll on her, leaving her helpless and, at times, hopeless.

In the next month, when his parents were struggling, unsuccessfully, to oversee Nick's agreement to eat more, he went back to see his childhood psychologist, Dr. David. Nick trusted Dr. David and remembered he found him to be helpful in past years when he was treated for obsessive-compulsive disorder (Obsessive Compulsive Disorder; OCD; *DSM*-5; American Psychiatric Association, 2013). That's why it was to Dr. David that Nick confided his secretive purge behavior that had developed as part of the eating disorder. As Nick later noted, Dr. David wasn't trained to work with eating disorders, so Nick found he couldn't really help him. Instead, Dr. David helped him move one step closer to effective, specialized eating-disorder treatment by advising they disclose Nick's vomiting behavior to his parents.

Nick was surprised that Dr. David wanted to tell his parents about the vomiting, although it seemed like déjà vu from the incident with his friends and the guidance counselor. On some level, Nick subconsciously knew he was out of control and worn out from wrestling with the eating disorder. He was determined, but tired. It was all getting so complicated. Dr. David explained to Nick that he normally held their therapy sessions in confidence, but the vomiting was a dangerous behavior he and Nick needed to address with Nick's parents in order to ensure his safety. Although exhausted, Nick's anxiety peaked, and once again the eating disorder motivated him to "game" his treatment team, if possible.

Meanwhile, after a few months of his parents' failed attempts to prod Nick into weight gain, and while Nick was also seeing Dr. David, Nick began treatment at a medical center with a pediatric outpatient eating-disorder program. There Nick saw a nutritionist and a physician who were well acquainted with eating disorders and their treatment. Nick and his parents were given guidelines to follow to increase Nick's nutrition intake. When they took this step, Nick's parents raised the level of care to specialized eating-disorder services. Evidence comparing treatment outcomes indicates Nick now stood a better chance of recovery than when he received non-specialized care (House et al., 2012; Spotts-De Lazer & Muhlheim, 2016).

Still, even with specialized care, Nick did not gain. Until Nick's purge behavior surfaced, his outpatient treatment team was very confused by his lack of progress. No wonder. Nick later said, "I was good at lying – I looked the doctors [at the hospital] straight in the eye and lied when asked about purging. I couldn't lose all the progress I had made [protecting the eating disorder]. They were getting confused at the eating-disorder clinic. They were thinking of other things that might be going on."

Joanne was a full-time, stay-at-home mom. During the day, Tim worked as a university researcher. Much of the load to feed Nick was on Joanne's shoulders. She noticed Nick seemed to be looking more skeletal. She felt tremendous pressure to restore her son's health. She was anxious. At the same time she was patient and dedicated to Nick's care. Day after day she sat with Nick at meals and snacks making sure he was nourished. Tim was also scared. On the outside he remained calm. Maybe because of male socialization or maybe because Tim was a logical and pragmatic person by nature, he patiently focused on how to fix the problem. In time, Joanne and Tim learned to collaborate with each other about how to best support Nick's recovery.

Tim began to provide hours of meal support with his son by either taking turns with Joanne, or joining her. Tim saw Nick's weight loss as a problem that would likely take a while to reverse, so he rolled with the weeks when there wasn't much progress, and he was encouraged by positive signs. He was not especially concerned about Nick's weight as long as Nick was moving ahead. Joanne and Tim were on their own trying to feed Nick to reverse the weight-loss trend once eating disorder-treatment began. Despite their best efforts, Tim, too, became discouraged as he and Joanne saw Nick fail to gain weight. They shoved food in Nick, sticking with food he would eat. Somehow nothing made a difference.

Nick thought his parents were too strict with their first attempts to get him to eat. His memory of this initial period of his parents trying to feed him was distinctly unhappy. Eventually caught in lies about his eating, his parents tightened their surveillance. Nick felt like his privacy had been invaded. His parents were policing him. He later told his psychotherapist, "It was like they watched everything I did. They patted me down and searched my pockets. I felt frustrated and dehumanized. I wanted them to stop staring at me and talk about something else besides my eating. I felt shackled. We got into power struggles. Eating was a battle of wills. It was like party divisions in Congress where one side shackles the other, and then neither side is willing to give. If they would have backed off a little bit, had a little faith and were less like police, maybe I would have given a little." Joanne later noted that Nick was in no way ready to let go of the eating disorder no matter how strict or lenient she and Tim were until he was much further into treatment. It was the eating disorder that had Nick believing lenience would have improved his chances of eating when his parents were at their most vigilant.

It is true that Joanne and Tim had difficulties mobilizing their anxiety into effective strategies to help Nick eat. To discourage vomiting after meals, they were advised to increase supervision to include an hour of staying with Nick after meals. As a result of this and repeated attempts to nourish Nick with more food, Joanne sometimes felt resentful toward her son. She felt trapped by the eating disorder. Like most parents, she and Tim were ill equipped to face the extreme behaviors Nick demonstrated in an effort to avoid eating, such as hiding food. They needed more help. Later on, in multi-family group treatment, Joanne and Tim came to understand that, for Nick, both anticipating and receiving food caused him high anxiety – thus Nick's food avoidance (Kaye, Wierenga, Bailer, Simmons, & Bischoff-Grethe, 2013). They learned anorexia is a neurobiological condition that neither they nor Nick intended, nor asked for. And they learned that Nick needed to acquire better emotional-regulation and distress-tolerance skills so he was less likely to rely on the eating disorder to cope.

Over time, with the help of other parents in MFGT, Joanne and Tim became more confident in managing Nick's eating at home. They found out from a nutritionist who met with multiple parents in the group format how to provide balanced meals. They discovered how to give consistent support without hostility and to gently but firmly guide. Finally, as treatment progressed, Nick slowly took increasing responsibility for his recovery. He became collaborative with his parents once they shared the same recovery goal. Ultimately, Nick began feeding himself in a healthful and balanced manner.

Both Tim and Joanne were curious to understand the factors that might have led to anorexia nervosa for Nick. Later, during MFGT, they discussed their confusion about what led Nick to develop an eating disorder. They learned that a common pathway to anorexia was a negative body image. However, from outward appearances, Nick didn't seem to be the least bit bothered by the way his body looked before the onset of the eating disorder.

Looking back, Nick was not shy in school. He had a strong desire to make friends. Everybody knew Nick. He was known as the thin kid who was friendly, affable, and had no issues with his body image leading up to middle school. In another district, Nick's thin physique might have caused him to be bullied as he navigated his social environment. But Nick's schools were wonderfully protected from bullying because of their excellent bullying-prevention measures. He didn't get teased for being thin. In fact, Nick seemed fully accepting of his body before puberty. He even joked about having a thin body. Once as a child, he jested with his mother, as he put up his skinny arms and grabbed his biceps, "I am bringing these to the gun show." Even when he was the last kid picked in gym class, he rolled with the punches.

Nick did always have an exceptionally fussy relationship with food. As a child, as far back as his parents could remember, certain things tasted good – but not many. And many things just smelled or tasted bad. Then there was texture. Stringy things like celery or certain meats felt uncomfortable to the point that Nick, as a 5-year-old, would just avoid them. "This is deee-gusting," he would say as he refused a stringy food. So Nick ate a very limited selection of foods. He was the kid who liked one kind of peanut butter on one kind of bread. He was overwhelmed by noise and smells. As a result, Nick's parents remembered spending large amounts of time in his early years trying to help him expand his eating. They had been professionally advised to increase the variety of food he ate. They tried. But gradually Nick's stubborn refusal to try new foods wore Joanne and Tim down. So Nick's family decided on peace at the dinner table over food fights. They confined themselves to giving Nick the foods he would eat.

Although not diagnosed as a child, it is likely Nick struggled with Avoidant/Restrictive Food Intake Disorder (ARFID; *DSM*-5; American Psychiatric Association, 2013). ARFID probably preceded Nick's treatment for Anorexia Nervosa: Binge-Eating/Purging Type (*DSM*-5; American Psychiatric Association, 2013). (Despite what the diagnosis implies, Nick, like Anna whom you'll meet later in this book, didn't struggle with binge eating. Binge eating is not a requirement for this subtype of anorexia nervosa.) There were several ways Nick showed signs of ARFID as a younger child. First of all, ARFID is more common in males (Fisher et al., 2014). And second, typical of ARFID, Nick had a strong aversion to the taste and sensory characteristics of certain foods. For example, once when Nick tried a blueberry, he reacted with an explosion of sensation to the taste and texture of that single berry. As part of his sensory overload with certain foods, he had trouble putting unfamiliar things in his mouth. So strong was his avoidance, that he would commonly choose hunger over unknown foods. Third, as with those with ARFID, Nick could put off eating for long periods of time rather than eat undesired foods. As a result, he suffered early nutritional imbalance.

Nick suffered social repercussions related to ARFID, too. Meals with other children were difficult because he ate such a limited range of foods. Unlike with anorexia, but typical of ARFID, Nick did not fear weight gain and was not dissatisfied with his body shape, weight, or size in his elementary school years. However, not typical of ARFID and despite his picky eating, Nick never failed to achieve expected pediatric weight gain as a pre-pubescent child. Until weight loss in his teens due to anorexia nervosa, there was no evidence that he failed to grow as expected.

Nick's early struggles with anxiety disorders and childhood obsessive-compulsive disorder may have predisposed him to both ARFID and anorexia nervosa. We know that children with anxiety disorders and obsessive-compulsive disorder are at a higher risk for both ARFID and anorexia nervosa (Fisher et al., 2014). As in Nick's case, ARFID usually occurs at a younger age than anorexia, typically under age 12. Even though ARFID doesn't involve body image concerns, it can evolve into anorexia (Norris et al., 2014; Norris, Spettigue, & Katzman, 2016). Looking back over his eating history, Nick, Joanne, and Tim later recognized Nick's extremely picky eating as ARFID, and how it contributed to later anorexia. There is little doubt this was how Nick's illness developed.

One way Joanne and Tim were able to distinguish ARFID from later anorexia in their son was Nick's relationship with particular foods. During intense periods of especially picky eating as a child, Nick ate few foods – only those he could tolerate based on texture, taste, smell, and so on. One food he ate plenty of was bread. But with the onset of puberty, anorexia, and his growing preoccupation with body image, bread dropped out of Nick's food choices because, now ensconced in body-image concerns typical of anorexia, he began to see bread as fattening.

Inside, Nick began to be bothered by his body during his puberty years. At the height of anorexia he wanted to weigh exactly 100 pounds. The body-image distortion present in the neural brain signature of anorexia was at work (Frank, 2015). Nick honestly thought he looked better at this very-low weight, and, once overtaken by the eating disorder, no amount of persuasion would influence him otherwise until his brain was better nourished. Nick was lost in the illness. He had a distorted view of himself as fat. His distorted views were fortified by an online community that promoted anorexia as a desirable lifestyle.

For all his outward joviality, Nick was a high-anxiety child. Alongside his food-avoidance issues, he was treated by Dr. David for OCD in the sixth grade. Perhaps Nick had a pre-existing vulnerability to anorexia typical of children with OCD (Altman & Shankman, 2009). Both anorexia and OCD share common traits – those seen in Nick: anxiety, an obsessive need to exert control, perfectionism, and following self-imposed rules to exactitude.

Four years after his treatment in sixth grade for OCD, Dr. David's attentions were turned to the eating disorder. When he insisted on sharing Nick's purging behavior with his parents, treatment bumped up to a referral from the specialized outpatient clinic Nick attended to a partial hospital program for eating disorders. With the perfect excuse that summer vacation was coming, plans were made for Nick to enter a partial hospital program in a nearby city – one Nick could commute to. Six months had passed since his friends insisted he tell his parents. Typical of eating disorders, it took time to navigate the gauntlet erected by the eating disorder.

Typical of how eating disorders progress, Nick felt increasingly disconnected from friends and family (Tantillo & Sanftner, 2010; Tantillo et al., 2013). He wanted to keep to himself. He was not able to see that the internal demands of the eating disorder pushed him further and further into isolation. Once more, Nick didn't see himself as separate from the illness. Rather, he saw himself and the world around him through the distorted lens of the illness. Only later would he be able to separate himself from the eating disorder. Still held hostage by the illness, Nick wanted nothing to do with the new plan for a higher level of care in a partial hospital program. He tried valiantly to prevent admission to the program by convincing everyone he was making progress. Now, at this point, he convinced no one. Although he would never admit it, his one secret solace was that he wasn't being sent to an even higher level of care – a 24/7 residential treatment center. Instead, he would get to live at home and attend full-day hospital programming.

Nick's brother was not told about the eating disorder because Nick was adamant that he be kept in the dark. Nick was intensely private and embarrassed. So admission to the partial hospital program was presented at home as Nick's attending an *eating camp*. This worked as a cover story because Jordan, Nick's brother, was also going to attend camp – a music camp. Jordan had always been aware that Nick didn't like all kinds of foods. So for him, Nick's eating camp seemed to be an extension of his brother's lifelong sensitivity and resistance to foods he didn't like. Jordan had always wished his brother could eat right and thought maybe this would fix things.

After the new round of revelations from Dr. David, Joanne and Tim were on high alert. Like many parents, Joanne and Tim had innocently assumed Nick wasn't purging. Joanne said, "I couldn't imagine our highly sensitive child tolerating vomiting." In fact, Joanne was shocked by Nick's purging and every new revelation as it occurred. She thought she knew her son well. She never dreamed he would lie about eating-disorder behaviors in the ways that he did. On the other hand she didn't understand until her participation in MFGT it was the eating disorder and not Nick who was lying to her.

Tim was not as shocked by the lies, or the various manifestations of the eating disorder. Like Joanne, he had read about anorexia. And he listened carefully to Joanne when she researched treatment options and diligently shared materials and information from MFGT. He knew deception was characteristic of the illness. Also, Tim was used to dealing with Nick's problems. From his perspective, things had been happening with Nick since pre-school. He had received treatment for hypersensitivity to sensory input, food avoidance, and OCD. Nick always got better. Tim believed he would do the same now. While Joanne rationally understood everything she read about eating disorders and their treatment, she found she was more emotionally reactive than Tim to Nick's illness. Her anxiety was often eased by Tim's confidence.

Slated to begin eating camp, Nick wasn't quite prepared for what happened next. He had his intake appointment and was officially admitted to the partial hospital program for eating disorders. On his first day of the program, he learned the bathrooms were checked after every use. Robbed of his ability to purge, Nick was highly perturbed. At this point, he remembers saying to himself, "Not a lot left to mask here – I won't talk or admit to anything." Nick was further dismayed to find out that he had to eat all that was put before him at regular program meals. His parents had warned the program staff about Nick's food "peculiarities." However, they were assured Nick would be eating the same program food as the other patients. Through all of this, the eating-disorder voice inside of Nick's head continued a relentless volley of blowback. "Why are you listening to this stuff? You should get some exercise done! Look up other ways to take care of this! Find ways to drain things from your stomach!" Meanwhile Nick's parents had long ago instituted sitting with him for an hour after meals at home. Similarly, at his treatment program, he was not allowed to go to the bathroom to purge. Nick felt cornered. He began to accept digestion of his food without getting rid of it. A bitter pill to swallow.

Nick generally loved people, but was anxious upon entering the partial hospital program, especially when meeting unfamiliar people. At first, he socially withdrew, because he thought everyone would judge him. In the first MFGT meeting, which was part of the partial hospital program, there were 30 people in the room he didn't know. He was nervous and resentful. Later, he realized the other patients participating in his partial hospital program were nice. He met one who came in and cheerfully said to him, "Hi! My name's Laura. How are you?" To Nick, she seemed friendly and nice – not some stereotype of a self-harming person who was morose and withdrawn, or angry and hateful. This was just the beginning. Nick eventually bonded with everyone in the program. A little short on friends at the time, Nick was happy to make new ones.

He was more able to recognize and consider giving up the eating disorder when he saw others like him – some his age – struggling. A natural "giver," Nick found he liked to help other patients. Once he said to one of the participants, "You can do this. You need to fight this thing!" Along the way, he figured out he needed to help himself if he was going to help others. If he was going to encourage his new friends, he needed to be a role model.

As mentioned already, part of the partial hospital program was the MFGT. Nick reluctantly started attending those meetings with his parents. MFGT is a group therapy modality in which patients and their families come together during recovery to share, offer support, and build connections with each other (Tantillo, 2006; Tantillo et al., 2013). Through practicing emotional and relational skills, they are guided to develop a sense of mutuality (mutual understanding, trust, and respect) with each other. Most importantly, they are empowered to build mutual connections by learning to accept differences as well as similarities among themselves. Based on relational-cultural theory (RCT; Miller & Stiver, 1997), MFGT helps patients and their families bond and connect to each other so they can disconnect from the eating disorder (Tantillo, 2006; Tantillo, MacDowell, Anson, Taillie, & Cole, 2009).

Nick said nothing at the first MFGT meeting. He had determined he hated MFGT and his whole treatment program. "I don't want to talk," he said. He did not like large groups of people, and he didn't want to be exposed in any way. He didn't want to share in front of others. In hindsight, he said, "It took a long time for me warm up. I didn't like it. It felt like too much exposure of personal detail, especially with other parents there." Over time, despite his initial reticence, Nick learned to connect with others. He liked the other patients and family members in the partial hospital program, who were generally good and nice people. In the beginning, he was determined to hate the patients, their parents, and the staff – but he couldn't. Everyone, including the staff, was friendly to him from the start, even though he was the only guy in the program.

It was not unusual for Nick to be the only male in an eating-disorder program, because these illnesses have traditionally been attributed to women and gone undiagnosed in men. When it comes to eating disorders, women are known to outnumber men by as much as 3:1 for college students (Eisenberg, Nicklett, Roeder, & Kirz, 2011), 4:1 among teens (Dooley-Hash, Banker, Walton, Ginsburg, & Cunningham, 2012), and 4:1 among children with early-onset eating disorders (Madden, Morris, Zurynski, Kohn, & Elliot, 2009). In the past decade, researchers have moved beyond old impressions that eating disorders occur mostly among women and that they are female problems. Even though Nick was the only male in the partial hospital program at the time of his treatment, many men and boys had attended his and other eating disorder programs before him. Even though eating disorders in men and women share many similar characteristics, there are also some important gender differences. Women are increasingly motivated to be muscular, as well as thin (Ricciardelli & McCabe, 2007). Nonetheless, men continue to be more concerned with muscularity than the number on the scale in comparison to women (Hoffman & Warschburger, 2017). While many men desire to "bulk up" in order to increase muscularity (Pope, Phillips, & Olivardia, 2002), some boys and men, like Nick, appear to be motivated to be slender to enhance muscle definition. Muscle definition is more visible in a thin body, compared to a large body.

Since MFGT included parents as well as patients, Nick found other reasons to feel more positive about participating. He saw his parents learning from other parents about what worked or didn't work with their kids. Happily for Nick, his parents were figuring out how to better support his eating and body-image issues. They stopped being the "Gestapo police" about his food at home, and they seemed more relaxed about Nick's slow progress. Nick was also learning a lot about how his parents felt about his problems by listening to other parents' thoughts and feelings. He had been wracked with guilt about the burden his illness placed on his parents, but felt less defensive about his parents' burden when he heard other parents sharing their feelings. He wasn't the only one whose parents seemed overwhelmed by their teenager's eating-disorder struggles. They were all overwhelmed together. To Nick's surprise, most of the other parents were relieved to be part of the program. They were happy to know they could do something to help.

Nick's parents, along with the others, also met as a group with a nutritionist before MFGT meetings. Here Nick's parents got more specific ideas about how to provide meal support. Portioning, timing, nutrient balance – all those issues and more were addressed. In all, Joanne and Tim's MFGT-inspired parent-support skills boosted Nick's recovery. Eating disorders are often cowed into submission when confronted by confident, better-eating-disorder educated, compassionate, and determined parents.

A key goal of MFGT is increased and restored connection – to self, the body, and others. This is in direct opposition to the intra- and interpersonal disconnection promoted by the eating disorder (Tantillo et al., 2013). Important to recovery in MFGT is building strategies to promote mutual connections (Tantillo, 2006). During group meetings, activities are introduced that promote the strengthening and deepening of relationships among patients, their families, and therapists. With this comes a growing sense of mutual trust and what Tantillo calls *perceived mutuality* among all group members – patients, families, and therapists (Tantillo et al., 2013; Tantillo & Sanftner, 2003). Connection to self grows in this context, because people come to know themselves through connections with others. At a brain level, interpersonal interactions stimulate our brain's neural circuits to help us make sense of what we're experiencing during interactions (body sensations, cognitions, emotions). The internal personal sensing of others thus helps strengthen connections in our own brains. In this way, interacting with others helps us integrate our own emotions, thoughts, and bodily states.

In Nick's initial session of MFGT, the group leader, Shelley, described the purpose and goals of the group, distributed a schedule and orientation material, and had all families and patients introduce themselves (Tantillo, 2006). Then psychoeducation about eating disorders – their nature, risk factors, maintaining factors, and treatment – was offered. As part of learning about eating disorders, Shelley recognized and validated the care burden placed on families by the illness. That was consistent with extensive research by Treasure and her colleagues (Gisladottir, Treasure, & Svavarsdottir, 2017; Goodier et al., 2014; Zabala, Macdonald, & Treasure, 2009), who have shown caregivers often need help because they suffer guilt and distress in their role as carers. As part of relieving this distress, one of the first goals in MFGT was to externalize the eating disorder illness from the patient (Tantillo, 2006). That goal is also common to other psychotherapies for eating disorders, including family-based treatment (FBT; Stiles-Shields, Hoste, Doyle, & Le Grange, 2012).

Shelley carefully explained the importance of placing the eating disorder illness outside the patient. The intent here is for both patient and family members to relieve themselves of blame for the illness. The MFGT model stresses *no one asked for the illness and neither patient nor family member caused the eating disorder*. Rather, the illness is an invader that found a vulnerable person, often with biological, psychological, and social risk factors. She instilled a sense of hope as she spoke. Accurate information and hope are essential to dispel the discouragement that many patients and families feel in the beginning of treatment. Shelley explained, "Just as the eating disorder invaded your loved one's brain, it can be separated from her or him as recovery progresses."

An example of an important MFGT activity is learning to identify points of tension and disconnection related to the eating disorder. Alone at first, in a room full of strangers, Joanne began feeling more and more comfortable in MFGT. Tim usually stayed at home tending to Jordan. Joanne and Nick, together at group, had always protected one another. This was one of the unspoken rules of their relationship. According to their rule, Joanne tacitly agreed not to reveal details about Nick to others, because exposure made him uncomfortable. However, Shelley encouraged group members to share their experiences. So try as she might to leave out details about Nick's life with the eating disorder, Joanne sometimes connected with group members by sharing what Nick thought was too much information. Like the time Joanne told the group, "Nick hid food we served him last night, and I was furious." On the way home in the car from the group that night, Nick was predictably fuming at his mother for disclosing particulars about his life. His anger was usually under wraps, but that night he was highly offended by his mother's indiscretion. He let her know. In the next MFGT meeting, Shelley could see the tension between Nick and his mother. Nick barely gave his mother eye contact and pulled away from her. Shelley took a chance and found a way to surface the tension.

In keeping with the goal of building a sense of mutuality among participants, Shelley was careful not to assume or tell Nick or his mother what they were feeling. She judiciously decided to use self-disclosure to convey how Nick and his mother had moved her emotionally. She checked into her own experience about what she felt as she watched Nick and his mother interact (Tantillo, 2004). In the spirit of being emotionally present to build mutuality, she disclosed to Nick, "When I see you struggle with your mom, it makes me feel sad – I see how much you are struggling. You clearly love each other and at the same time, it seems like the eating disorder is working hard to keep you apart from each other." At this, Nick felt Shelley's sadness and asked himself, "Shelley feels sad. Do I feel sad? I feel tears coming. I think I do feel sad." By being vulnerable herself, Shelley enabled Nick to break through the numbing, deadening effect of starvation on his emotions (Kaye et al., 2013). It pushed Nick to name his own experience as well as identify an important tension between him and his mother.

Another tenet of MFGT, based on relational-cultural theory, is learning to build mutuality with others by not only tolerating differences between self and others, but also actually growing from acknowledging those differences. A point of tension between Nick and his mother was privacy versus openness. Nick was a private person who learned to share in group – but in the end he still valued his privacy. As already noted, in the early weeks of treatment, Nick sometimes became angry with his mother for sharing in group. More quickly than Nick, Joanne became comfortable sharing the ways she was affected by the eating disorder. It was more important to her to share and to hear from others in MFGT.

Eventually, Nick and his mother acknowledged this difference between them. By doing so, they were engaging in *relational repair*, another goal of MFGT (Tantillo, 2006). They learned to acknowledge and appreciate rather than fear their differences. Nick stopped trying so hard to control his mother's openness by getting angry. He collaborated with her about what to tell and what not to tell. He respected her need to build a sharing community with group members while still taking care of himself. Joanne also respected Nick's privacy by being careful not to share personal details that Nick asked her not to. Reflecting on their increased mutuality and connection, Shelley pointed out to the group, "It's good to name and understand your differences. The eating disorder probably used differences between us to keep itself going by creating conflict and disconnection." Turning to Nick and his mom, Shelley said, "The eating disorder has likely been thriving on disconnection between the two of you over the issue of privacy."

Identifying points of tension and disconnection generated by the eating disorder was an ongoing goal of MFGT. Besides the issue of privacy for Nick and his mom, there were many more points of tension. One of the most important was Nick not asking his parents for help because he thought he was a burden. He was so compliant with nutrition restoration efforts, sometimes his parents barely knew he was struggling inside. Like many people with an eating disorder, Nick was sensitive to his parents' feelings, especially if they seemed upset. Nick avoided asking his mother for help. He didn't want to inconvenience her. He saw his mother get upset about matters related to the eating disorder and was aware of all the time and attention his special needs required. It seemed to be taking a toll. In MFGT, this topic, previously avoided, was brought to the surface so relational repair could take place. Nick's mother excused him from his need to take care of her. She assured him that her vulnerable negative feelings did not need to be fixed or accommodated by him.

Considering Nick and his mother, Shelley asked the group, "Have any other parents felt concerned their children are not asking for help because they're trying not to burden their families?" A dad in the group quickly identified the same point of tension with his daughter. He found his daughter Natalie was fiercely independent about healing herself without her parents' help. He suspected she overheard him and her mom complaining about all the money and time expended for her treatment. Natalie agreed she had heard them complaining, so to spare them, she took the stance she didn't need their help. Her Dad said once he realized she was feeling like a burden to them, he apologized for complaining. He assured her that he and her mom wanted to help, and they were grateful to support her treatment despite what she overheard. It took some time for Natalie to trust her dad meant what he said, but she became willing to work on asking for help.

In MFGT, parents validate and help other parents and patients. Joanne and Nick saw the similarity with Natalie's situation and were relieved to be sharing this point of tension with other family members. Upon hearing Natalie's story, Nick felt encouraged to allow himself to be vulnerable enough to ask his parents for help. Further, because Nick was very invested in helping other group members – especially the patients – he soon adopted a stance of setting an example for recovery that also helped him make changes. Nick increasingly projected an attitude of, "If I can do it, you can do it." For example, he supported Natalie in trusting her parents enough to ask for help.

Another facet of MFGT was identifying family rules that created points of tension and disconnection. For Nick, a number of family rules were identified and reviewed for whether or not they supported tolerance of difference, emotional expression, or conflict management in the family. Or did the rules support disconnection? One rule that maintained disconnection was already discussed: protect Mom from pain by hiding symptoms. Here are some more rules in Nick's family that pointed to a need for relational repair: (1) avoid conflict in order to avoid potential hurt feelings; (2) feed Nick whatever few foods he will eat because he doesn't eat enough (accommodating the eating disorder); (3) Mom should protect Nick from food anxiety; (4) go inward with your distress instead of outward, and conceal, don't feel; (5) protect Nick's little brother by not answering his questions about what's going on with Nick; and (6) eliminate all tension because it's uncomfortable. All these family rules were surfaced in

MFGT and challenged in constructive ways in order to build connection both amongst all family members, but especially between Nick and his own inner life.

In MFGT, strategies for addressing these rules were provided. For example, a strategy for expressing buried, unspoken feelings like fear and anxiety was to pass out a feelings word list to help people find the words to express their feelings. Another strategy was to ask group participants to help other participants who were struggling to identify their feelings. For example, Shelley said to the group, "Nick is being really brave to try to say how he feels. Who else in the group would like to share feelings they might have had in a similar situation?" Joanne later noted that she learned through role modeling the therapists at MFGT how to ask Nick about his feelings on car rides back home from MFGT. Recalling how other patients had talked about their feelings, Joanne would ask Nick, "Did you feel that too?"

As a result of family rules created by the eating disorder, carer distress was complex for Nick's family. Nick never gave Tim and Joanne any lip when they plated his food and set it down in front of him. He didn't resist when they asked him to spend an hour with them after dinner in order to prevent any temptation to purge. Throughout all this, Nick offered no overt resistance. He did everything they asked. Nonetheless, Joanne felt resentment. She felt trapped by the disorder and initially felt she should not share this. Care was so labor intensive, Joanne eventually recounted, "I felt closed in by it all. I felt like the world had shrunk to a very small place, and I felt disconnected from the rest of humanity." Nick's parents were grateful Jordan was away at camp for some of the worst feeding experiences – those where Nick silently struggled with obvious distress to eat normal food at home.

Nick's illness had a large impact on his brother. Joanne said, "Jordan could see I was sad a lot." She lamented, "I didn't have the time or patience for him that I usually had. Nick was also impatient and withdrawn from him. He knew Nick was getting help with his eating, something which had always been problematic." Joanne realized Jordan didn't appreciate the gravity of the situation, because she and Tim deliberately downplayed it. Joanne recalled, "Jordan thought my sadness was due to my mother's illness, which was something else that was upsetting him." They didn't want to overwhelm Jordan. They were worried, because he had a high-anxiety personality, like Nick. That's why they weren't always forthright with him. Joanne later thought maybe they could have been clearer with him.

Despite the complexity of their caregiver distress, thankfully neither Tim nor Joanne suffered guilt, which is common in many parents of those with eating disorders (Fox, Dean, & Whittlesea, 2017). They had devoted so many of their resources – time, money, caring, and treatments – to Nick's earlier problems in life, they were confident they would continue to do so with the new problem – the eating disorder. For them, this was just another problem to be solved – even when it frustrated them over the long weeks of treatment. They had become experts in seeking the best care for Nick through earlier efforts around OCD, anxiety, and ARFID. Their confidence continued to grow with the help of MFGT and partial hospitalization programming.

One day, a few weeks into his participation in MFGT, Nick threw out the cover to his iPad – the cover he had so carefully hidden his food in. He cleaned shelves in his room of food he had hidden. During the hour after dinner when he sat with his parents, he helped them find topics of discussion he enjoyed and that helped distract him – like a favorite – politics and political debate. Inspired by increasing trust in his parents and their backing off from their policing practices, Nick slowly took charge of his own recovery.

Recently, in thinking about his recovery journey, Nick said, "The recovery is going very slowly. At first my head seemed like it wasn't working properly. I couldn't figure things out." Compared to healthy adolescents, research using MRI brain scans indicates adolescents with anorexia show higher levels of brain activity in temporal and parietal areas during performance of cognitive tasks. Like Nick, they find they have to work harder to perform cognitive tasks, especially those that use working memory (Castro-Fornieles et al., 2010). Processing information, focusing attention, planning, and decision-making require more effort.

Further, this brain deficit is linked to a well-established finding that those with anorexia have difficulty quickly and productively adapting to change (Kaye et al., 2013; Sultson et al., 2016; Zastrow et al., 2009). As Nick restored his nutrition, he noted that his concentration and memory improved, and his thinking seemed sharper. As a result, his coping skills improved with practice. His improved cognitive functioning made him clearer and more effective in his ability to reflect on how the eating disorder was affecting him and how it affected his relationships with people. This experience also strengthened his sense of perceived mutuality in relationships, because he could better understand how he affected others and was able to be more emotionally vulnerable, allowing others to influence him too (Tantillo et al., 2013).

During his course of MFGT, Nick made real and lasting friendships. Originally a bit shy, he eventually opened MFGT meetings and was eager to participate in group exercises. He considered both staff and participants friends, sometimes texting group members in between to see how they were doing. Nick once proclaimed, "Now I have 15 new names in my phone contacts!" This kind of relational-skills building was highly encouraged by staff. MFGT created a healing community for Nick. Later he was able to take his improved social-connection skills and build a stronger community for himself at school. As part of his social awakening, he entered his first romantic relationship with a girl he met. Nick was very excited about this development. He even went to his junior prom with her.

Recounting his work in treatment, Nick noticed something different about the staff in MFGT. "It really helped when the therapists admitted they didn't understand something." When Shelley would say, "I can't know for sure how this must be feeling, because I don't have an eating disorder," Nick was impressed by her humility. Further, she wasn't trying to tell him how he felt, like some therapists had in the past. Nick commented, "I like the loose professionalism – I can chat with the staff about things other than eating disorders." For example, Nick found out one of the therapy interns was moving to a different city and talked to her about that. Another therapist had absolutely opposing political views to his in a number of areas. He liked that the staff shared bits about their lives. It made them human.

In the end, Nick improved significantly. He stepped down to an intensive outpatient program in the same treatment facility, where he attended a few evening meetings a week for 3 hours of group and meal support. Then he moved to outpatient psychotherapy, first once a week, then every other week. He missed his friends from the recovery programs he attended, but he still saw Shelley for follow-up individual psychotherapy to ensure he maintained the gains he made during higher levels of program care. At last Nick was more connected with himself and others and less connected with the eating disorder. He was able to carry his enhanced ability to connect with self and others into life outside of treatment by making new friends and deepening family connections.

Question

My 16-year-old son has been diagnosed with an eating disorder. I would like him and his father to participate in something like MFGT therapy, but they don't like groups. What can I do?

Answer

If you can find this resource in your community, or even a parent support group, explain to your teen (a minor under age 18) that receiving treatment for an eating disorder is not negotiable. As parents, you intend to do everything in your power to make sure he receives the best treatment available. You have chosen a program that includes groups, and he will attend with you. Explain that interacting with other teens and their families has many proven benefits. When in treatment groups, he can choose when and whether to talk, but he will participate with you.

With regard to your husband, encourage him to come and observe. Let him know that interacting with other patients and their families will provide support, education, and some specific parent skills that are needed to speed up your son's recovery. Tell him you want his support to pursue treatment and that your son's treatment will be most effective if both of you agree to participate.

Question

I'm afraid if my son is part of a group focused on eating disorders, the eating-disorder behavior of other participants will be contagious. Will he get ideas from being in a group and become sicker?

Answer

There is ample evidence that multi-family group therapies, and therapy groups in general, are useful for treating adolescent eating disorders (Downey, 2014). An argument is sometimes made that participants in group treatment for eating disorders often share a high degree of perfectionism, low self-esteem, competitiveness, and a tendency to compare to one another (Vandereycken, 2011). Further, you're right to be cautious. Just like with pro-eating-disorder websites, blogs, and chats, therapy groups can potentially become insular and self-stigmatizing, and breed an eating-disorder subculture. Those problems, if not managed, could have negative effects on group dynamics and enhance rather than reduce eating-disorder behavior.

It is important to point out that perfectionism and competitive comparisons for those with eating disorders occur outside of group therapy in everyday adolescent interactions. Those interactional problems, including the ones mentioned above, are exactly what can be addressed and managed in a specialized group-therapy setting. To create a safe space, common ground rules for eating-disorder group-therapy participants include not discussing numbers, such as weight, clothes size, calories, or time spent exercising. Further, specifics of eating behaviors, food, exercising, and purge behavior are typically forbidden topics. Unhelpful alliances that promote a pro-eating-disorder culture are discouraged. Raising consciousness and engendering hope and solidarity in recovery are encouraged. Those who are doing well are promoted as positive role models. The pain and misery of not doing well are met with compassion and recognition for what they are – not something to be admired or pursued.

Question

As a parent, I'm embarrassed to enter MFGT with other parents. My teen doesn't want others to know about the eating disorder either. We're inclined to agree this is best kept within our immediate family and our treatment team.

Answer

A common misperception is that eating disorders are the fault of someone in the family, or represent a family weakness. This causes embarrassment, shame, secrecy, and isolation. Research has shown no one is to blame for eating disorders. Neither parents nor patients cause them. Eating disorders are a result of multiple social, psychological, and biological factors coming together in ways that are difficult to predict. Beyond risk factors, science cannot identify why some young people develop eating disorders. An initial hurdle for parents and patients is coming to terms with their blamelessness. When they do, they are usually more relaxed about sharing with others for mutual support and sharing.

Professionals leading multi-family groups are well aware of the false stigma attached to having a child with an eating disorder. They are sensitive to parents' concerns and spend time debunking false stereotypes to relieve embarrassment and guilt. Because group participants are encouraged to allow themselves to be vulnerable with one another, group leaders also stress confidentiality to protect privacy among group participants.

Parents need mutual support and a sense that they are not isolated in the process of fighting an eating disorder. Particularly when in the thick of the distress of a newly diagnosed eating disorder, parents benefit from mutual support and sharing ideas. Parents coming together can engender hope, enhance parent strengths, improve parent self-knowledge and reflectiveness, and improve family communication about the eating disorder. It is important to remember that the eating disorder works against those things and wants patients and families to remain disconnected from themselves and others.

Perhaps one of the most persuasive arguments for parents taking a chance to come together with other parents is the benefit to their child. Hollesen, Clausen, and Rokkedal (2013), Marzola et al. (2015), Eisler et al. (2016), and others have found clear benefit to teens who participate in MFGT. Benefits include better self-affirmation; less self-blame; improved mood; healthier BMI; and a reduction in restrictions, eating concerns, weight concerns, amount of exercise, and drive for thinness.

References

Altman, S. E., & Shankman, S. A. (2009). What is the association between obsessive-compulsive disorder and eating disorders? *Clinical Psychology Review*, 29(7), 638–646.

American Psychiatric Association. (2013). *Diagnostic and statistical manual of mental disorders* (5th ed.). Arlington, VA: Author.

Castro-Fornieles, J., Caldú, X., Andrés-Perpiñá, S., Lázaro, L., Bargalló, N., Falcón, C., & Junqué, C. (2010). A cross-sectional and follow-up functional MRI study with a working memory task in adolescent anorexia nervosa. *Neuropsychologia*, 48(14), 4111–4116.

Dooley-Hash, S., Banker, J. D., Walton, M. A., Ginsburg, Y., & Cunningham, R. M. (2012). The prevalence and correlates of eating disorders among emergency department patients aged 14–20 years. *International Journal of Eating Disorders*, 45(7), 883–890.

Downey, J. (2014). Group therapy for adolescents living with an eating disorder: A scoping review. *SAGE Open*, 4(3). Online publication. doi:10.1177/2158244014550618

Eisenberg, D., Nicklett, E., Roeder, K., & Kirz, N. (2011) Eating disorders symptoms among college students: Prevalence, persistence, correlates, and treatment-seeking. *Journal of American College Health*, 59(8), 700–707.

Eisler, I., Simic, M., Hodsoll, J., Asen, E., Berelowitz, M., Connan, F., … Landau, S. (2016). A pragmatic randomised multi-centre trial of multifamily and single family therapy for adolescent anorexia nervosa. *BMC Psychiatry*, 16(1). Online publication. doi:10.1186/s12888-016-1129-6

Fisher, M., Rosen, D., Ornstein, R., Mammel, K., Katzman, D., Rome, E., … Walsh, B. T. (2014). Characteristics of avoidant/restrictive food intake disorder in children and adolescents: A "new disorder" in *DSM*-5. *Journal of Adolescent Health*, 55(1), 49–52.

Fox, J. R. E., Dean, M., & Whittlesea, A. (2017). The experience of caring for or living with an individual with an eating disorder: A meta-synthesis of qualitative studies. *Clinical Psychology & Psychotherapy*, 24(1), 103–125

Frank, G. (2015). Advances from neuroimaging studies in eating disorders. *CNS Spectrums*, 20(4), 391–400.

Gisladottir, M., Treasure, J., & Svavarsdottir, E. K. (2017). Effectiveness of therapeutic conversation intervention among caregivers of people with eating disorders: Quasi-experimental design. *Journal of Clinical Nursing*, 26(5–6), 735–750.

Goodier, G. H. G., McCormack, J., Egan, S. J., Watson, H. J., Hoiles, K. J., Todd, G., & Treasure, J. L. (2014). Parent skills training treatment for parents of children and adolescents with eating disorders: A qualitative study. *International Journal of Eating Disorders*, 47(4), 368–375.

Hoffman, S., & Warschburger, P. (2017). Weight, shape, and muscularity concerns in male and female adolescents: Predictors of change and influences on eating concerns. *International Journal of Eating Disorders*, 50(2), 139–147.

Hollesen, A., Clausen, L., & Rokkedal, K. (2013). Multiple family therapy with anorexia nervosa: A pilot study of eating disorder symptoms and interpersonal functioning. *Journal of Family Therapy*, 36(S1), 53–67.

House, J., Schmidt, U., Craig, M., Landau, S., Simic, M., Nicholls, D., ... Eisler, I. (2012). Comparison of specialist and nonspecialist care pathways for adolescents with anorexia nervosa and related eating disorders. *International Journal of Eating Disorders*, 45(8), 949–956.

Kaye, W. H., Wierenga, C. E., Bailer, U. F., Simmons, A. N., & Bischoff-Grethe, A. (2013). Nothing tastes as good as skinny feels: The neurobiology of anorexia nervosa. *Trends in Neurosciences*, 36, 110–120.

Madden, S., Morris, A., Zurynski, Y. A., Kohn, M., & Elliot, E. J. (2009). Burden of eating disorders in 5–13-year-old children in Australia. *Medical Journal of Australia*, 190(8), 410–414.

Marzola, E., Knatz, S., Murray, S. B., Rockwell, R., Boutelle, K., Eisler, I., & Kaye, W. H. (2015). Short-term intensive family therapy for adolescent eating disorders: 30-month outcome. *European Eating Disorders Review*, 23(3), 210–218.

Miller, J. B., & Stiver, I. P. (1997). *The healing connection: How women form relationships in therapy and in life*. Boston, MA: Beacon Press.

Norris, M. L., Robinson, A., Obeid, N., Harrison, M., Spettigue, W., & Henderson, K. (2014). Exploring avoidant/restrictive food intake disorder in eating disordered patients: A descriptive study. *International Journal of Eating Disorders*, 47(5), 495–499.

Norris, M. L., Spettigue, W. J., & Katzman, D. K. (2016). Update on eating disorders: Current perspectives on avoidant/restrictive food intake disorder in children and youth. *Neuropsychiatric Disease and Treatment*, 12, 213–218.

Pope, H., Phillips, K. A., & Olivardia, R. (2002). *The Adonis complex: How to identify, treat, and prevent body obsession in men and boys*. New York, NY: Simon & Schuster.

Ricciardelli, L. A., & McCabe, M. P. (2007). Pursuit of muscularity among adolescents. In J. K. Thompson & G. Cafri (Eds.), *The muscular ideal: Psychological, social, and medical perspectives* (pp. 199–216). Washington, DC: American Psychological Association.

Rodgers, R. F., Lowy, A. S., Halperin, D. M., & Franko, D. L. (2016). A meta-analysis examining the influence of pro-eating disorder websites on body image and eating pathology. *European Eating Disorders Review*, 24(1), 3–8.

Spotts-De Lazzer, A., & Muhlheim, L. (2016). Eating disorder and scope of competence for outpatient psychotherapists. *Practice Innovations*, 1(2), 89–104.

Stiles-Shields, C., Hoste, R. R., Doyle, P. M., & Le Grange, D. (2012). A review of family-based treatment for adolescents with eating disorders. *Reviews on Recent Clinical Trials*, 7(2), 133.

Sultson, H., van Meer, F., Sanders, N., van Elburg, A. A., Danner, U. N., Hoek, H. W., … Smeets, P. (2016). Associations between neural correlates of visual stimulus processing and set-shifting in ill and recovered women with anorexia nervosa. *Psychiatry Research: Neuroimaging*, 255, 35–42.

Tantillo, M. (2004). The therapist's use of self-disclosure in a relational therapy approach for eating disorders. *Eating Disorders*, 12(1), 51–73.

Tantillo, M. (2006). A relational approach to eating disorders multifamily therapy group: Moving from difference and disconnection to mutual connection. *Families, Systems, & Health*, 24, 82–102.

Tantillo, M., & Sanftner, J. (2003). The relationship between perceived mutuality and bulimic symptoms, depression, and therapeutic change in group. *Eating Behaviors*, 3, 349–364.

Tantillo, M., & Sanftner, J. L. (2010). Mutuality and motivation: Connecting with patients and families for change in the treatment of eating disorders. In M. Maine, D. Bunnell, & B. McGilley (Eds.), *Treatment of eating disorders: Bridging the gap between research and practice* (pp. 319–334). London, UK: Elsevier.

Tantillo, M., MacDowell, S., Anson, E., Taillie, E., & Cole, R. (2009). Combining supported housing and partial hospitalization to improve eating disorder symptoms, perceived health status, and health related quality of life for women with eating disorders. *Eating Disorders*, 17, 385–399.

Tantillo, M., Sanftner, J., & Hauenstein, E. (2013). Restoring connection in the face of disconnection. *Advances in Eating Disorders*, 1(1), 21–38.

Vandereycken, W. (2011). Can eating disorders become contagious in group therapy and specialized inpatient care. *European Eating Disorders Review*, 19, 289–295.

Zabala, M. J., Macdonald, P., & Treasure, J. (2009). Appraisal of caregiving burden, expressed emotion and psychological distress in families of people with eating disorders: A systematic review. *European Eating Disorders Review*, 17(5), 338–349.

Zastrow, A., Kaiser, S., Stippich, C., Walther, S., Herzog, W., Tchanturia, K., … Friederich, H. C. (2009). Neural correlates of impaired cognitive-behavioral flexibility in anorexia nervosa. *American Journal of Psychiatry*, 166(5), 608–616.

4 Anna

Resistance to Recovery

Anna fainted at school. It happened in the school bathroom. She had been feeling weak and dizzy and when she fell and hit her head. Her friend, Tyler, saw her slump down and stayed with her in the bathroom. Alarmed, Tyler shouted at another student, "Go get the school nurse as fast as you can." Anna was dizzy and confused as she struggled to consciousness but managed to stay still when Tyler told her to not move until the nurse came. Embarrassed and upset, Anna tried to persuade people trying to help her that she was fine. Nonetheless, Anna was transported to the hospital in an ambulance with a suspected concussion. Anna's parents were called to meet the ambulance at the hospital. Shocked, Kelly and Justin, Anna's parents, left their respective workplaces and broke speed limits getting to the hospital. There the emergency room physician who first examined Anna determined she didn't have a concussion but she was clearly ill.

After ruling out a number of possibilities, it was a positive that the emergency room (ER) physician considered Anna's presenting symptoms, e.g., sudden diarrhea and fainting, might be the result of an underlying eating disorder (Mascolo, Trent, Colwell, and Mehler, 2012). The ER physician knew that in someone so young without signs of other illnesses, bulimic purge behavior was a possibility. He asked Anna about self-induced vomiting or laxative use. Anna didn't admit to either. Kelly, Anna's mother, was suspicious of an eating disorder and had observed dietary restriction. She told the ER physician so. Given the evidence, he decided to keep Anna overnight on a medical unit for observation.

No sooner had this happened than Kelly received a call from the school nurse. It seems Tyler, too frightened by Anna's fainting to keep Anna's confidence, reported to the school nurse that she had been with Anna when she purchased over-the-counter laxatives after school one day a few weeks ago. Tyler knew Anna had been taking laxatives before school each day in order to lose weight. Earlier on the day Anna was taken to the hospital, Tyler reported Anna had rushed to the bathroom after lunch in the cafeteria with stomach pain and a bout of sudden diarrhea. She guessed it was from Anna's laxative use and followed Anna to the bathroom only to get there in time to see Anna faint to the floor. Kelly reported all that Tyler said to the hospital social worker who was part of the team evaluating Anna. In the hospital, Anna was infused with fluids and electrolytes to stabilize her dehydrated condition resulting from laxative abuse. After a day of observation and electrolyte repletion and before discharge from the hospital the electrical activity of Anna's heart was assessed using an EKG to make sure her heart's electrical activity was normal after treatments. It was determined that Anna was medically stable enough to be discharged. Dr. Brody, a staff psychiatrist at the hospital, was called in when an eating disorder seemed likely. She determined Anna was abusing laxatives, was malnourished due to restriction of intake, and had little insight into her condition. Taking into consideration multidisciplinary input, the hospital social worker prepared to make post-discharge recommendations for an eating disorder evaluation and medical follow-up.

Meanwhile, Kelly and Justin were becoming increasingly alert to Anna's discomfort with her body, something that had been growing worse over the past year or two. For example, Kelly often caught Anna turning and twisting in front of the hallway mirror obviously inspecting her body around the waist area. Kelly and Justin had been trying to intervene in small ways. Kelly was acutely aware that Anna disliked her body and found herself watching any language around the house that suggested body dissatisfaction. Kelly had noticed Anna picking at her dinner and often leaving the table in the middle of a meal to head for the bathroom. Suspicious of vomiting, Kelly asked her about it. Anna retorted with, "Are you kidding? I hate throwing up. You are so paranoid." That had left Kelly sensing Anna's defensiveness about anything that suggested she might have an eating disorder, but now what? She didn't know what to do to help her daughter.

Soon after Anna was admitted to the hospital and the damage the eating disorder (called Ed by the family) had done to her body had been assessed, the hospital social worker told Kelly and Justin what to do: the hospital who evaluated Anna highly recommended residential or specialized hospital care to address Anna's potential for further dangerous behavior. They were informed of the gastrointestinal and cardiovascular complications of purge behaviors, such as vomiting, laxative abuse, and diuretic abuse. Anna was medically stable for now, but the doctors were concerned for her future. Yikes. After hearing this and before Anna was released, Kelly and Justin both did some intense reading about various treatments for eating disorders and decided together that an intensive home-based method, Family Based Treatment (FBT, Lock & Le Grange, 2015), with outpatient medical management might be the best way for them to help her. Anna met some of the main criteria for FBT: she was still fairly young; was medically stable, thank goodness; and had been ill with anorexia for less than 3 years. The timing was on their side. Additionally, after her overnight stay in a medical hospital for dehydration, fainting, and, as was discovered, related mild heart arrhythmia, Anna was embarrassed, contrite, and seemed superficially more willing to work on getting rid of Ed.

Another important aspect of their decision was that Kelly and Justin were both available to tag team a home-feeding program. They fully intended to follow through with weekly medical evaluations with their local doctor in order to keep tabs on Anna's precarious health. They read the positive recommendations for FBT written by parents who had tried the approach (Maudsley

Parents, n.d.), but what drove their attraction to this intervention the most was their fear of sending their daughter to a hospital or live-away treatment facility. Not only did Anna not want to be sent away, but the 4 hours of travel each way to the nearest facility for delivery, pick-up, and family-therapy involvement seemed impossible if they also were to care for Molly, their younger daughter. The geographic distance would also limit Kelly's and Justin's active and more continuous involvement in Anna's treatment. A disadvantage of residential treatment is that it limits parental involvement, education and practice in preparation for discharge and transition to family and community life.

As mentioned already, the reason Anna was hospitalized was that she had passed out and hit her head. Despite her protests, and unwillingness to reveal bulimic behavior she passed out on the floor because she had been abusing laxatives for some time. Since eating disorders are the harbingers of lies, Anna didn't know, nor did she care to know, the truth about the dangers and, more importantly, the ineffectiveness for weight loss of laxatives as well as vomiting.

Laxatives are an ineffective way to flush food because they work on the large intestine and not the small intestine where most of the nutrients are absorbed. Anywhere from roughly 15% to 75% of those with bulimia nervosa turn to laxative abuse (reviewed in Yen & Ewald, 2012). Yet only 10-12% of calories ingested are lost through laxative abuse (Turner, Batik, Palmer, Forbes, & McDermott, 2000). Further, laxatives can be unsafe when used for reasons other than medically recommended treatment. Laxatives flush liquids, electrolytes, and nutrients out of the body. Important minerals and vitamins may be washed away before they are properly absorbed. Iron deficiencies, or hypocalcemia, are examples of poor nutrient absorption related to laxative abuse. Self-induced vomiting and laxative abuse along with diuretic abuse all result in the dangerous loss of potassium-containing fluids (hypokalemia), as well as rebound edema (water retention). Hypokalemia is not typical of weight loss behavior by itself, so the presence of low potassium levels in the presence of restrictive eating disorders correctly suggests purge behavior. Further risks of laxative abuse include muscle weakness, lassitude, cardiac arrhythmias, hypotension, and falls. Electrolyte imbalance and dehydration can result in death through cardiac arrhythmias, a situation that has been publicized in well-known media cases, for example the documentary film, *Someday Melissa*, produced by Melissa's mother Judy Avrin (Avrin & Cobelli, 2011). Anna put her body at dangerous risk for malnutrition, dehydration, and electrolyte imbalance every time she used laxatives to manage her weight (Baker & Sandle, 1996; Kovacs & Palmer, 2004).

We cannot say what percentage of nutrient intake is lost with self-induced vomiting. It depends on the frequency and technique of vomiting and individual differences in metabolism and gastric-emptying time (slowed when accompanied by chronic restriction behavior), as well as other factors (Saren, 2016). There are a large number of gastrointestinal and cardiovascular consequences of self-induced vomiting. The most common gastrointestinal complications are reflexive vomiting without self-stimulation, pharyngeal (throat) soreness due to chronic irritation, dental erosions usually discovered by dentists, painless swelling in the salivary glands, esophageal damage from exposure of the esophagus to vomited acidic gastric stomach contents, and, over time, spontaneous reflux into the esophagus of acidic gastric contents. Swelling in the salivary glands is not seen in all patients with self-induced vomiting and is usually not visible until a few days after a binge-purge episode.

Anna's parents knew she had lost weight and that she had become very picky about the food she ate. At 15, she ate with her family at dinner only because Kelly insisted. If Kelly and Justin didn't pressure Anna every night to eat with them, she would eat alone in her room. She was increasingly secretive about her intake. Ed had such a grip on Anna she was completely unwilling to discuss topics related to food. Nevertheless, the brief hospital stay was a wake-up call for her parents. Anna, under the influence of the eating disorder, was desperate enough to make herself this dangerously ill in order to manage her weight.

Anna's inner life was far more of a struggle than Kelly, Justin, or Molly would ever begin to suspect. Anna heard the rants of Ed in her mind regularly. It verbally abused her, calling herself "fat," "ugly," "stupid," "worthless," "obese," and "disgusting," among other names, and railed swear words at her. Anna compared herself to sizes she used to be, saying things to herself like, "I'm not as skinny as I was when school ended last spring." The inner demands of Ed for further levels of "skinny" were increasing, rather than decreasing, as Anna lost weight. Looking back, Anna said, "I couldn't be satisfied with my body – every time I set a new weight goal, like 110 pounds, it was only good for a while. I figured if I got to 110 pounds, I could do even better. So I would try to go down to an even lower weight – like 105 pounds. I couldn't win, but I didn't see at the time that Ed would never be satisfied. No weight was ever good enough for very long." Anna's anxiety about body size and whether or not bones were properly protruding accelerated as she yielded more to the internal pressures from Ed to try harder to have a perfect, smaller body.

Anna measured her thighs with her hands every morning. It was important to her that she could wrap her two hands around the widest part of her thigh without losing contact with the other hand. If her thighs were bigger than the circle of her touching hands, she was too fat. Then there was the pinch test for the other dreaded body part – her stomach. Anna demanded of herself that, when she sat down, there were no folds of skin that showed themselves; if she could pinch some of her flesh with her fingers, she was "disgusting." She told herself she would rather be dead. Then there were her collarbones. It was critical that her skin be stretched over these so that, when inspected in a mirror, they stuck out clearly defined – like shiny knobs. Any sign of "padding" around these important bones meant she was "ugly" and "too fat." These kinds of body checking behaviors are common in individuals with ED's (Fairburn, 2008). The eating-disorder illness, a berating taskmaster, was hard at work controlling Anna's thoughts and actions.

Anna's struggle with a restrictive eating disorder was riddled with perfectionism. Underlying her pursuit of a thin body was an immature attempt at self-imposed control—a trial run at adult maturity. She felt it was important to "not make trouble" by trying to become perfect or "good." She was prone to be over-responsible and self-reliant in order to take care of or protect others. She imposed perfectionistic controls on herself demanding that she "get it all right." When so many other aspects of life didn't yield to Anna's adolescent demands for control and perfection, she turned to controlling the pursuit of perfect eating. A perfect body seemed to be comparatively within reach. For Anna a perfect body began with a flat stomach. She wanted a thin appearance as defined by thin media images in magazines, newspapers, videos, and TV. Anything less was failure. The fat and bulk brought on by puberty were repulsive to her and demanded correction. Anna's fear of fat was maintained by her fear of failure to be thin and the societal stigmatization of obesity (Rudd Center; www.uconnruddcenter.org/weight-bias-stigma). Unfortunately Anna's pursuit of a perfect body was ill-fated and ultimately deluded because like most young people with eating disorders her weight management activities, e.g., restrictive eating and laxative abuse, became out-of-control. This was the opposite of the self-imposed control she wished for.

Here are some questions to ask to determine if perfectionism, as applied to the pursuit of the ideal body, has become a problem:

1. When I look in the mirror, do I see only flaws?
2. Is there an ideal way to eat and dress?
3. Is there a perfect body size?
4. Do I feel bad about myself when I eat foods I think are unhealthy?
5. Is my value as a person determined by the way I eat?
6. Is my worth as a person determined by the way I look?
7. Is there always some flaw or imperfection in the way I look or eat that can be corrected?
8. Do I avoid foods I used to enjoy because it is more important to eat the right foods than to enjoy food?
9. Do I avoid taking risks with new foods or forms of exercise because they might distract me from achieving my perfect weight?
10. Do I tend to make up rules for food, eating, clothes, or exercise?

With regard to dietary restriction, salt was Anna's enemy, as were too many fluids. Her logic was that both of these substances resulted in fluid retention, and she feared bloating. "Fat," "ugly," "gross," "obscenely humungous," "dirty," and "disgusting" were Anna's mantras. They repeated themselves in her head as she walked through her day. The words were like chanting, abusive cheerleaders who wanted Anna to win against the urge to eat or sit or be too lazy. Concentration in school became more of an issue. Fear of failure at school became complicated by inner chants expounding on body hatred. Both co-existed in Anna's head. Chants of "you are hideous" were met by chants of "better pay attention because if you don't you might fail this class."

Although she often thought she would prefer to figure out a way to die in order to get away from her inner fat thoughts, Anna usually ended up craving exercise and planning how to restrict her food. Anna obsessed about finding chances to secretly run up and down her home's basement steps barefoot. She did it quietly so no one would hear her behaving in such a bizarre way. Anna said to herself, "I will hate it if they try to stop me. No noise allowed!" especially after her parents became aware of her eating problems. After her hospitalization, Anna went into new levels of covert activity around her family and friends. When the family sat down to watch TV, she chose to stand as much as possible. Burning maximum calories was essential.

When eating a meal with the family while trying to appear "normal," Anna would become silent, preoccupied by the anxiety of consuming food. There is ample neurological evidence that the sight of many foods generates anxiety in those with anorexia (Ellison, Foong, Howard, Bullmore, Williams, and Treasure, 1998; Frank & Kaye, 2012; Kaye, Wierenga, Bailer, Simmons, & Bischoff-Grethe, 2013; Levinson & Byrne, 2015; Treasure, Cardi, & Kan, 2012). A stranger at her family's table, she quietly, in her head, loathed the dense substances she took in. Calculating the "damage," she thought obsessively about how she could "get rid" of what she had just put in her body. Exercising was one way to unload the fearsome density. Getting away from the table before too many calories were absorbed was critical. "I have to go to the bathroom," Anna would say. Of course no one would stop her from going to the bathroom since that was a basic human right. Anna's forays to the bathroom were a new means to avoid eating – with any luck, the rest of her family would be finished when she got back. While in there, she could exercise in the small space. She did it fairly quietly and then covered her clandestine activity with a noisy, prolonged flush. That's when Kelly suspected vomiting and asked her about it. Vomiting had never appealed to Anna, however. In her desperation, she had succeeded in doing it a few times, but hated vomiting and preferred laxative abuse. Nonetheless, the fact she had used vomiting to appease Ed put her at risk for returning to it in moments of desperation.

Anna discovered stimulant laxatives, the most common kind abused by those with eating disorders (Mehler, 2011). Frustrated by the need to exercise for long periods of time to burn the calories she consumed, she perceived laxatives as offering a quicker alternative. Easy reading on social networks and blogs about how to be skinny with a flat stomach taught Anna the advantages of these over-the-counter medications. She used them to strip her body of any bloat in her stomach by flushing her intestines. The flat stomach that resulted when she emptied her bowels was thrilling. Easily obtained at the local drug store, Anna stocked up on Exlax, Miralax, and Senokot, which she hid under her mattress and carried with her in her backpack. Of this Anna said, "I was really good at hiding things by the time I got to the laxatives. I was highly accomplished at stealth." She was soon using at least one dose a day, despite uncomfortable stomach cramping and frequent trips to the bathroom.

Anna was desperate to have a flat stomach and thighs she could encircle with her hands. In retrospect, she realized it was a trivial obsession, but her brain had been hijacked by Ed, and she was obsessed to achieve this degree of perfection above all else in her life. It moved her to use laxatives in addition to food avoidance, exercise, and occasional self-induced vomiting. Progress at reaching those goals was gauged, in part, by the numbers on the bathroom scale. Anna's love-hate relationship with those numbers grew more intense as her need for reassurance that she was thin enough heightened.

Unfortunately, Anna's thin goals were elusive at best and any evidence of accomplishment gave way to stricter standards for being thin. Thus, Anna was caught in a never-ending cycle of (1) a drive for thinness, followed by (2) her repertoire of thin-achievement behaviors (including compensatory purging and exercise), followed by (3) momentary anxiety reduction (if the mirror, the scale, and the encircling fingers fed her the right results), followed by (4) increasingly stricter size standards, followed by (5) guilt, and circling back around to a sterner drive for thinness (see #1 above).

Initially, before Anna's hospitalization, Kelly was afraid of Anna's fierceness. Her daughter could be savage in defense of her quest for thinness. Kelly didn't like to see that side of her daughter. She was also afraid she would drive Anna into more Ed behavior if she upset her. She was afraid to confront her. She resorted to subterfuge to try and make her fears about Anna's issues known.

Whereas when Anna was a young girl Kelly might have dropped a comment in front of her like, "I don't like these jeans on me because I look too big," she now edited her body-reflection issues through a "word-police" filter that operated on the following principles: "No negative body-image talk allowed. No thin talk. All bodies are fine just the way they are. Anna is beautiful just the way she is. No talking about junk food or bad foods." Fashion magazines that had been lying around were thrown away. In those indirect ways, Kelly tried to create a healthier environment for Anna and persuade her to stop hating her body and attempting to make it smaller. She went out of her way to compliment Anna on how beautiful she was. She convinced Justin he should be paying more affirming attention to Anna so that she would feel better about herself. Dutifully, he made it a point to talk to Anna every night about how her day had gone.

All of Kelly and Justin's ideas and help were well-intended and represented steps in the right direction, but were coming a little late in the game. They didn't realize that Ed often takes on a life of its own – that it has self-reinforcing properties that a healthy home environment can mitigate, but not defeat without more help. By the time the call came from Anna's high school, Anna's condition had worsened to a point of brain and body impairment that shocked Kelly and Justin.

Kelly and Justin were stunned that they hadn't known what Anna was up to. They had not been aware of her laxative use, much less occasional vomiting. They felt blindsided, like they had somehow dropped the ball on caring for their daughter. She had never been much trouble as a young girl, so of course they took her good behavior for granted. They were overwhelmed to find out how dangerous their daughter's clandestine behaviors were. They quickly learned from the emergency-room physician who treated Anna that laxative use removes water and electrolytes from the body. Finally, when cornered by her friend's revelation and pressed by the ER physician on day 2 in the hospital, Anna verbally admitted to using laxatives daily. The previous morning, she had used Senokot, a particularly dangerous one, because it causes the muscles of the intestines to contract and expel their contents. Diarrhea, in turn, causes water loss. Water loss had likely lowered Anna's blood pressure, increased her heart rate, and caused her to pass out. Anna, following Ed's demands, lied to the ER physician when he asked about self-induced vomiting.

Further investigation in the hospital revealed that Anna had lost considerable weight – beyond what could be accounted for by dehydration. A check by the hospital with her pediatrician's electronic record showed Anna's weight was 20% below her last check up the year before. Given that Anna was a physically maturing teen, she should have increased her overall weight, height, and body mass index (BMI). Instead her weight and BMI had decreased.

When they were first given the news, Kelly and Justin were justly overwhelmed with anxiety for their daughter's condition. They didn't have a clue how to manage it at this dangerous level. Further, Kelly could see that Anna, although humbled and frightened by her medical emergency, remained defensive about her behaviors. As she recovered in the hours after her discharge from the hospital, she seemed angry that she had "given up" her secret about laxatives to the ER physician. Further, she seemed to minimize the seriousness of her medical condition, although she agreed to further treatment.

With their pediatrician's support and careful oversight, Kelly and Justin embarked on the demanding journey of home-based treatment. They familiarized themselves with the neurobiological research about Anna's diagnosis, Anorexia Nervosa: Binge Eating/Purging Type (American Psychiatric Association, 2013). Like Anna, some people with this diagnosis do not binge eat but purge even after a small or normal meal is eaten. Because of their research, Kelly and Justin had a better understanding of their child's resistance to restoring healthy eating. For example, Kelly read Kaye, Bailer, Klabunde, and Brown's (2010) research report that indicated that those with eating disorders "tend to resist treatment and lack insight about the seriousness of the medical consequences of AN [anorexia nervosa]" (p. 1). These authors further reported that:

> brain imaging studies suggest that people with AN have lower-than-usual drive in a number of the systems that respond to hunger and appetite, which may explain how it's possible for them to pursue emaciation to the point of death. Normally when people become hungry, neural networks around the brain become more active, making food taste more rewarding and driving the motivation to eat. People with AN may get mixed messages from various parts of the brain, which may explain why they often have obsessions with food and cooking yet don't have enough motivation to eat.
>
> (p. 4)

Kelly and Justin read all of this and more. What they learned was frightening, but at the same time reassuring, because the illness their daughter suffered was somewhat easier to comprehend the more they exposed themselves to the information. They no longer expected their daughter to cooperate with them when they told her to eat. They also understood that Anna's resistance to treatment was normal, given her condition. They began to see that it was the eating disorder, Ed, not Anna, that mounted persistent resistance.

They were beginning to understand the enormous task in front of them, too, as they embarked on trying to restore nutrition to a daughter who not only resisted eating, but was also truly anxious and disabled when it came to eating. Anna was at first relieved to avoid being sent off to the hospital when she heard her family was going to use FBT at home. When she was finally back after 2 days of emergency care at the hospital, she was glad of it. However, she grew dismayed and resentful as she increasingly understood her parents' firm resolve to restore her eating to previous levels. From her perspective, working with their new FBT therapist, Dr. Wollen, gave enormous power to her parents (Lock & Le Grange, 2015). At the behest of Ed, she had devoted considerable energy to avoiding her parents' detection of her food-restriction, exercise, and laxative-use. Now all her efforts were lost. Not understanding that she was overwhelmed by a powerful eating disorder, she blamed herself and felt like a failure.

As the eating disorder increasingly eclipsed her brain, Anna increasingly perceived her parents as enemies. That her parents were taking charge of what she ate was impossible. However, the thought of going to a hospital was even more impossible. What she didn't realize at the time was that she would occasionally wish for hospitalization because her parents were relentless. Coached and encouraged by Dr. Wollen, they firmly and persistently learned to feed her meal after meal. Anna did not realize she would become depressed, hateful, guilty for disappointing her mom and dad over and over, and anxious beyond anything she had experienced before.

Their first meeting with the FBT therapist was alarming. Dr. Wollen charged Kelly and Justin with restoring Anna's nutrition – basically, her health. After reviewing both the dangers of Anna's laxative abuse, as well as her malnourished status, Kelly and Justin were tasked with the seemingly impossible directive that they assist Anna in discontinuing her access to laxatives and returning to normal eating. Kelly thought it might be easier to wrestle a rattlesnake. Anna became silent and angry. She glared at both her parents, as well as the therapist. Justin reconsidered the magnitude of the task ahead. It might be easier to hospitalize Anna, he thought. At least she would be safe. He couldn't imagine what his family, including young Molly, would experience as they subdued the eating disorder that ravaged Anna. Dr. Wollen explained that in the first phase of FBT treatment, Kelly and Justin would need to temporarily take charge of Anna's eating and make sure they thwarted other eating-disorder behaviors, such as over-exercise and laxative abuse. He explained that in the later two phases of treatment, food and weight control would gradually be returned to Anna, and normal adolescent issues would be addressed.

The initial session with Dr. Wollen ended very positively in that it reinforced Kelly and Justin's resolve to beat down Ed and free their daughter from its captivity. Much to everyone's surprise, Molly, age 12, was directed to attend each session. She was frankly angry with her sister for upsetting their parents. She didn't see why she needed to attend family sessions, especially when she had after-school sports that were going to be interrupted. It was Anna's problem, not hers, and she resented the intrusion into her schedule, as well as the many ways in which Anna was swallowing up her parents' time and attention, if not money, for treatment. During the first session, Dr. Wollen made it clear that Anna was sicker than Molly had thought. At one point, he mentioned something about "treating Anna like you would if she had been diagnosed with cancer, or diabetes." Now Molly was not only angry, but afraid for her sister.

Following the FBT manualized treatment protocol (Lock & Le Grange, 2015), Kelly and Justin determined how much food Anna needed to start eating. They gave her a few days to adjust, but ramped up her intake soon after. They were told early aggressive treatment had the best outcome. Research has shown that early weight gain by session four of FBT treatment is an important predictor of higher weight gain by the end of treatment (Doyle, Le Grange, Loeb, Doyle, & Crosby, 2010; Lock, Couturier, Bryson, & Agras, 2006; Madden et al., 2015). Everyone in the family knew they were operating against the threat of hospitalization, because when Kelly and Justin had asked the therapist about possible inpatient care, Dr. Wollen had indicated that hospitalization would be necessary if medical instability reoccurred. It all depended on the progress they made. Everyone expected Anna's weight to not only stop dropping, but to increase each week.

Dr. Wollen weighed Anna in his office at the beginning of each session when he met with her briefly alone. Further, there were periodic medical-management checks with the pediatrician during which time Anna was weighed in a gown. The need for weekly records of laxative-abuse behavior to the FBT therapist seemed unnecessary, as Anna vowed she had been frightened into health and away from purge behavior following the unpleasant and terrifying stay and medical interventions she experienced in the hospital. Nonetheless, not trusting Ed's wily ways, Dr. Wollen required a daily log of purge behavior, even if zero purge behavior was recorded.

At first, Anna tried to convince her parents that she had to increase her nutrition slowly or she would suffer from refeeding syndrome, something she had researched on the Internet. *Refeeding syndrome* occurs when malnourished patients receive nutritional rehabilitation and a potentially fatal shift occurs in fluids and electrolytes.

> These shifts result from hormonal and metabolic changes and may cause serious clinical complications. The hallmark biochemical feature of refeeding syndrome is hypophosphataemia [an abnormally low level of phosphate in the blood]. However, the syndrome is complex and may also feature

> abnormal sodium and fluid balance; changes in glucose, protein, and fat metabolism; thiamine deficiency; hypokalaemia [an abnormally low level of potassium in the blood]; and hypomagnesaemia [an abnormally low level of magnesium in the blood] (Mehanna, Moledina, & Travis, 2008, p. 1495).

Patients at greater risk for refeeding syndrome include those with cardiac problems, the chronically undernourished, and those who have had little intake for more than 10 days. Refeeding syndrome is more apt to occur when a high amount of intake is consumed over a short period of time, outpacing the body's ability to transition from a catabolic state (starvation with resulting tissue loss) to an anabolic state (refeeding leading to weight gain and tissue growth) (Mehler & Anderson, 2010). Given the snail's pace at which Anna stemmed her weight loss and began to gain, both the pediatrician and the therapist assured Kelly and Justin that refeeding syndrome was an unlikely concern. Should anything like it manifest, the pediatrician promised he would manage it, or, if needed, refer Anna to a higher level of care.

Running out of arguments, Anna was increasingly frustrated as her parents did not back down. To get rid of her parents' persistent feeding, she could be heard saying things like, "I hate you," or "You're killing me." Of course, she also simply put her head down, clamped her jaws shut, and refused to eat, arms crossed tightly across her body. Session two of FBT is the Family Meal, part of the manualized protocol (Lock & Le Grange, 2015). This took place with Anna and her family in the therapist's office. Molly, Kelly, Justin, and Anna sat on the couches and chairs surrounding a small table in Dr. Wollen's office. Justin served the food, portioning out normal amounts for everyone. He knew lasagna was a difficult food for Anna and fully anticipated she would need lots of encouragement to battle Ed and tolerate the inevitable and excruciating anxiety she would experience upon eating. A multitude of ED thoughts (e.g., "You are a pig if you eat this! You are so disgusting! They just want to make you fat!") pushed Anna to display avoidant behaviors like shoving the food around her plate and arguing with her parents that she was not hungry, or had "eaten enough. Her parents, however, refused to give in to Ed.

Shored up by the FBT therapist, Kelly and Justin persevered during the Family Meal. When Anna had not started eating the lasagna that Justin served her, Dr. Wollen encouraged Justin and Kelly by saying to them, "I'm glad to see the two of you prepared a meal that will move Anna toward improved eating. Do you think Anna has eaten enough of the meal you prepared to restore her health?" Justin and Kelly realized this was exactly the kind of situation they would face at home when prompting Anna to eat. Working together they considered what strategies might work best to encourage Anna to eat. Dr. Wollen reinforced their idea to take a direct approach. Justin clearly and firmly stated to Anna, "You need to eat the lasagna on your plate." Hearing her father's clear instruction relieved Anna of making a choice to eat or not. She picked up her fork and ate a bite of lasagna. It was a start.

Recent research (White et al., 2017) looked at the effectiveness of various strategies parents use to prompt children to eat during the Family Meal portion of FBT. Although the research sample was small (18 families whose teens received inpatient treatment prior to FBT), the two strategies found to be associated with the best outcomes at the end of treatment were direct eating prompts ("You need to eat these potatoes") and non-direct eating prompts, such as encouraging eating. Parents providing their child with informative comments ("It is protein that will help you build muscle"), parents offering their child choices about what to eat, and parents' physical movement to encourage food consumption were not as effective as these two strategies.

Lock, Le Grange, Agras, and Dare (2001) identify goals for the Family Meal in FBT. They include:

1 Evaluate the efficacy of parent strategies used to re-nourish.
2 Provide feedback to the family to assist increasing nourishment.
3 Coach parents to deal with the challenges of encountering eating-disorder behavior (e.g., help parents remain calm and patient even when their child resists eating).
4 Empower parents to take charge of renourishment efforts.
5 Empower siblings to assist their ill sibling to face challenges after eating.

With these goals in mind during the Family Meal, Dr. Wollen set about to reinforce parent unification, parent patience and persistence in re-nourishing, and parent empowerment to creatively develop strategies for feeding. He helped them ignore Anna's attempts to deflect away from the eating task at hand ("We have to go, I have to study for my test tomorrow.") and kept them focused on re-nourishing Anna (Fitzpatrick, Darcy, Le Grange, & Lock, 2015; Lock & Le Grange, 2015).

In subsequent sessions, after the Family Meal, Kelly and Justin celebrated their successes at home, noting what worked best. Both parents learned ways to calm themselves down, because when anorexia is in the room during a meal there is inevitable distress and the potential to have conflict with Anna. They became masters at regulating their own anxiety and frustration at meals, so they could role model calmness for Anna and avoid arguments. Along the way, they also learned to help Anna soothe herself and calm down after eating a portion of her meal, so that she could better tolerate completing her meal.

At home, Anna's mother or father would sit with her for an hour at meals if needed, coaxing her and reassuring her that they were not going away. Anna remained disturbed by her parents' persistent, seemingly unwavering attempts to feed her. Since breakfast was difficult for Anna, she was often late getting to school. Kelly made it clear to her that her health came first. School came second. A doctor's note to the school excused Anna from frequent tardiness in the first month of home-based feeding. Gradually Justin and Kelly identified a goal of reducing the time to consume breakfast to 30 minutes. When this was accomplished after a month, Anna was no longer late for school.

Much to Anna's chagrin and embarrassment, each day she was also removed from school by her father for lunch. Kelly and Justin learned to in no way trust Ed's grip on their child. They knew that if given the chance, Anna would skip her lunch, or at least skimp on any lunch they sent with her to school. The FBT therapist made it clear that all meals and snacks were to be supervised until Anna showed she could take responsibility for feeding herself in a normal fashion. That meant that in the 2 months of FBT Phase I, every day Justin showed up in the school parking lot and waited for his daughter to come eat with him on the front seat of the car. Kelly prepared full, nutritious lunches. Justin served them from a brown paper bag.

Surprisingly, Anna showed up every day without fail. She knew her parents were very serious in their resolve to get her to restore her weight and eat the foods her family ate on a regular basis. Anna learned to focus her attention on reducing the amount of food she was served. She tore little pieces of sandwich off the edges and let them slip quietly to the floor. She inspected any meat for ribbons of fat so that she could try to remove them. Justin caught on to the latter behavior quickly and forbid Anna to open her sandwiches and pick them apart. Anna tried to take little bites. Since she was full most of the time, eating slowly was easy. According to Ed, the longer she could prolong her lunches the better, even though it meant she missed lunch with her friends. Although she wanted to be with her friends, slowing down her eating and dealing with her anxiety trumped that desire.

Anna sometimes imagined how much easier the hospital might have been. At least then she wouldn't have had to deal with her parents suspecting her of under-eating several times a day. Further, it was clear that Molly, even though scared for her sister, hated her. Getting away from her family in the hospital might have been better. Molly was slow to come around to having any kind of compassion for her sister. She rolled her eyes at dinner when Anna argued with her parents about eating one more bite of rice. Anna could do without Molly's complaining and judgmental presence. The FBT therapist addressed Molly's feelings. She didn't want to be the focus of therapy, and she didn't want attention on her. However, at some point during every family session, the therapist checked in with her.

During one session, something in Molly's voice triggered Dr. Wollen to ask if she were angry. Molly teared up at this and reluctantly admitted her anger. "Of course I'm mad. She's a brat and yells at Mom and Dad. I hate eating with her. She tries to boss my parents around when they make her eat. I just want her to stop acting this way." The therapist showed Molly he understood how she felt and validated her feelings. He helped Kelly and Justin understand Molly's reactions as well. Kelly and Justin had always been open about what was going on. However, Molly couldn't hear beyond her stubborn anger and fear. She couldn't process the fact that Anna wasn't trying to be bad or misbehaving – she was sick. Dr. Wollen helped Molly admit to her fear for Anna and her family. Her fear was what really drove her anger.

Slowly, Molly was brought around to her new role in fighting the illness that had so rudely invaded her family. Now Molly, along with her parents, tried not to criticize her sister when she rebelled, but to understand that for Anna, food actually didn't taste good, and it actually scared her. With her increased patience and eventual support for Anna's efforts, Molly began to feel sorry for her sister. Consistent with FBT (Lock & Le Grange, 2015), she was instructed by Dr. Wollen to refrain from "helping" her parents to try to get Anna to eat in an effort to take some of the stress off them. Instead, she was mobilized in therapy to turn her attention to expressing support for her sick sister when she struggled to eat. Aligning herself with her sister, she said things like, "You look really mad at Mom and Dad. This must be really hard."

Over time Kelly felt increasingly confident about their involvement in Family Based Treatment, but she occasionally doubted if she and Justin were doing the right thing. Sometimes she worried maybe Anna was more stubborn than they thought. Then she remembered it was Ed, not Anna, that was rebellious and stubborn. One winter night as the family was gathering for dinner, Anna refused to sit down with them, but instead ran out of the house without her coat. Justin went after her, concerned for her safety. He was prepared to call the police if necessary. It seemed like Anna was depressed and hateful most days. What if she became suicidal? On days like that, Justin also had his doubts about their progress. When Anna ran out of the house, she was actually hiding up the street behind a culvert. When her father drove by slowly, she couldn't bear to see him looking for her. She felt both furious and guilty at the same time. She stood up from her hiding place, walked to the car, and sullenly got in. Anna and her father went home that night, where she ate her dinner, one disgusting bite at a time.

While Kelly and Justin had to be forceful at times to ensure Anna regained her health, it is important to point out "the goal of parent control in FBT is circumscribed to those areas that maintain the ED, such as food, eating, and exercise" (Katzman, Peebles, Sawyer, Lock, & Le Grange, 2013, p. 438). Dr. Wollen made it clear he wasn't suggesting Kelly and Justin take over Anna's entire life. The focus of FBT is "not on limiting adolescent autonomy, but on limiting the impact of the ED on the adolescent" (p. 438). Parental control was limited to those areas that had a direct impact on renourishment and inhibited eating-disorder behaviors. For example, Anna was not allowed to have any digital devices in her bedroom after bedtime. That limit did not shift during any phase of FBT treatment; Anna's required bedtime, as well as her turning over her digital devices, remained in force. Because it did not interfere with eating restoration, Anna was allowed to see her friends at their houses, as long as she came home for supervised meals with her parents.

Through Kelly and Justin's persistence in re-nourishing their daughter, Anna's eating began to stabilize. While Anna's increased intake and weight gain brought Kelly and Justin joy, the process was very taxing for Anna. At first as Anna started to refeed her body, her stomach hurt because her gastro-intestinal track had slowed so much from under-eating. The process of readjusting to eating adequate food was painful. She was both anxious and in pain from diarrhea, bloating, and feelings of nausea. The therapist and the pediatrician both assured Kelly, Justin, and Anna that gastric discomfort was normal during the nutrition-restoration process. Unused to her parents persisting in the face of physical pain, Anna was soon depressed and tired from the daily grind of eating enough.

Then there came a week when Anna didn't gain weight. She did not lose, but she did not gain. The FBT therapist reassured them that, while it was a cautionary sign about eating enough, they could reapply their efforts the next week. During their session, Kelly and Justin were encouraged to strengthen their nutrition restoration tact so that Anna would gain weight the following week. They worked out a plan in the session to double their efforts and increase the amount of food in Anna's afterschool snack so she would gain the next week. While Kelly and Justin were keeping an eye out for any possible laxative use, vomiting, or clandestine exercise, they knew anything was possible, even if it didn't seem likely. They were getting more savvy at "catching" or discovering anorexia behaviors (e.g., secret exercise behavior in the bedroom) and were increasingly effective at curtailing them.

During this session Anna said she didn't know why she had not gained weight that past week. As far as she was concerned, she had eaten more food than she eaten in months, was stuffed at every meal, and groaned at the news she hadn't gained. She also insisted she had not used laxatives since her scare in the emergency room a few months earlier. However, the desperation to restrict was strong, and Kelly and Justin knew it. Anna repeated several times that she was not purging – no use of laxatives and no vomiting. She knew no gain meant doubled efforts on the part of her parents, and that seemed like an awful possibility. Finally, on further questioning, Anna admitted she had been exercising in her room at night. Her fear of weight gain was depressing and intolerable, and she was angrily desperate. The therapist was careful not to take a punitive approach. He encouraged Anna's parents to react with compassion at Ed's strength and its influence on their daughter. Anna agreed not to exercise, since it resulted in her parents' efforts to feed her more.

Each family session began with a weight check and some individual time for Anna with the therapist, followed by a family session focused on reviewing the week's progress, any setbacks, and specific plans for ways to be successful with nutrition restoration over the next week. Eventually, when Anna was in a healthy-weight range – determined by her growth-chart trajectory for height, weight, and BMI – plans began to be made to place eating back in Anna's care. Anna still felt defeated, but became resigned to her parents' persistence on staying in a healthy weight range.

Prior to arriving within this healthy weight range, Anna found herself arguing regularly with her pediatrician, her family therapist, and her parents about what her healthy-weight range should be. She thought it was unfair that she would be held to her growth-chart history and some calculations done by her pediatrician to determine her genetic healthy weight. Anna's parents understood that she was still very persuaded to defend and protect Ed and, because of that, any argument she could generate to reduce weight expectations would be expected.

Her treatment team presented her with a different perspective than the perspective she was operating under – the eating disorder's.

Based on research into eating disorders, the Academy for Eating Disorders (AED; Academy for Eating Disorders, 2012) recommends the following on the part of physicians: "Measurement of height, weight, and determination of body mass index (BMI); record weight, height, and BMI on growth charts for children and adolescents, noting changes from previous height(s) and weight(s)" (p. 8). Anna argued, "As long as I'm healthy and all my blood tests are normal, I should be allowed to remain at my weight," a too-low weight. However, research has found normative height and weight charts are too simplistic. They do not account for different genetic body types. One girl at Anna's height might be healthy and menstruating at one weight, while another girl might be malnourished, not menstruating, and unhealthy at that weight. Each body is different and needs to be considered according to its own history and activity level. Although no one ever wins an argument against an eating disorder, Anna's arguments, reflecting its mindset, were consistently met with facts about healthy, genetically-determined weight ranges and medically sound definitions of good health.

In addition to closely monitoring and communicating weight changes to Kelly, Justin and Dr. Wollen, Anna's pediatrician was careful to use language that externalized the illness from Anna (Katzman et al., 2013), thus removing blame for the illness from both her and her parents. He and the FBT therapist both stressed that no one was to blame for the illness and that causes of the illness were difficult to determine. In keeping with this, in Phase I of FBT, Dr. Wollen stayed focused on eating and weight management and remained agnostic with Anna's family regarding the causes of the illness. There was no discussion of "psychological problems" or adolescent or family stressors that might have somehow contributed to the eating disorder. These would have distracted Kelly and Justin from the important work of re-nourishing their daughter. Anna would also need to be physically re-nourished before benefiting from any future emotional work.

In Phase II of FBT, Kelly and Justin maintained control of managing Anna's eating-disorder symptoms until Anna, worn out from resisting, demonstrated she could eat well and gain and maintain weight on her own. Phase II of FBT is intended to gradually return control of food and weight management to the young patient, and, toward the end of this phase, to begin exploring adolescent-development issues that may be related to the illness. In Phase II, Anna and her parents negotiated gradual weaning from parental nutrition management. For example, Anna negotiated autonomy in preparing her afterschool snack, checking with her parents after preparation to ensure she met her parents' watchful expectations. By this time, Anna had observed what her parents' nutritious snacks were for 2 months, day after day during Phase I of treatment. She was well aware of what foods to choose and what portions to choose based on their examples. The question was, would she be able to confront Ed enough to feed herself well?

During Phase II, Justin and Kelly resigned themselves to insisting Anna maintain healthy nutrition and body weight even when some of Anna's attempts at autonomy failed. For example, at first as Anna resumed gradual control over her food, there was an independent eating experiment that fizzled. Anna lobbied to eat lunch at school with her friends. Her parents, properly cautious, suggested trying 1 day a week without parental supervision. Anna thought she could handle 2 days. That was too many, as it turned out.

Anna found that Ed still commanded her obedience at a level she thought she was past. On the second day of unsupervised lunch, her friend Brittany, who was sitting next to her, was eating a salad and water for lunch. The anxiety of eating more than someone nearby was overwhelming. Anna said to herself, "I can't do this. I can't eat all the stuff my parents packed in my lunch when Brittany is having salad for lunch." Temporarily defeated by Ed, Anna threw half her sandwich away. However, she had collaborated enough with her parents at this point that she honestly reported her experience to her mother. They both agreed Anna would not eat with under-eating friends. Anna ate with a good friend, Ellie, who knew about her struggles and her recovery – a friend who could encourage her. Ellie ate normal amounts and types of food at lunch – a sandwich, chips of some kind, and fruit. She didn't talk about being "fat" and didn't label chips "junk." She provided a supportive atmosphere for Anna to normalize her eating. Further, Anna and her family agreed to only 1 day a week of unsupervised lunch until Anna felt more confident. With time, the number of days of unsupervised lunch with friends like Ellie increased as Anna became more confident in pushing back on the eating disorder.

The gradual and vigilant maneuvers to wean Anna from parental supervision took place over 10 weeks after the completion of Phase I. Thus Phase II of FBT was completed. Anna returned to her previous exercise activities when she showed her parents she could tolerate and take responsibility for increasing her intake commensurate with increased exercise and caloric needs. Anna's life and her food intake were normalizing.

Anna and her family moved into the final phase of FBT, Phase III, they began to focus on some of Anna's adolescent issues. For example, Anna raised the problem of wishing her parents would focus more on their own lives and not be so fearful for her safety. During FBT, Kelly and Justin had become so accustomed to frequently checking up on Anna to make sure she was not engaging in eating-disorder behavior, they were having difficulty letting go of their vigilance. Once they realized Anna was well on her way to recovery and now deserved privacy and less oversight, they negotiated a system in which Anna put a sign on her bedroom door indicating she was okay and needed some time alone. In this way, Anna's normal adolescent wish for autonomy over her personal space and time was honored.

Another issue addressed in Phase III was Anna's penchant for seeking perfection. Anna was attached to perfection in school grades and perfection in body image. In a healthier frame of mind, Anna saw there was no such thing as perfect and striving for it in any arena of her life was hurtful to her recovery. The pursuit of perfection, she learned, created anxiety, which in turn fueled Ed. Wanting to starve Ed of oxygen, she began to work on accepting her genetically determined body and her less-than-perfect academic grades. She was given homework to practice being imperfect, e.g., folding her clothes the wrong way, purposefully skipping days of exercise, and sending an email with an intentional typo. That took time and practice and, overall, represented a major paradigm shift for Anna.

While Kelly and Justin had learned not to trust Anna's recovery until she had demonstrated an ability to take personal responsibility over the almost 4 months of Phase II and Phase III, they were encouraged and empowered by their skill in defeating Ed. The ability to collaborate with their daughter against Ed seemed next to impossible in the beginning. However, online support from websites like Maudsley Parents (n.d.) and F.E.A.S.T. (n.d.) bolstered them and gave them fresh ideas. It seemed that there was no problem they encountered with Anna that some other parent doing home-based feeding hadn't also encountered. Further, the expert guidance and coaching by their FBT therapist proved invaluable, especially when they steered off course. Progressing through the three phases of treatment, Anna gradually gained insight into the ways in which Ed had besieged her life. She gradually understood and absorbed the work and vigilance it took to get well and stay well.

Question

What is the role of the pediatrician in Family Based Treatment? I'm used to the physician giving directions and making decisions, and I'm confused by being charged with making health decisions for my child.

Answer

Parents are often confused when they are charged by an FBT therapist to make critical decisions about how to move their child into recovery. Pediatricians who support FBT will indeed empower parents to take charge of key decisions, like calorie goals. For many, this represents a paradigm shift from a model in which physicians are expected to make authoritative decisions. It isn't that parents can't seek nutrition and medical consultation. It's that parents will be asked to make common-sense decisions about nutrition and exercise activity and to help discover their own answers. This is so that parents build confidence in fighting the illness. As previous research has shown, it's critical to the success of Family Based Treatment that pediatricians like Anna's be included in the treatment team for medical management. Pediatric care supporting FBT can be challenging. Here are some of the specific ways in which pediatricians can best support FBT therapy with a patient, as outlined by Katzman et al. (2013):

1 Become familiar with the FBT model of treatment.
2 Function as a consultant to the parents and the FBT therapist, deferring to the parents and the primary therapist. The key to FBT success is

empowering parents to make decisions that are in the best interest of their child. For example, if parents ask the pediatrician about calorie intake or exercise restriction, the pediatrician might respond with, "What do you think is best for your child?" Pediatricians learn to work with parents as they struggle to do their best.

3 Assess medical stability at every visit and hospitalize for safety when necessary. If hospitalization occurs, help parents see this as a restoration to medical stability and not a failure on their part.
4 Support the FBT therapist's not providing a specific meal plan. Inform the family that the amount of caloric intake needed to restore health is different for different individuals, and whatever amount and type of intake is needed to restore health will depend on regular health assessments (e.g., weight checks). In other words, intake goals are a moving target.
5 Share timely reports with the treatment team. For the pediatrician, it is useful to provide regular reports about medical status and relevant evaluation information that can be used in FBT sessions.
6 Mirror FBT terminology to show consistency and support with FBT therapy (e.g., for Anna, reminding Justin and Kelly it's Ed, not Anna, that is frustrating them). FBT goals include de-pathologizing the child and externalizing the illness from the patient.
7 Involve parents at each pediatric visit. Share weight, height and vital sign information with them. Set realistic weight goals based on growth history and support weight increase with age.
8 Prepare parents that their child may seem worse in the beginning (Phase I of FBT) and that parents and providers alike are unpopular with the struggling patient in the early stages of treatment. Parents are often upset in the early stages of treatment because of unpleasant blowback from Ed.
9 "Normalize parental stumbles when they occur" (Katzman et al., 2013, p. 435, Figure 2). The goal is parent empowerment and support even when parent mistakes are made.
10 Help parents not set expectations too high for FBT. Reiterate FBT does not work for everyone. Research shows 50–60% of young people with anorexia nervosa recover after one year of FBT treatment and another 15–20% do not (Lock, Le Grange, Agras, Moye, and Bryson et al., 2010). On a positive note, reflect that research has shown that FBT is more protective against relapse than individual therapy (Lock et al., 2010).
11 Be cautious not to respond to early distress in treatment with a recommendation to switch to a higher level of care (except in the case of medical instability), as parents need to not be undermined. Further, there is little evidence that another facility would have better outcomes and, ultimately, a child needs to come home from higher levels of care, often to another round of home-based feeding.
12 Support, in Phase II of FBT treatment, FBT-guided adolescent eating autonomy while encouraging weary parents to not settle for less than achievement of a healthy-weight range and other bio-indicators of health.

13 Decrease the frequency of medical visits as soon as it is safe to do so, recognizing that a decrease in medical visits will not likely parallel a similar decrease in FBT-session frequency.

Question

I am concerned about parental control of adolescent eating as part of Family Based Treatment. Exerting control over an adolescent's food intake seems counter-intuitive to parents' need to support adolescent autonomy. Further, how can parental control be effective if it promotes a negative, not a positive, alliance between my daughter and the treatment team?

Answer

As indicated in Anna's story, the goal in FBT is for parents to unite against an illness in their child, not to come together against their child, or their child's autonomy. Were anorexia an issue of self-discipline and making bad-versus-good choices, encouraging adolescent autonomy from the outset might be appropriate. However, anorexia is an illness and not a choice. And while there are cases where adolescents with anorexia are able to normalize their own eating, given guidance, the premise of FBT is that most young people with anorexia are not able to manage recovery on their own. They need parents to temporarily take charge of renourishment until they have enough strength, perspective, and confidence to see and fight the illness on their own.

The eating-disorder illness directs anger and hostility toward the treatment team and the parents. The more strength it has, the more this happens. Therefore, in the beginning of treatment, parents often feel worse and the patient, under the influence of the eating disorder, often feels negative toward the treatment team and parents. Nonetheless, treatment-team members need to be careful not to argue or negotiate with the eating disorder. Ideally, they remain kind, understanding, and compassionate when talking with their resistant patient. They set their sites on the two things the eating disorder does not want – renourishment and recovery. The young person under the influence of the eating disorder is usually anxious, depressed, and angry at the prospect of recovery goals being achieved. Therefore, the illness is strongly motivated to derail the therapy process and will attempt to do so. In the beginning of treatment especially, there is usually a negative-seeming alliance with the patient. That is to be expected.

In a large meta-analysis of the relationship between the therapeutic alliance and treatment outcomes in eating disorders (Graves et al., 2017), symptom reduction was found to be the best predictor of the therapeutic alliance, regardless to treatment type, patient age, or eating-disorder diagnosis. Early symptom reduction "enhanced" both the therapeutic alliance and positive treatment outcomes.

Other research examined the therapeutic alliance for parents and children undergoing FBT. As might be expected, mothers' and fathers' alliance with the therapist were similar and significantly higher than adolescent alliance, especially early in treatment (Forsberg et al., 2014). Despite the strong early alliance between therapist and parents and the weaker alliance between adolescents and therapists, neither had an impact on treatment outcomes. Other research indicated a therapeutic alliance with adolescent patients undergoing FBT was not predictive of weight outcomes, but was predictive of important psychological recovery (Rienecke, Richmond, & Lebow, 2016). Counter to common perception, LoTempio et al. (2013) found that adolescent patients undergoing FBT for anorexia could and often did form an alliance with their therapist. This might be expected since, as FBT therapy progresses, adolescents are increasingly likely to see and acknowledge their symptoms. Further young patients come to understand that their treatment team and their parents were not working against them. Rather, they were working for them.

Question

What if eating-disorder symptoms return after an initial success with Family Based Treatment?

Answer

Patients and their parents learn to use tools and strategies developed during FBT therapy. Once these tools are learned, they are available for use in the future should eating-pathology return. Also, optional, as-needed "tune-up" sessions are often available from FBT therapists and other affiliated team members (i.e., pediatricians, psychiatrists, and consulting dietitians).

Rarely, but sometimes, a return to restriction on the part of a patient may recur in Phase II of FBT. Lock and Le Grange (2015) explain that both parents and patients collaborate in Phase II of FBT to develop healthy, independent eating in the patient. The therapist's job is to "help to make sure that the timing, as well as the tempo, of this process is appropriate" (p. 189). If the patient begins dieting again and loses weight, it is important that the patient not be blamed. Rather, as Lock and Le Grange point out, that the therapist's and the parents' decision to return independence to the patient was premature. Lock and Le Grange speak to the relapse that might occur during the process of FBT: "It is relatively uncommon for a return to starvation to occur if the transition to independent eating has been negotiated mutually and carefully" (p. 189). If a temporary setback does occur during the second phase of FBT, parents should "swiftly reestablish control over eating" (p. 189). Lock and Le Grange go on to say, "Once this temporary setback has been overcome and the handing over of the feeding responsibilities to the patient has been successfully negotiated, the therapist returns to a focus on adolescent issues related to food and weight" (p. 190).

Research examining the maintenance of FBT-treatment gains confirm that relapse rates after a year of post-treatment remission are rare (Le Grange et al.,

2014). Research showed remission rates after FBT remained stable for up to 4 years post-treatment (Le Grange et al., 2014; Lock, Couturier, & Agras, 2006). In the case of difficulty, such as relapse encountered during the FBT process, various adjunct therapies are have been proposed. For example, Bhatnagar and Wisniewski (2015) propose using Dialectical Behavior Therapy (DBT) as an adjunct to FBT (FBT-DBT) for youth whose emotional dysregulation undermines treatment success. Hopf, Hoste, and Pariseau (2015) reviewed various adjunct parent-group interventions aimed at providing parent support and reducing the negative impact on FBT of caregiver burden and parental criticism. Wagner, Diamond, Levy, Russon, and Litster (2016) proposed shifting to the use of Attachment-Based Family Therapy (ABFT) when patients were unsuccessful in Phase II of FBT, or experienced relapse after the completion of FBT and didn't want to return to FBT. Both FBT and ABFT focus on parents as the solution to overcoming anorexia. However, while FBT stays focused on parents' restoring nutrition in their child, ABFT focuses on improving the trust and emotional climate in the parent-child relationship ("attachment repairing") so that adolescents are more willing to allow their parents to help them overcome the eating disorder. More than can be enumerated here, there are a number of proposed, explored, or utilized methods to address relapse with FBT if and when it occurs.

References

Academy for Eating Disorders. (2012). *Eating disorders: Critical points for early recognition and medical risk management in the care of individuals with eating disorders* (2nd ed.). Retrieved from http://aedweb.org/web/downloads/Guide-English.pdf

American Psychiatric Association. (2013). *Diagnostic and statistical manual of mental disorders* (5th ed.). Washington, DC: Author.

Avrin, J. (Producer), & Cobelli, J. (Director). (2011). *Someday Melissa* [Motion picture]. USA: Someday Melissa.

Baker, E. H., & Sandle, G. I. (1996). Complications of laxative abuse. *Annual Review of Medicine*, 47, 127–134.

Bhatnagar, K., & Wisniewski, L. (2015). Integrating dialectical behavior therapy with family therapy for adolescents with affect dysregulation. In K. L. Loeb, D. Le Grange, & J. Lock (Eds.), *Family therapy for adolescent eating and weight disorders: New applications* (pp. 305–327). New York, NY: Routledge.

Doyle, P. M., Le Grange, D., Loeb, K., Doyle, A. C., & Crosby, R. D. (2010). Early response to family-based treatment for adolescent anorexia nervosa. *International Journal of Eating Disorders*, 43(7), 659–662.

Ellison, Z., Foong, J., Howard, R., Bullmore, E., Williams, S., & Treasure, J. (1998). Functional anatomy of calorie fear in anorexia nervosa. *The Lancet*, 352(9135), 1192.

Fairburn, C.G (2008) Cognitive behavior therapy and eating disorders. New York: The Guilford Press.

F.E.A.S.T. (n.d.). Families empowered and supporting treatment of eating disorders. Retrieved from http://members.feast-ed.org/

Fitzpatrick, K. K., Darcy, A. M., Le Grange, D., & Lock, J. (2015). In vivo family meal training for initial nonresponders. In K. L. Loeb, D. Le Grange, & J. Lock (Eds.), *Family therapy for adolescent eating disorders and weight disorders* (pp. 45–58). New York, NY: Routledge.

Forsberg, S., LoTempio, E., Bryson, S., Fitzpatrick, K. K., Le Grange, D., & Lock, J. (2014). Parent-therapist alliance in family-based treatment for adolescents with anorexia nervosa. *European Eating Disorders Review*, 22(1), 53–58.

Frank, G. K., & Kaye, W. H. (2012). Current status of functional imaging in eating disorders. *International Journal of Eating Disorders*, 45(6), 723–736.

Graves, T. A., Tabri, N., Thompson-Brenner, H., Franko, D. L., Eddy, K. T., Bourion-Bedes, S., & Thomas, J. J. (2017). A meta-analysis of the relation between therapeutic alliance and treatment outcome in eating disorders. *International Journal of Eating Disorders*, 50(4), 323–340.

Hopf, R. B., Hoste, R. R., & Pariseau, C. (2015). Parent support as an adjunct to family therapy. In K. L. Loeb, D. Le Grange, & J. Lock (Eds.), *Family therapy for adolescent eating and weight disorders: New applications* (pp. 139–154). New York, NY: Routledge.

Katzman, D. K., Peebles, R., Sawyer, S. M., Lock, J., & Le Grange, D. (2013). The role of the pediatrician in family-based treatment for adolescent eating disorders: Opportunities and challenges. *Journal of Adolescent Health*, 53(4), 433–440.

Kaye, W. H., Bailer, U. F., Klabunde, M., & Brown, H. (2010). Is anorexia nervosa an eating disorder? How neurobiology can help us understand the puzzling eating symptoms of anorexia nervosa. Retrieved from http://eatingdisorders.ucsd.edu/ research/ biocorrelates/PDFs/Kaye2010NeurobiologyofAN.pdf

Kaye, W. H., Wierenga, C. E., Bailer, U. R., Simmons, A. N., & Bischoff-Grethe, A. (2013). Nothing tastes as good as skinny feels: The neurobiology of anorexia nervosa. *Trends in Neurosciences*, 36(2), 110–120.

Kovacs, D., & Palmer, R. L. (2004). The associations between laxative abuse and other symptoms among adults with anorexia nervosa. *International Journal of Eating Disorders*, 36(2), 224–228.

Le Grange, D., Lock, J., Accurso, E. C., Agras, W. S., Darcy, A., Forsberg, S., & Bryson, S. W. (2014). Relapse from remission at two- to four-year follow-up in two treatments for adolescent anorexia nervosa. *Journal of the American Academy of Child & Adolescent Psychiatry*, 53(11), 1162–1167.

Levinson, C. A., & Byrne, M. (2015). The fear of food measure: A novel measure for use in exposure therapy for eating disorders. *International Journal of Eating Disorders*, 48(3), 271–283.

Lock, J., Couturier, J., & Agras, W. S. (2006). Comparison of long-term outcomes in adolescents with anorexia nervosa treated with family therapy. *American Journal of Child and Adolescent Psychiatry*, 45(6), 666–672.

Lock, J., Couturier, J., Bryson, S., & Agras, S. (2006). Predictors of dropout and remission in family therapy for adolescent anorexia nervosa in a randomized clinical trial. *International Journal of Eating Disorders*, 39(8), 639–647.

Lock, J., Le Grange, D., Agras, W. S., & Dare, C. (2001). *Treatment manual for anorexia nervosa. A family-based approach*. New York, NY: Guilford.

Lock, J., & Le Grange, D. (2015). *Treatment manual for anorexia nervosa: A family-based approach* (2nd ed.). New York, NY: Guilford.

Lock, J., Le Grange, D., Agras, W. S., Moye, A., Bryson, S. W., & Jo, B. (2010). Randomized clinical trial comparing family-based treatment with adolescent-focused individual therapy for adolescents with anorexia nervosa. *Archives of General Psychiatry*, 67(10), 1025–1032.

LoTempio, E., Forsberg, S., Bryson, S. W., Fitzpatrick, K. K., Le Grange, D., & Lock, J. (2013). Patients' characteristics and the quality of the therapeutic alliance in family-based treatment and individual therapy for adolescents with anorexia nervosa. *Journal of Family Therapy*, 35(S1), 29-52.

Madden, S., Miskovic-Wheatley, J., Wallis, A., Kohn, M., Hay, P., & Touyz, S. (2015). Early weight gain in family-based treatment predicts greater weight gain and remission at the end of treatment and remission at 12-month follow-up in adolescent anorexia nervosa. *International Journal of Eating Disorders*, 48(7), 919–922.

Mascolo, M., Trent, S., Colwell, C., & Mehler, P. S. (2012). What the emergency department needs to know when caring for your patients with eating disorders. *International Journal of Eating Disorders*, 45(8), 977–981.

Maudsley Parents. (n.d.). *Maudsley parents: A site for parents of eating disordered children.* Retrieved from www.maudsleyparents.org

Mehanna, H. M., Moledina, J., & Travis, J. (2008). Refeeding syndrome: What it is, and how to prevent and treat it. *BMJ*, 336(7659), 1495–1498.

Mehler, P. (2011). Medical complications of bulimia nervosa and their treatments. *International Journal of Eating Disorders*, 44(2), 95–104.

Rienecke, R. D., Richmond, R., & Lebow, J. (2016). Therapeutic alliance, expressed emotion, and treatment outcome for anorexia nervosa in a family-based partial hospitalization program. *Eating Behaviors*, 22, 124–128.

Rudd Center. (n.d.). www.uconnruddcenter.org/weight-bias-stigma

Saren. (2016). On the efficacy of self-induced vomiting (purging) [Web log post, May 13]. *Science of eating disorders: Making sense of the latest findings in eating disorders research.* Retrieved from www.scienceofeds.org/2016/05/13/on-the-efficacy-of-self-induced-vomiting/

Schaefer, J. (2003). *Life without Ed: How one woman declared independence from her eating disorder and how you can too.* New York, NY: McGraw-Hill.

Treasure, J., Cardi, V., & Kan, C. (2012). Eating in eating disorders. *European Eating Disorders Review*, 20(1), e42–49.

Turner, J., Batik, M., Palmer, L. J., Forbes, D., & McDermott, B. M. (2000). Detection and importance of laxative use in adolescents with anorexia nervosa. *Journal of the American Academy of Child and Adolescent Psychiatry*, 39(3), 378–385.

Wagner, I., Diamond, G. S., Levy, S., Russon, J., & Litster, R. (2016). Attachment-based family therapy as an adjunct to family-based treatment for adolescent anorexia nervosa. *Australian and New Zealand Journal of Family Therapy*, 37(2), 207–227.

White, H. J., Haycraft, E., Madden, S., Rhodes, P., Miskovic-Wheatley, J., Wallis, A., … & Meyer, C. (2017). Parental strategies used in the family meal session of family-based treatment for adolescent anorexia nervosa: Links with treatment outcomes. *International Journal of Eating Disorders*, 50(4), 433–436.

Yen, M., & Ewald, M. B. (2012). Toxicity of weight loss agents. *Journal of Medical Toxicology*, 8(2), 145–152.

5 May

Boyfriend Abuse

Jarold left his girlfriend May's house just before dinner – her family hadn't invited him to stay. He wondered about that. He didn't know if he truly loved May, but she seemed to like him a lot, and that's what really mattered. She showed him this by agreeing to do whatever he asked, which to him was the most important thing. Nevertheless, as he pulled out of her driveway in his father's car, he began to wonder. Even though he had just left her side, he was suspicious about what May was up to. Too bad he was driving, or he could text her. Maybe he could text at the traffic light. No luck – green lights all the way. As he pulled into his driveway, he felt an increase in his urgency to find out where she was and what she was doing. Maybe she had already texted him. He checked. No text from May. Jarold wished May could remember what he told her. He wanted her to text and ask if he made it home okay whenever he left – let him know that she was thinking of him.

Jarold would make sure to tell May she had slipped up, that she had forgotten to text him again. If she really cared, she would have remembered. He tightened his grip on the steering wheel. He was angry May had forgotten. When the car was stopped in front of the garage, Jarold pulled out his phone and banged out a message. She had better be with her phone. He became angrier as he imagined May not carrying her phone with her as she moved around the house. "Why haven't you called?" he pounded onto the keys of his phone. No response. What was she thinking? Was she playing games with him? Maybe she was talking to someone else – her mother maybe. He tried to be friendly to May's mother. The truth was, he hated the woman because she had told May – more than once – that she spent too much time with him. It would take a while before he could get May to stand up to her. Weeks maybe. Where was she? Why wasn't she answering? He needed her to answer him now. For the fifth time, he texted, "Where are you?" No answer.

The next day, May was waiting for Jarold at the front door to their school. Lots of other kids were passing by saying "Hi" and "What's up?" to May. Jarold approached her from the oncoming crowd with a glare, grabbed her wrist, and pulled her toward him so he was inches from her face. "I thought I told you to call me after I left – to make sure I got home okay." May looked frightened as he hissed at her so early in the morning. "I have texted you all night, and you never picked up! I'm not sure this relationship is working! You don't give a s–t about me!" May started to cry. She said weakly, "I forgot to recharge my phone. I didn't know it was dead until this morning. I'm sorry." "Forget it!" Jarold said sharply and walked away, turning his back on her. May was devastated. "Did he just break up with me?" she screamed in her head. She panicked. She felt the color drain from her face. She was terrified he was leaving her.

May's friend Drew saw her standing near the door alone, looking pale and sick. "What's wrong?" Drew asked as he approached May. "Jarold's t'd at me." "Again?" Drew said. May and Jarold had been going out for several months, and Drew had run interference for them before. He was frustrated. He wished May wasn't so shaken up by Jarold, and he wished Jarold would treat May better. "I'll tell him you're freaked when I see him next period." May got more worried. "No – don't." May knew from past experience that Jarold would be angrier if he knew she told someone what was going on. He'd informed her in an almost scary way that their problems were their business and nobody else's.

Since going out with Jarold, May was learning to cope with her feelings in ways that weren't obvious to anyone. At lunch that day, she escaped to the school library. Alone with her lunch and her phone, she desperately texted Jarold in hopes he would forgive her for not answering the evening before, even though she knew Jarold would ignore her until he was ready to see her. "I'm so sorry. ILU [I love you]. I miss u. AML [all my love]. Love 4ever." She only ate part of her lunch, because her appetite was lost to anxiety. Overwhelmed with worry, she automatically started thinking about ways to relieve her stress. Almost without consciously deciding, she knew she needed to throw up her lunch. No way she could keep it down. She hated herself so much. Her thoughts turned to self-loathing. "I am the fattest, ugliest girl at this school," she told herself. "I'm too disgusting for Jarold to even look at me. No wonder he treats me this way. I deserve it." At least she could do something to make herself thinner and more attractive to Jarold.

May entered a stall in the most deserted bathroom she could find. Some girl was taking her time texting by the mirror. May waited quietly. She was focused on vomiting as soon as she could. "If that girl would just leave," May thought to herself. "Please hurry up. Leave. Leave. I have to get rid of this lunch. My disgusting stomach is sticking out." The agony of waiting to be alone in the bathroom was both annoying and exhilarating. When she was sure she was alone, May quickly dislodged the contents of her stomach into the toilet. Very practiced, May was quick and thorough. She rinsed her mouth out so she didn't smell of vomit and felt the first moments of relief from her day of pain and anxiety. She was grateful for the small comfort she could count on from purging. Later, May noticed her eyes were bloodshot from crying and vomiting. "Better not let this show – especially to my mother," May thought.

Although her daytime practices around food gave her some comfort, May's daily dietary restraint gave way to nagging, nighttime hunger, followed by secretive, nighttime binge eating. Rummaging through her kitchen after everyone was in bed, May dipped into cereal, cake, bread, cookies, and ice cream. Her nighttime binges resulted in ravaging guilt, more vomiting to "get rid of it," and a renewed commitment to compensatory restricting the next day. A repeated cycle of daytime restricting followed by nighttime binge eating and purge behavior had begun.

For 3 days, May never left her phone, and for 3 days, Jarold never called. Finally, on the 4th day after her phone went dead, Jarold called. "What's up?" he said casually. Equally casually, she relied, "Nothing – just hoping you'd call. I've missed you so much." "Yeah – I missed you too. Can I come over?" Jarold asked. "OK – I'll tell my Mom we're gonna do homework." "Be right over, babe – I missed you so much."

Jarold and May were caught in an emotionally, physically, and verbally abusive dating relationship. For May, her abusive attachment to Jarold provided an important context for her potential eating disorder. Findings from the 2013 National Youth Risk Behavior Survey found that among 9,900 students who dated, 20.9% of female students and 10.4% of male students experienced some form of physical or sexual teen dating violence during the 12 months before the survey (Vagi, Olsen, Basile, & Vivolo-Kantor, 2015). One in three high school adolescents is verbally abused by a dating partner, a statistic that rises in college (Hattersley-Gray, 2012). Further, the risk of many self-harm behaviors, including unhealthy weight-management practices such as vomiting and laxative use, is higher in adolescent girls who have been abused by their partners (Silverman, Raj, Mucci, & Hathaway 2001). As was the case for May, intimate partner abuse among adolescents is associated with increased levels of clinical depression (Ackard, Elsenberg & Neumark-Sztainer, 2007; Roberts & Klein, 2003; Vagi et al., 2015).

It may be the painful humiliation associated with emotional, physical, or sexual abuse, or a combination of all three that leads to increased self-harm behaviors. Not wanting to risk exposure limits ways for girls like May to seek help. Left to their own devices, young people caught in abuse become isolated in their torment and fear. For example, even after May and her parents began psychotherapy, May's shame and secrecy inhibited disclosure of both her abusive relationship with Jarold and her vomiting. Even direct questioning by her therapist was at first responded to with deception. May was unwilling to disclose what deeply embarrassed her. Girls in May's position have difficulty generating the traction needed to self-empower and overcome their suffering. They turn to self-harm behaviors like vomiting and laxative use, because those behaviors give relief. As such, self-harm behaviors are attempts at self-regulation gone awry. The brain's dopamine system discovers and motivates that which is salient and ensures that rewarding behaviors will continue (Wise, 2004).

May had come to believe that she could not exist without Jarold. She protected and defended him with steadfast loyalty. She talked to her parents about how troubled she was about Jarold's home situation. His parents were divorced. He lived with his mother Lynn and her boyfriend Jed, with whom Jarold had a tense, conflicted relationship. Jarold wished he could live with his father who had moved halfway across the country and rarely called. Hurt and rejected, Jarold had become bitter toward his mother's boyfriend. Jed had once slapped Jarold when he yelled at his mother. May saw that Jarold was under a lot of stress. She hoped her more loving family could replace his dysfunctional one. She frequently told her parents how wonderful Jarold was and wanted them to like him.

May's mother Jenny was increasingly suspicious of May's relationship with Jarold. May used to have many friends, but since dating Jarold, her old friendships had gone unattended. May seemed to love being smothered by Jarold. He clearly monopolized her time and demanded her attention. Once Jenny overheard May defending herself to Jarold about having a friend sleep over after school on a Friday. He demanded an intense loyalty that felt like possessiveness and extreme jealousy to Jenny. She worried about her daughter, but felt sorry for Jarold at the same time. May's father Ken was impressed with Jarold's polite bearing toward him. Ken observed the boy's innocent behavior watching TV with his daughter downstairs. At first he tried to befriend Jarold, asking him to help move things with him in their garage, or engaging him in conversation about school. Jarold seemed to respond to Ken's overtures and made himself at home in May's family.

Meanwhile, May had never felt quite so loved. A few months earlier, the first time they were alone on a date, Jarold had said he loved her almost immediately. Murray (2000) in her book, *But I Love Him: Protecting Your Daughter from Controlling, Abusive Dating Relationships*, describes saying "I love you" too soon as "the all-time great hook for a teenage girl" (p. 29). The words were romantic and magical to May. She had never been in love before. The promise of her first boyfriend was enticing and seductive. Before long, Jarold and May talked 1 to 2 hours a day – often by text, sometimes by phone.

May had always been insecure about her body. Far from the long, lanky, thin ideal, May had short, sturdy, muscular legs and a long waist that was thicker than she wanted. In her 2011 study, Smolak reported that 40% to 60% of schoolgirls aged 6 to 12 were unhappy or concerned about the unattractiveness of their bodies. Further, this body shame could and sometimes did become a life-long struggle. Evidence indicates that early body dissatisfaction continues. Bucchianeri, Arikan, Hannan, Eisenberg, and Neumark-Sztainer (2013) followed a large sample of boys and girls for over 10 years and found participants' body dissatisfaction increased between middle and high school, and increased further during the transition to young adulthood as BMI increased with age.

May's mother was Korean. Her father was White. She thought she looked more Korean than White. She liked her thick black hair. She didn't like her stomach, her thighs, or her buttocks. Each feature was subjected to a culturally determined set of standards for beauty. May was not unusual in this way of viewing her body. When she was at school, she compared herself to girls who were popular and thin. She compared herself to the pretty girls who most resembled those she saw on television. Walking down the hallway between classes, she kept her eyes on the stomachs and legs of slender girls whose bodies she admired. Sadly, the more May compared herself to other girls, the worse she felt about herself.

Like May, women and men in previous research studies have shown a bias in perceiving women's bodies according to their individual sexual parts rather than the whole (Gervais, Vescio, Förster, Maass, & Suitner, 2012). The media further amplifies this bias. The result is that many women objectify themselves by dissecting their personal appearance into its relevant areas (e.g., size of hips, size of thighs), then determining what efforts need to be made to close the gap between the ideal-appearing body part and their perception of the actual body part. May had long ago internalized an idealized model of beauty peddled to her via the media through thousands of daily exposures to advertisements.

May was obsessively engaging in body comparisons at school. Recent research has shown that, in general, adolescent body comparisons are associated with unhealthy weight-management behaviors. These are precursors to eating disorders (Myers & Crowther, 2009). Peer influence on intention to engage in unhealthy weight-related behaviors is strongest when adolescent girls compare themselves to their slim peers (Rancourt, Choukas-Bradley, Cohen, & Prinstein, 2014). May's engagement in body comparisons to other girls was a reflection of her low body esteem and her desire to close the gap between what she thought her body looked like and what she wanted her body to look like. While she intended to compare herself to others in order to self-evaluate and garner *thin-spiration*, the net result was poorer body esteem and greater body dissatisfaction. The more she compared, the worse she felt about herself. She scanned the Internet to find the fastest diet tips in order to lose the most weight. But when she tried to restrict, she became hungry and ate too much. Then she felt guilty and a failure, despairing she would never achieve her ideal body type.

The Internet was also her source of information on vomiting. May read a blog, fascinated by a thin-looking girl who championed her skills at weight management. She suggested tips for losing weight by secretly vomiting after meals – including tips for how to hide the evidence from parents. This seemed like the perfect solution to May – she could eat what she wanted normally, then get rid of it and not gain weight, and even lose weight. She set a weight goal of 110 for herself – many pounds below where she currently was.

Already self-conscious and anxious about her body, May was especially sensitive to any comments others might make about her appearance. The day she and Jarold first connected beyond "Hi" at school, he commented on how pretty she was. She lit up at the suggestion a boy might find her attractive. Jarold was cute, she thought. Her friend Ashley encouraged her to talk to him, because she heard from Jarold's friend that he liked May. No question May wanted a boyfriend. She felt left out when other girls talked about kissing boys they liked. At 14, she saw her life improving.

How could someone as nice and attractive and smart as May end up in an abusive relationship and be courting an increasingly serious eating disorder? It is already known that there are multiple causes for eating disorders, and sometimes, as in May's case, eating disorders are maintained because they provide some sense of purpose, skill, and distraction from internal turmoil. Costin (2007), a well-known spokesperson for those recovering from eating disorders, points out that eating disorders can serve many functions, such as comfort, distraction, self-punishment, blaming oneself instead of others (e.g., an abuser), and discharging negative feelings. This is not to mention the obvious unhealthy weight-management function of these behaviors – to avoid society's discrimination against other-than-thin bodies.

As noted by researcher Dias (2003), "what is not acknowledged is the extreme fat prejudice in Western society, and the intolerance for a diversity of sizes and shapes that may drive women and girls to extreme behaviors to avoid discrimination" (p. 37). However, given similar cultural exposure, background, and personality characteristics, some individuals like May develop eating disorders and some do not. To complicate the etiological picture, research suggests individual biochemical and genetic factors may help to determine which individuals, although similar in many ways, will or won't develop eating disorders (see Maeve's story for more details on this).

In addition to sociocultural factors, family dynamics can provide fertile ground for someone predisposed to an eating disorder. May's father came from a large family in which he felt both loved and overwhelmed by the constant hubbub of siblings sharing the bathroom, the dining room table, the family TV, and, last but not least, his parents. As number five in the line-up of six children, he sometimes felt like he was raised more by his two older sisters than his busy parents. Too harried to tend to the individual wants and desires of their younger children, Ken's parents relied on the older sisters to get him to bed and back up in the morning. As a child, Ken longed for parents who took turns reading to him before bed. As an adult, Ken wanted a different kind of marriage and family. He wanted lots of time for his children. In fact, he would even be fine with an only child if it meant giving him or her his undivided attention.

Jenny came from a first generation Korean family. She was an only child. Originally, her parents were not supportive of her marriage to Ken, a Caucasian American. Jenny's parents had hoped for a marriage to a Korean man – preferably educated and from a good family. They spoke to Jenny about how Korean grandchildren would make them happy. Jenny felt responsible for her parents' happiness. But like most Americans, she was raised in an individualistic culture in which men and women married for love, not family tradition. Like many Asian American women, Jenny married outside her race. Long ago, she had determined she would make her own decision about whom to marry. She and Ken met in college in California. Jenny's closeness to her family was appealing to Ken. It reminded him of what he wanted for his own future family – someone devoted to him, his future children, and a life together. He was able to cast aside his Korean in-laws' disappointment that he wasn't Korean.

Predictably, May was raised in a family that doted on her and her younger brother, Danny. Ken and Jenny were true to their values. They married, worked hard while childless, and saved their money. They planned for Jenny to be home with their children at least part-time until they started pre-kindergarten. May was cherished. However, during a wellness visit, her pediatrician observed that May was immature in assuming age-appropriate responsibility for her self-care, and implied she was a bit shy for her age. The doctor advised that she needed a bit more autonomy from her parents. "How can you parent too much?" Ken thought. Had he and Jenny made themselves too available? Was his intense relationship with May a compensation for his own loving, but benignly neglectful relationship with his parents? No matter, Ken and Jenny would continue their genuinely loving and involved relationship with May, a complicated melding of love, control, and protection in a balance that may have unwittingly, along with other factors, helped set the stage for May's crisis in adolescence.

By 14, May suffered with more than her fair share of adolescent social anxiety. She had a high degree of sensitivity and anxious concern about humiliating herself in the eyes of others by saying or doing something wrong or inappropriate. This is especially likely to occur in teens who, like May, were behaviorally inhibited as children (Chronis-Tuscano et al., 2009). May experienced a high need for approval combined with a growing need for autonomy. These needs pressed on her every nerve as she entered an era of adolescent "big emotions." Now her brain's fast-growing limbic system made her emotions, including her interpersonal insecurities, seem 10 times as strong – and 10 times as hard to handle.

At home, when May would occasionally close her bedroom door wishing for alone time, Jenny and Ken would become uncomfortable for no particular reason other than they felt shut out. They didn't understand that teenagers typically want a degree of privacy, and a common way to accomplish that is to close their bedroom doors. When May was confused about something, Jenny would come to her side, immediately sensing something was wrong. She would then ask what was wrong. If May didn't want to talk about it, Jenny would become distressed and push May to talk. At the same time, when May was really upset, she struggled to manage her feelings and would often seek out her parents for help. Sometimes Jenny would rub her back. If May was anxious and distressed, Ken would reassure her that everything would be okay and try to help her breathe slowly and regain her composure. If May became disturbed about something at school, she was unable to calm down without her parents' help. She had little confidence, and didn't know how to self-soothe or self-regulate. If she did try to manage herself, or keep a secret, she felt guilty for shutting out her parents. The unwitting message to May from her parents was, "You need someone to take care of you." May's self-esteem grew poorer as the gap grew between her chronological age and the developmental level of maturity expected in someone her age. May's autonomy and self-regulation skills were increasingly out of sync with those of her peers.

Then along came Jarold. He championed independence from all parents and seemed so grown-up to May. And he adored her – something she was used to. May welcomed the intense attention he gave her. It wasn't until she was so anxiously attached to Jarold and fearful of being without him that she began to realize how often they fought and how critical he was of her in many ways. If Jarold wanted more control, he just needed to manipulate May into a place of insecurity and fearfulness. He would say something like, "Wear the red shirt tomorrow – it looks better than the tight one you wore today." To this statement, May thought, "Does he think I look fat today? Why did he say my shirt is tight?" To Jarold she would say, "I thought you liked my outfit today. Do I look fat or something?" May was easy to take advantage of around her appearance, and Jarold knew it.

The more Jarold and May drew close, the unhappier she seemed. She became desperate to look good for Jarold. She wanted her parents to stop harping about losing all her friends because she was too dependent on Jarold. She pulled inside, away from her parents – until she needed them to help her manage her feelings. Jarold would try to comfort May when she cried over her conflicts with him, but he couldn't manage it for very long. He became angry when she couldn't pull it together and when he saw her leaning on her parents. He wanted May to lean on him, and him alone. Caught in the tension between Jarold and her parents, May began to restrict her eating and found comfort in secretly binge eating and vomiting.

In addition to trying to self-regulate through binge eating and purging, May occasionally experienced urges to cut herself. Although she hadn't actually begun yet, she'd given it a lot of thought and was on the verge of cutting when she entered treatment. She had already made a plan for what she would use. With cutting, physical pain replaces emotional pain, and the physical pain goes away. Upon being injured, the brain releases "feel-good" endorphins and neurotransmitters. This biological process is a protective response to pain from injury. Thus, the body's neurotransmitter response to pain is, in essence, abused by those who cut to find relief. Once endorphins are secreted by the brain, the brain begins the process of ensuring the behavior that led to the brain reward will be repeated (Jacobson & Gould, 2007). This cycle of cutting for relief from emotional pain is caught up in the reward circuit of the brain and may become compulsive or addictive. The pattern is repeated again and again until it is consciously and deliberately broken.

The ongoing pattern of cutting in the face of intense emotions can be diagnosed as Nonsuicidal Self-Injury Disorder (NSSID), a diagnosis in need of further study in the fifth version of the *Diagnostic and Statistical Manual of Mental Disorders* (*DSM*-5; American Psychiatric Association, 2013). It includes self-cutting, burning, or hitting – all forms of direct injury to the body. Lifetime prevalence rates for nonsuicidal cutting range from 13% to 23% (Jacobson & Gould, 2007) with the highest rates by far occurring among teens – 17% to 18% in community samples (Muehlenkamp, Claes, Havertape, & Plener, 2012; Swannell, Martin, Page, Hasking, & St. John, 2014) and up to 40 % in clinical samples (DiClemente, Ponton, & Hartley, 1991). Along with eating disorders, teens use, or in the case of May, have the potential to use these self-harm strategies to cope with painful feelings. May's self-harm behaviors were tucked away from both Jarold and her parents.

Two things were clear to Ken and Jenny as they watched their daughter become increasingly isolated from old friends and more depressed and anxious. First, the relationship with Jarold was too dependent and too abusive. May's psychological pain seemed to be related to her tumultuous relationship with the young man. She seemed to be upset a lot after interactions with him. The second thing Ken and Jenny knew was that May was increasingly self-conscious about her body and preoccupied with how she looked. True, May said she loved Jarold. True, he gave her plenty of attention. Yet, May hated the way she looked more than ever, despite the fact that she had a boyfriend who said he adored her.

At first Jenny and Ken blamed Jarold and viewed him as the cause of all May's problems. They would hear May arguing with him at least weekly on the phone, and sometimes she was crying. One time when they argued, Ken asked May to give him the phone, because May seemed so upset. He told Jarold whatever was going on would have to wait until the next day. Ken sensed disrespect and anger coming from Jarold when he responded to Ken with: "Right!" just before hanging up the phone.

May seemed preoccupied with finding ways to be with Jarold. She started to sneak phone calls and more than once broke the house rule that Jarold couldn't be at their home when a parent wasn't there. May's brother, Danny, told on her. Unused to May's breaking house rules, Jenny and Ken were angry and hurt they couldn't trust her any longer. She seemed to be under some kind of spell. She regularly began to find reasons not to eat with the family. At first she wouldn't eat desserts with them anymore, claiming they made her fat. Since May's family was enmeshed in many ways, her desire to depart from family foods and family meals was quickly noticed. May was focused on pleasing Jarold and was determined to be thinner than the girls at school who sometimes flirted with him. Instead of feeling guilty for defying her parents' wishes and preferences, May seemed to be distancing from them more and more.

At first, Jenny was hesitant to seek help for May. When she talked to her own parents about these problems, they advised her to become stricter. They believed May's issues could be resolved with parental discipline, self-discipline, and better motivation. They believed it would make the family look weak to seek outside professional help for such a private matter. On the other hand, Ken was desperate to get professional help because he felt he was losing his daughter. More inclined to think like her parents, Jenny reluctantly went along with Ken, because she could not deny they had been unable to pry May away from Jarold, or to get her to be her old loving self toward the family. So they started psychotherapy together. They wanted their daughter fixed. They made an appointment to see a social worker, Ms. Wright, who met with the family and then with May alone. Ms. Wright found May to be depressed, secretive, and willing to meet with her, but not willing to share much.

The idea that Ms. Wright would quickly fix May, or tell them what to do to fix her, faded shortly after starting therapy. When May came home from school shaken from another fight with Jarold (the time her phone had died), Jenny and Ken became discouraged. Therapy had begun, yet May wasn't fixed. When she made an excuse for her swollen red eyes and inability to concentrate on her homework, they realized something remained very wrong. Jenny and Ken began to understand there were no quick fixes and the process of change might be slower than they had hoped.

Ms. Wright recognized she needed more alone time with May to understand her experiences with Jarold. After discussing confidentiality with May and upon noticing May's bruise disclosed to her by Ken, Ms. Wright asked May if someone had grabbed her, or hurt her. At first May hesitated, but the directness of the question, along with May's need for approval resulted in her admission. She told Ms. Wright of her argument with Jarold at school – only she justified Jarold's action as her fault: "I should have just told him I couldn't talk because my phone was dead. He thought I blew him off because I didn't pick up my phone. I would have been angry, too." May was in the habit of defending Jarold if anyone questioned his behavior. She was terrified of being without him – of him breaking up with her, or moving on to some other girl.

Sensing May's distress, Ms. Wright asked May if she had done anything to harm herself. May said, "No – I don't want to kill myself." Ms. Wright clarified. "Thank you for sharing that. I also want to ask about other ways that you might hurt yourself, because you might be trying to cope with difficult feelings, or stress." May defensively repeated that she didn't want to kill herself. Ms. Wright said, "I will give you some examples of other ways people sometimes hurt themselves, and you can tell me 'Yes' or 'No.'" May answered "No" to questions like, "Do you cut yourself?"

Then Ms. Wright asked May a series of eating-disorder questions from the SCOFF questionnaire (Morgan, Reid, & Lacey, 2000), a brief assessment tool for anorexia and bulimia. She asked, "Do you skip meals, or eat very light meals because you want to lose weight?" "Sometimes," answered May. Ms. Wright asked, "Do you ever make yourself vomit or use laxatives or diuretics (water pills) to get rid of food or liquids because you feel too full?" "Well – sometimes I vomit if I'm too full." "Tell me more about that," Ms. Wright said. May went on to explain that sometimes at night, after she skipped meals, she found herself eating two or three bowls of cereal after dinner. Ms. Wright asked, "So, do you worry you have lost control over how much you eat?" "Well – yes – sometimes I feel like I can't stop till my stomach hurts," May reluctantly answered. May thought about the intense hunger that resulted from a day's eating restriction. All the willpower May could muster dissolved into shame and guilt after succumbing to her body's hunger by eating several bowls of cereal, usually at night.

Direct questions from Ms. Wright were hard for May to dodge. She was used to her parents beating around the bush to find out about her life. She usually circumvented them with vague answers. Ms. Wright's questions were direct and specific. She was specialty-training in the field of eating disorders. When Ms. Wright asked the following question from the SCOFF questionnaire, "Would you say that food dominates your life?" May said, "For sure." Ms. Wright went on to ask, "Do you think of yourself as fat when others say you are too thin?" She told Ms. Wright she felt fat much of the time and how much she wanted to be thinner even though others reassured her she already was. Ms. Wright finished asking questions from the SCOFF with, "Have you lost more than 14 pounds in the last 3 months?" May responded with, "I wish but probably not." May had responded to 4 out of 5 questions from the SCOFF with a "Yes." Her responses suggested she struggled with bulimia nervosa.

In addition Ms. Wright administered the Eating Disorder Inventory-3 (EDI-3; Garner, 2004) to help arrive at a diagnosis and clarify some of the psychological underpinnings of May's eating problems. May's scores on the three EDI-3 Risk Scales indicated she was at high risk for drive for thinness, body dissatisfaction, and bulimia. Further results of the EDI-3 Psychological Scales indicated May had significant low self-esteem, self-alienation, interpersonal insecurity, poor awareness of internal emotional states, emotional dysregulation, and perfectionism. These characteristics underpinned the development of May's eating disorder, or helped maintain it. Based on interviews and the administration of the EDI-3, May was diagnosed with Bulimia Nervosa, Moderate (binge eating 4–7 times per week; *DSM*-5). She was vomiting 5–6 times per week and had done so for at least 3 months. That was because she experienced an ongoing, berating voice in her head that criticized her for having a body that was too large and unshapely. When she binge ate she experienced both comfort and deep guilt and shame because she feared binge eating would lead to weight gain. She relieved her guilt by vomiting. It was her means of compensating.

Ms. Wright stressed with Ken and Jenny how important it was for May to see her pediatrician as soon as possible. In bulimia, medical complications (usually reversible) are a result of the mode and frequency of purging (i.e., vomiting and laxative abuse). May needed to undergo a medical exam, including a laboratory evaluation and EKG to screen for a number of medical sequelae of bulimia. These include electrolyte acid-base imbalance (e.g., hypokalemia), heart arrhythmia, gastrointestinal disorders (e.g., dysphagia, dyspepsia, and esophageal tears), parotid gland enlargement, anemia, dental erosion from stomach acid exposure, edema, and blood-pressure abnormalities (Westmoreland, Krantz, & Mehler, 2016). Ms. Wright obtained a signed release from May and her parents to receive the pediatrician's report about her weight, physical exam, and lab work in order to corroborate May's report of her weight and symptoms.

Ms. Wright spent extra time determining the function served by May's vomiting. May told Ms. Wright that after the recent fight with Jarold at school, she could hardly stand the food in her stomach, and she had vomited at school that same day. "Did you feel better afterwards?" Ms. Wright asked. "How did you know?" asked May. Ms. Wright explained that vomiting, like many forms of self-harm behavior, often gives temporary relief, but becomes difficult to stop, because the brain is rewarded by relief and will seek the same relief again. This made sense to May. If only insight were cure.

Based on her clinical interview, Ms. Wright also diagnosed May with Major Depressive Disorder, Single Episode, Moderate With Anxious Distress (*DSM*-5). An administration of the Reynolds Adolescent Depression Inventory-2 (RADS-2; Reynolds, 2002), a commonly used self-report measure of depression in adolescents, clarified the severity of May's depression. Her overall scores revealed she was more depressed than 90% of girls in her grade, on average, suggesting she was significantly depressed. Major Depressive Disorder symptoms include depressed mood most of the day every day, loss of energy every day, sleep problems, chronic feelings of worthlessness and unjustified guilt, diminished ability to concentrate and make decisions, and suicidal ideation without a plan or specific intent. Along with depression, Ms. Wright thought there was a possibility May suffered from Acute Stress Disorder or, possibly, Posttraumatic Stress Disorder (*DSM*-5). May was exposed to physical danger with Jarold and, although May defended him and minimized the episode, she reacted with distress. Ms. Wright reserved judgment on the latter diagnosis until later.

After obtaining a fuller clinical picture of May's difficulties, Ms. Wright informed her that because of some of the things she described, May was at emotional and physical risk. She would need to invite May's parents in and talk with them so that the right additional help and support could be arranged. May felt panicky. She said, "Isn't coming here and telling you enough? Why do we need to tell them?" Ms. Wright responded, "You can tell them, or I can, but they need to know, because they care about you and want what's best for your safety. As I explained, what you say in here is confidential, except where your safety is a concern." May said, "But they will make me break up with Jarold. They already are starting to hate him." Ms. Wright assured May that she understood how much May was attached to Jarold, and she would not support her parents forbidding contact with him, or insisting that she break up with him. Rather, she told May she would suggest to Jenny and Ken that they allow her to make any decisions about whether or not to stay with her boyfriend. However, because there was an injury, May should understand that her parents might want to take legal or other action to protect her from any future emotional or physical abuse by Jarold. Further, because of the vomiting behavior, there were other immediate risks to her health that would need to be assessed by a specialty-trained physician. Ms. Wright explained the issue of electrolyte imbalance and other medical complications when vomiting occurred, so that May could understand the need for medical monitoring.

May worried she had revealed too much in therapy. It scared her that someone who was going to talk to her parents knew that much about her private life. She was frightened that someone knew her carefully protected secrets about her relationship with Jarold. Now, regretting all that she had revealed, May said Ms. Wright could tell her parents if they had to know, but she wanted to wait outside while it happened. Ms. Wright knew how the continuation of May's good relationship with her parents was riding on them working through this situation together and convinced May to stay in the room while they both talked to her parents. Jenny and Ken were startled to hear that Jenny had lied to them about Jarold's anger at her in school and his grabbing her arm. They were more startled to hear their daughter had an eating disorder. May's duplicitous behavior was suspected, but the reality rendered her parents shocked, sad, and angry. Jenny felt particularly embarrassed and guilty, because all this had happened under her own roof, and she had not known. "What kind of parent am I that I could let this happen?" she asked.

It was no surprise that May's parents didn't realize she was ill with bulimia nervosa. She was deceptive, because the eating disorder encourages this behavior. May was doing her best not to expose her vulnerabilities. No one was to blame. Jenny and Ken were not bad parents. May did not ask to walk into an abusive relationship, nor did she ask for an eating disorder. A complex confluence of internal and external factors came together to create the perfect storm that led May into her problems. It is difficult to separate the various factors that influenced May to eat in restrictive ways. First, there was the influence of peers who wanted to be model-thin and eat healthy. May further internalized this thin ideal through viewing Internet sources along with the daily barrage of media messaging about women's bodies. Then, there were May's personality and individual characteristics, like depression, striving for perfect control, body dissatisfaction, a high need for approval, poor ability to self-regulate, and low self-efficacy. Further, there was genetic stacking for clinical depression and anxiety.

When Ms. Wright asked about their family history, Jenny and Ken reported a number of possibly relevant heritable characteristics. There was a genetic proclivity for anxiety and depression in both families. Jenny called herself "an anxious perfectionist," and Ken had two brothers who suffered from depression. *Perfectionism* is a personality disposition that is reflected in the belief that mistakes or flaws are unacceptable. When evaluating one's own behavior, the perceived flaws are those most noticed. Success and failure are seen as absolutes, and the world is seen as black or white and either-or. This form of cognitive rigidity is a hallmark characteristic of perfectionism (Wade & Tiggemann, 2013). There is no compromise, no gray area, and no "good enough." The world becomes a rigid and rule-bound place with the mistaken impression that all in life is "controllable." Those prone to perfectionism are driven to achieve and are critical of themselves when they don't. They have difficulty recognizing their successes, because the nature of perfectionism is to rigidly focus on flaws, real or imagined. This was in May's mother's nature and, unbeknownst to either of them, passed along to May as a natural approach to the world. As explained in Anna's story, perfectionism about weight and external appearance, especially in the wake of body disatisfaction, provides fertile ground for eating disorders (Boone, Soenens, and Luyten, 2014).

Schaefer (2003), known for writing *Life Without Ed*, identified her own battle with perfectionism as the core of her struggle with her eating disorder

(Ed). Unfortunately for girls like May, perfectionism, as research has shown, can be a predictor of negative outcomes for eating disorders, especially anorexia nervosa (Bardone-Cone, Sturm, Lawson, Robinson, & Smith, 2010). Perfectionist tendencies make it harder to recover. Once May applied the principles of self-imposed perfection to body size and foods consumed, she was on her way to a more difficult future with ritualized eating and, ultimately, an eating disorder.

So many factors played a part of May's problems. For example, as Ken and Jenny would soon learn, their well-meaning parenting provided love and support, but not enough encouragement for May to learn to soothe herself or solve her own problems. She became overwhelmed when emotionally distressed and avoided or numbed her negative feelings through eating-disorder behaviors (dietary restraint, binge eating, and vomiting). Her urges to cut (later revealed to Ms. Wright), rather than applying effective coping skills, were further self-defeating strategies to manage her pain.

Ken and Jenny quickly became aware that trying to figure out who was to blame, or what caused May's eating disorder and their part in an abusive relationship with Jarold, was not useful in helping their daughter. They needed to acknowledge that whatever mistakes were made, it was more important to move forward into recovery. As pioneering strategic family therapists point out (Haley, 1973), being agnostic with regard to the cause of psychological disorders in treatment can be helpful, because the main focus can then be on current problem solving, rather than on past blame for the issues at hand.

Treasure and other eating-disorder researchers (Whitney, Murray, Todd, Whitaker, & Treasure, 2005) pointed out that carers like Jenny and Ken often blame themselves for contributing to their loved ones' eating disorders. In doing so, they may be prone to unhelpful responses, such as defensiveness, guilt, anxiousness, and even anger in the face of the eating disorder and during treatment interventions. It is the job of treatment professionals to prepare parents for collaborative participation in treatment. One of the ways Treasure (Treasure & Alexander, 2013) has successfully done this is with the use of animal metaphors with which parents can easily identify and provide more helpful support to their children who have eating disorders. These include a *jellyfish* for overly emotional, under-controlled parent responses; an *ostrich* for avoidant responses; a *kangaroo* for over-protective and over-functioning responses; a *rhinoceros* for overly forceful, often angry responses; and a *terrier* for persistent, nagging, and critical responses. On the helpful side, the *dolphin* stays alongside and guides through recovery, and the *St. Bernard* is a steady, calm, empathetic helper. Although Treasure's metaphors were developed to help carers cope with eating disorders, much of the wisdom of her animal metaphors can be applied to coping with a variety of psychological disorders, including the type of depression and trauma-bonding displayed by May in her abusive relationship with Jarold.

Ken could see himself as occasionally resorting to rhinoceros behavior. When he found out about May's vomiting behavior and the coercive nature of her relationship with Jarold, he felt helpless and frustrated. He became critical and confrontational with his daughter. Part of his response was driven by Jenny's feeling overwhelmed in the face of unpleasant truths about May. He felt protective of his family and wanted to make things right. Jenny found herself somewhere between a jellyfish and a general parenting method she shared with Ken, the kangaroo. It was all so complicated. Jenny would burst into tears from anxiety as she pleaded with May to eat foods she had given up. When Jenny later discovered May was eating large amounts of the family's snack supply in the kitchen at night, she insisted May stop binge eating after she and Ken went to bed. May, feeling guilty, would become angry with her mother. This only caused Jenny to become more overwhelmed. At the same time, Jenny wanted to save May from both bulimia and Jarold.

With the help of Ms. Wright, Ken and Jenny discovered a key dynamic in their relationship with May. It was as if they both had pouches like a kangaroo, and they had repeatedly allowed her to jump into them as they tried to protect her from life's bumps and bruises. If she had stress, they tried to soothe her. If she panicked about something, they sat with her until she calmed down. If she seemed hurt by Jarold, they repeatedly blamed him and saw her as a victim. Now that they knew she vomited to manage her weight and appearance, they wanted to watch her every move. They wanted to walk on eggshells not to upset her. Their kangaroo behavior had denied May opportunities to learn to cope with forces both inside and outside herself. She had spent too much time in Jenny and Ken's pouches.

May needed to learn strategies of mindfulness: *self-regulation, distress tolerance*, and *interpersonal effectiveness*, skill sets noted in Dialectical Behavior Therapy (Linehan, 1993). She had fallen behind in these skill acquisitions, in part because she had not practiced them much prior to adolescence. Ken and Jenny needed to learn to step back and allow May to struggle more with her feelings, her relationships, and her place in the world. She needed to learn more effective coping strategies and self-responsibility skills in order to effectively make her way in life, outside the kangaroo pouch. This meant Jenny and Ken had to retreat at just those moments when they wanted to scoop May up and protect her. To aid May and the family in this work, Ms. Wright referred them to an adolescent Dialectical Behavior Therapy (DBT; Linehan, 1993, 2015) skills-training group at a nearby clinic.

DBT-skills training is evidence-based and has been shown to be effective in building mindfulness skills (skills to accept the present moment), skills to regulate emotions (cope with pain and distress), and skills to effectively navigate interpersonal relationships (e.g., to effectively ask for what one does or doesn't want; Mehlum et al., 2014). Although May was initially resistant, Ms. Wright empowered the parents to insist and encourage May to take advantage of an opportunity to develop more effective coping skills. Over the course of 18 weeks, May and her parents participated in a once-a-week, multi-family DBT skills group that covered the following four modules: *mindfulness, emotion regulation, distress tolerance*, and *interpersonal effectiveness*. A fifth module, *walking the middle path,* was recently added to address the special problems of teens and their families (Benedek, 2016; Miller, Rathus, & Linehan, 2007; Rathus, Campbell, Miller, & Smith, 2015). In this fifth module, family members learn to validate (accept) each other and engage in effective behavioral modification to support change. The term *middle road* is apt because it helps families consider multiple perspectives, reduce black-and-white thinking, and generate balanced (not extreme) solutions to an adolescent's family's dilemmas (Rathus et al., 2015).

Learning DBT skills has been found to improve caregiver skills and improve the effectiveness of DBT-skills training for all family members (Harvey & Rathbone, 2014; Powell, 2014; Wilks et al., 2016). By participating in the group, Jenny and Ken were not only informed of the skills May learned, but they could also use the skills themselves (e.g., manage their reactivity to May) and encourage her to use her new knowledge. In all, family DBT-skills training helped to provide May with a safe and validating space in which to recover.

Ken and Jenny's DBT knowledge became especially useful when Jenny and Ken were challenged by the need to step back from May's relationship with Jarold. Ms. Wright advised them that trying to forbid May from seeing Jarold would undermine her need to find her own way with her relationship. May's deception to her parents about the cause of the bruise on her arm was difficult to accept, as was her bulimic behavior, but they had to learn to trust her to figure out how to take care of herself. In order to address high-priority safety issues, and before beginning to focus on bulimia, Ms. Wright said to Jenny and Ken, "I know you want to take responsibility for protecting May from her abusive relationship with her boyfriend, and I encourage you to take legal action to protect her if appropriate. Take her to the nearest hospital emergency room if she harms or threatens to harm herself. Call the local police if she runs away, and you can't find her, or she or Jarold threaten or harm you. Otherwise, May will have to learn the skills that will enable her to choose to make the changes necessary to end her destructive relationship on her own. You won't be able to completely control her behavior as much as you wish." Ken and Jenny learned in DBT that May needed to take responsibility for addressing dilemmas created by her relationship with Jarold.

May and her parents' DBT-skills training was separate but complementary to their work with Ms. Wright. As part of setting up a collaborative treatment plan with May and her family, Ms. Wright recommended Cognitive Behavior Therapy (CBT; Beck, 2011) adapted for the treatment of bulimia (Fairburn, 2002). More specifically, she recommended CBT adapted for adolescents with bulimia (CBT-A; Lock, 2005). CBT-A is a modified CBT treatment protocol for adolescent bulimia. Consistent with Lock's manualized CBT-A protocol, Ms. Wright continued to meet weekly with May over a period of 6 months. At the end of each individual session, she met for a check-in with Ken, Jenny, and May (Lock, 2005). Her sequenced focus was to normalize May's eating (first stage); to problem solve, identify emotions, and correct distorted thoughts and beliefs related to the eating disorder (second stage); and to prevent relapse (third stage).

Although evidence shows CBT-A is an experimental treatment and may not be as effective for reducing binge-and-purge behavior as evidence-based Family Based Treatment for bulimia (FBT-BN; Le Grange, Lock, Agras, Bryson, & Jo, 2015), CBT-A afforded the opportunity for Ms. Wright to keep specialty-trained focus on bulimia, while at the same time providing an opportunity to attend to May's other adolescent issues (e.g., her troubled relationship with Jarold). Further, with CBT-A, Ms. Wright kept May's parents involved in each session. Family involvement in treatment has been shown to be an important factor for successful bulimia treatment (Le Grange, Lock, Loeb, & Nicholls, 2010; Schmidt et al., 2007). By applying both parent-involved DBT and CBT-A, Ms. Wright was able to provide a more comprehensive treatment plan that included the eating disorder and other behaviors, like involvement with an abusive dating partner.

May's parents' check-in at the end of each session with May and Ms. Wright accomplished a number of objectives (Lock, 2005). First, Ken and Jenny were kept in the loop with regard to what was being discussed. Second, because their observations of May were regularly solicited, they were empowered as part of a collaborative treatment effort. Third, in the context of family check-ins, May's parents were encouraged to provide compassionate and positive support for May's initially faltering efforts to resist the eating disorder. Fourth, a number of parent-involved interventions to provide a healing home environment were negotiated with May.

For example, May had a history of skipping breakfast, skimping on lunch, and starting to binge eat in the evening. Her parents learned to assist her with meal planning, provide her with three meals and two snacks a day, and make sure she attended all her appointments. They sat with her at meals because she asked them to. She said, "It would actually help me a lot if you would sit with me at breakfast, because I hate eating breakfast, but I know I have to." At first, this was a stretch for Ken and Jenny, because their household was often chaotic in the morning. However, once in place, eating breakfast as a family both helped May normalize her eating and brought structure and order to the household. May also negotiated with her parents for at least one of them to sit with her after dinner for an hour so she was not tempted to vomit. At first it was awkward, because May had hidden her purge behavior from her parents and now was openly admitting it. Toward the end of therapy, this level of support was no longer needed because May was more able to resist the demands of the eating disorder. The focus on bulimia with Ms. Wright was in many ways a welcome relief for May's family, because it gave them a break from their previous over-focus on the issues with Jarold.

Individual sessions with Ms. Wright included keeping food logs, including records of binge and purge behavior. May was only partially compliant with food logs (e.g., "I forgot to write down a few days"), but this improved once she met for a consultation with a dietitian and recognized the importance of keeping a record of her eating. She needed to be accountable to herself as well as the dietitian as she worked on normalizing her eating (Lindgren, Enmark, Bohman, & Lunström, 2014).

While May lost little weight in her pursuit-of-clean-eating dietary changes, her increasing daytime pickiness with food suggested the need for her to work with a dietitian to balance her nutrition with a wider variety of foods. Jenny and Ken had accommodated her previous restrictive eating habits, even changing their own eating behaviors to mimic her needs. "After all, what could be wrong with a healthier diet?" they had asked themselves. They did not suspect May was motivated by body-size management more than healthy eating. Ms. Wright advised them that accommodating the eating disorder by changing their own eating habits would simply encourage eating-disorder behavior. Jenny and Ken went back to eating their normal meals. Although they were scared they would leave May behind, they understood that May needed to confront her anxieties about eating (e.g., face her fear foods). They needed to be patient with her as she struggled to restore three meals and two snacks into each of her days.

Sometimes when May was struggling with mashed potatoes at dinner, they had to restrain themselves from getting angry. They learned to understand that May had become terrified of mashed potatoes – a food she associated with "getting fat." As Kaye et al. (2013) have pointed out, people with bulimia nervosa have inhibitory deficits that make it difficult to control food intake despite an over-arching drive to restrict. Those with bulimia:

> have a seemingly relentless drive to restrain their food intake, an extreme fear of weight gain, and often have a distorted view of their actual body shape. Loss of control with overeating usually occurs intermittently and typically only some time after the onset of dieting behavior.
>
> (Kaye, Strober, & Klump, 2002, p. 224)

Jenny and Ken had to dispel any illusion that May would easily or quickly stop binge eating or be able to eat their usual family foods. They learned that bulimia nervosa is a brain-based disorder in which appetite regulation and body image are disturbed and don't function normally (Kaye, 2008). They were disappointed to find out that Prozac (fluoxetine), a drug they believed might be an answer, rarely eliminated binge-and-purge behavior on its own, though it is approved for treatment of bulimia nervosa (Green, 2007; Walsh et al., 2000). However, once a visit with a psychiatrist confirmed Prozac might be helpful to May, they were encouraged that it might assist in reducing May's obvious depression and anxiety and might increase her ability to resist the demands of the eating disorder to binge and purge. Combined psychological treatment and medication can produce better outcomes for bulimia nervosa.

With regard to Jarold, Ken and Jenny decided not to give May an ultimatum to break up with him. They did talk to her about safety, given the amount of verbal fighting they overheard on the phone. They used "I" statements about their concerns. They drew up a safety contract in which May agreed to plans of actions if she felt threatened when she was with Jarold. Ken and Jenny also contacted Jarold's mother and talked to her about their concerns with the hope that they could establish a collaborative parental relationship.

Still, Jenny and Ken knew that if they wanted May to stay open with them about her relationship with Jarold, they would need to listen without becoming critical, even though they desperately wanted her to leave him. They didn't want May to start lying to them about having contact with Jarold, or to hide any big problems with him. They came to understand, with Ms. Wright's support, that May was choosing to be with Jarold, and that meant she was allowing herself to be emotionally abused (Roberts & Klein, 2003). As Murray (2000) points out to parents of girls who have abusive boyfriends:

> because your daughter internalizes what you think of her, you do not want to give her the message that you feel she is being victimized by her boyfriend. Instead, why not give her the message that she is strong, powerful, and able to make good decisions?
>
> (p. 15)

Ms. Wright encouraged May to attend meetings at a local advocacy center so May could learn the difference between healthy relationships and unhealthy, addictive ones. This helped May see the difference between being loved, and being possessed and abused.

Breaking up with Jarold happened in its own time. He became bored with her since he never really loved her in the first place. And May discovered the driving forces in their relationship were anxiety and fear, not love. She was no longer satisfied being Jarold's girlfriend.

Overcoming bulimia and thoughts of wanting to self-harm took longer than breaking up with Jarold. May's obsessiveness and attachment to identities that were in many ways disconnected from anything substantial meant long, hard work. Sneaking around at night to binge eat in order to soothe her negative affect took longer than giving up vomiting. The effort it took to compete to be the thinnest girl in the cafeteria was too exhausting. The frustration and feelings of helplessness after nights of binge eating followed by repeated attempts to restrict food became intolerable. She finally let go of eating-disorder behaviors, tired of being obsessed with food, weight, and body-size control. There were setbacks and slow movements forward. She made a project of decreasing vomiting behavior that was successful over 6 months of CBT-A, and, eventually, May no longer engaged in vomiting. She rarely thought about cutting herself anymore. Most importantly, she found an identity in new interests, like the track team and an Up With Girls Club at her school.

No longer at risk for an abusive relationship because of previous vulnerabilities, May gained strength and personal confidence. Jenny and Ken's anxieties diminished, although it was several months before they could relax. They, too, had been traumatized by May's difficulties. Yet their small family of four was stronger than it ever had been because they were able to work through all that had happened, together.

Question

I have heard that abuse by an intimate partner can contribute to eating disorders. Why does this occur if the abuse has nothing to do with eating?

Answer

Studies of college and high school girls like May who have experienced dating violence were more likely to report uncontrolled eating, use of vomiting and laxatives to purge, fasting and skipping meals, and use of diet medications (Ackard & Neumark-Sztainer, 2002; Bonomi, Anderson, Nemeth, Rivara, & Buettner, 2013; Romito & Grassi, 2007). Wong and Chang (2016) interviewed women who had experienced intimate partner violence (IPV) and found five reasons why victims of IPV may turn to altered eating behaviors. First, the anxiety, stress, and frustration of partner violence can result in physical symptoms like gastrointestinal distress (i.e., stomach in knots, poor appetite, and nausea), which affects the ability to eat. Second, abusive partners can control eating as a form of abuse (e.g., forced feeding, ridicule of healthy eating, limiting food choices and amounts, and controlling money for purchasing food). Third, victims may use food to soothe or cope with emotions (e.g., eating for pleasure when distressed, using food to fill a feeling of emptiness, and using food for comfort). Fourth, victims may use food to harm themselves after abuse. They punish themselves because of a sense of guilt or shame. Or they might internalize their abuser's criticisms of their eating and body (i.e., these women "make themselves as unattractive as their abusers made them feel"; p. 3498). Fifth, some victims used weight, eating, or not eating to challenge their abusers because these were areas that could not be completely controlled. Eating and weight control thus expressed self-reliance, confidence, or defiance. Wong and Chang's interview data demonstrated multiple and complex pathways from partner violence to problem-eating behaviors.

Question

How can parents restrain themselves from outbursts of anger and frustration when their child continues to engage in eating-disorder behaviors?

Answer

Carers of people with eating disorders routinely experience distress due to the burden of the caregiving role (social isolation, fatigue, insufficient information, and lack of skills and resources). Their distress is exacerbated by reluctant teens impervious to the impact of their serious illness on others. Further, parents may mistakenly blame themselves or their child for the illness. (Remember, the illness is no one's fault.) Despite their carer distress, parents are often advised to reduce expressions of hostility and criticism when supporting their child in recovery. This is because too much of either of those by parents toward their ill child, although understandable, can hinder treatment success (Rienecke & Richmond, 2017; Treasure & Nazar, 2016; van Furth et al., 1996). Hostile expressions communicate unhelpful blame toward the young person with the eating disorder.

When the eating disorder is placed outside the child and is viewed as no one's fault, it is easier to remain calm and noncritical in the face of the eating disorder. It is a painstakingly slow road to recovery, and a positive, compassionate approach can ease the way. For example, would a parent be angry toward a child because he or she was uncomfortable during a chemotherapy treatment for cancer? The answer is "of course not." Everyone understands that no one is to blame for a child having cancer. It is easy to understand the need for compassion in that example because chemotherapy is uncomfortable. The same is true for eating disorders and their treatment.

Many carer or parent interventions and family therapies have been developed to train parents in effectively responding to eating disorders and, thus, reduce their hopelessness, despair, and negative affect. Psychoeducational programs have improved carer coping by teaching them about the nature and treatment of eating disorders (Haltom, Ribeiro, & Potter, 2012). In addition, treatment modalities based on the Maudsley Model (collaborative-care, group-skills training; Sepulveda, Lopez, Todd, Whitaker, & Treasure, 2008; Treasure, Smith, & Crane, 2007); Multifamily Therapy Group (Eisler et al., 2016); and Family Based Treatment for anorexia and bulimia (FBT; Le Grange & Lock, 2009; Lock & Le Grange, 2015) have helped to increase parent skills to manage eating-disorder illnesses. Maudsley collaborative-skills training teaches effective meal support and positive, noncritical communication. Similarly, FBT assists parents in providing nutritional support to overcome illness without hostility. Hibbs, Rhind, Leppanen, and Treasure (2015) reviewed research on interventions for the caregivers of those with eating disorders. They found skills-training programs taught in workshops and in self-help or guided self-help formats (either online, by phone, or in books) reduced carer distress and reduced critical communications with patients. Materials from these programs are accessible.

Treasure's (Treasure & Alexander, 2013) animal metaphors mentioned above in May's story assist parents to recognize unhelpful and helpful patterns of communication in a light-hearted, non-threatening way. For example, May's father, Ken, recognized sometimes he behaved like a rhinoceros, argumentative and forceful. An alternative, using Treasure's animal metaphors, is adopting the attitude of a dolphin parent. A dolphin sticks close to its young and nudges, gently leads, guides, or follows, as needed.

Rhind et al. (2014) developed a program for carers of those with eating disorders called Experienced Carers Helping Others (ECHO). Areas of educational focus included bigger picture (remaining positive with a long-term view), self-care (taking time for self and family), biting-your-tongue (controlling the urge to inquire and avoid repetitive nagging conversations), insight and acceptance (the ability to accept and manage negative emotions), emotional intelligence (ability to disçuss and manage feelings), and frustration tolerance (ability to sidestep conflict, yet remain firm and understanding). Encapsulated in these educational factors are skills parents of those with eating disorders can use to reduce critical, argumentative, and hostile expressions.

Question

My son refuses to receive any treatment or see his pediatrician for his dieting and self-induced vomiting behavior. What do we do?

Answer

As indicated in May's and other stories in this book, eating disorders are life-threatening illnesses that need to be treated and medically evaluated. When parents feel overwhelmed by their child's refusal to comply in their own treatment, it is important that they recognize this is due to the influence of the illness. They should remain firm in their resolve to seek professional help. While it would be preferable to have a willing young person when obtaining medical evaluation for them, this is often not the case. Many people with eating disorders either don't believe there is a problem, or they "normalize" their behavior. They sincerely don't believe they need an evaluation or treatment. For example, a teen like May confronted with dieting and purge behavior might say, "I'm fine. Everybody diets, and I throw up because I'm too full." Despite this kind of defensive statement, it is up to parents and carers to confidently insist that eating-disorder behaviors be evaluated by a specialty-trained professional.

Despite the availability of evidence-based treatments, less than 25% of people with eating disorders seek treatment (Hart, Granillo, Jorm, & Paxton, 2011). One study found 0% treatment seeking in a sample of middle school adolescents (Meyer, 2001). A recent study by Ali et al. (2016) found the most prominent barriers to help-seeking for eating disorders were:

> stigma and shame, denial of and failure to perceive the severity of the illness, practical barriers (e.g., cost of treatment), low motivation to change, negative attitudes toward seeking help, lack of encouragement from others to seek help and lack of knowledge about help resources.
>
> (p. 9)

In addition, young people are particularly afraid of weight gain and have body size and shape concerns. Most likely you will see included here one or more of the reasons your child does not want an evaluation or treatment.

You, as a parent or carer, may also experience or sympathize with one or more of these barriers to getting help. If so, it is important to overcome them. Then it is important to insist your child receive an evaluation by a specialty-trained treatment professional and follow-up with treatment, if recommended. Parents of even the most out-of-control children often have more authority with their child than they think. Ultimately, young people respect and feel safer with parents who take charge when they are ill, or potentially ill.

References

Ackard, D. M., Elsenberg, M. E., & Neumark-Sztainer, D. (2007). Long-term impact of adolescent dating violence on the behavioral and psychological health of male and female youth. *The Journal of Pediatrics*, 151(5), 476–481.

Ackard, D. M., & Neumark-Sztainer, D. (2002). Date violence and date rape among adolescents: Associations with disordered eating behaviors and psychological health. *Journal of Child Abuse and Neglect*, 26(5), 455–473.

Ali, K., Farrer, L., Fassnacht, D. B., Gulliver, A., Bauer, S., & Griffiths, K. M. (2016). Perceived barriers and facilitators toward help-seeking for eating disorders: A systematic review. *International Journal of Eating Disorders*, 50(1), 9–21.

American Psychiatric Association. (2013). *Diagnostic and statistical manual of mental disorders* (5th ed.). Washington, DC: Author.

Bardone-Cone, A. M., Sturm, K., Lawson, M. A., Robinson, D. P., & Smith, R. (2010). Perfectionism across stages of recovery from eating disorders. *International Journal of Eating Disorders*, 43(2), 139–148.

Beck, J. S. (2011). *Cognitive behavior therapy: Basics and beyond* (2nd ed.). New York, NY: Guilford Press.

Benedek, E. P. (2016). DBT skills manual for adolescents. [Review of the manual DBT skills manual for adolescents, by J. H. Rathus, & A. L. Miller]. *Journal of Nervous and Mental Disease*, 204(4), 326.

Bonomi, A. E., Anderson, M. L., Nemeth, J., Rivara, F. P., & Buettner, C. (2013). History of dating violence and the association with late adolescent health. *BMC Public Health*, 13(1), 1–12.

Boone, L., Soenens, B., & Luyten, P. (2014). When or why does perfectionism translate into eating disorder pathology? A longitudinal examination of the moderating and mediating role of body dissatisfaction. *Journal Of Abnormal Psychology*, 123(2), 412–418.

Bucchianeri, M. M., Arikian, A. J., Hannan, P. J., Eisenberg, M. E., & Neumark-Sztainer, D. (2013). Body dissatisfaction from adolescence to young adulthood: Findings from a 10-year longitudinal study. *Body Image*, 10(1), 1–7.

Chronis-Tuscano, A., Degnan, K., Pine, D., Pérez-Edgar, K., Henderson, H., Diaz, Y., … Fox, N. (2009). Stable early maternal report of behavioral inhibition predicts lifetime social anxiety disorder in adolescence. *Journal of the American Academy of Child & Adolescent Psychiatry*, 48, 928–935.

Costin, C. (2007). *The eating disorders sourcebook: A comprehensive guide to the causes, treatments, and prevention of eating disorders.* New York, NY: McGraw-Hill.

Dias, K. (2003). The Ana Sanctuary: Women's pro-anorexia narratives in cyberspace. *Journal of International Women's Studies*, 4(2), 31–45.

DiClemente, R. J., Ponton, L. E., & Hartley, D. (1991). Prevalence and correlates of cutting behavior: Risk for HIV transmission. *Journal of the American Academy of Child and Adolescent Psychiatry*, 30(5), 735–739.

Eisler, I., Simic, M., Hodsoll, J., Asen, E., Berelowitz, M., Connan, F., ... Landau, S. (2016). A pragmatic randomised multi-centre trial of multifamily and single family therapy for adolescent anorexia nervosa. *BMC Psychiatry*, 16(1), 422.

Fairburn, C. G. (2002). Cognitive behavioral therapy for bulimia nervosa. In C. G. Fairburn & K. D. Brownell (Eds.), *Eating disorders and obesity: A comprehensive handbook* (pp. 302–307). New York, NY: Guilford Press.

Garner, D. M. (2004). *Eating disorder inventory-3 (EDI-3). Professional manual.* Odessa, FL: Psychological Assessment Resources.

Gervais, S., Vescio, T., Förster, J., Maass, A., & Suitner, C. (2012). Seeing women as objects: The sexual body part recognition bias. *European Journal of Social Psychology*, 42(6), 743–753.

Green, S. (2007). Anorexia and bulimia: Dying to be slim. *Drug & Market Development*, 18(4), 16–18.

Haley, J. (1973). *Uncommon therapy: The psychiatric techniques of Milton H. Erickson.* New York, NY: Norton.

Haltom, C., Ribeiro, R., & Potter, N. (2012). Collaborative professional education for carers of those with eating disorders. *European Eating Disorders Review*, 20(4), 311–314.

Hart, L. M., Granillo, M. T., Jorm, A. F., & Paxton, S. J. (2011). Unmet need for treatment in the eating disorders: A systematic review of eating disorder specific treatment seeking among community cases. *Clinical Psychology Review*, 31(5), 727–735.

Harvey, P., & Rathbone, B. H. (2014). *Dialectical behavior therapy for at-risk adolescents: A practitioner's guide to treating challenging behavior problems.* Oakland, CA: New Harbinger.

Hattersley-Gray, R. (2012). Dating abuse statistics. *Campus Safety Magazine*, December 10. Retrieved from www.campussafetymagazine.com/safety/dating-abuse-statistics/

Hibbs, R., Rhind, C., Leppanen, J., & Treasure, J. (2015). Interventions for caregivers of someone with an eating disorder: A meta-analysis. *International Journal of Eating Disorders*, 48(4), 349–361.

Jacobson, C. M., & Gould, M. (2007). The epidemiology and phenomenology of non-suicidal self-injurious behavior among adolescents: A critical review of the literature. *Archives of Suicide Research*, 11(2), 129–147.

Kaye, W. (2008). Neurobiology of anorexia and bulimia nervosa. Purdue Ingestive Behavior Research Center Symposium. Influences on eating and body weight over the lifespan: Children and adolescents. *Physiology & Behavior*, 94(1), 121–135.

Kaye, W., Strober, M., & Klump, K. L. (2002). Neurobiology of eating disorders. In A. Martin, L. Scahill, & C. J. Kratochvil (Eds.), *Pediatric psychopharmacology: Principles and practice* (pp. 224–237). New York, NY: Oxford University Press.

Kaye, W. H., Wierenga, C. E., Bailor, U., Simmons, A.N., Wagner, A., & Bischoff-Grethe, A. (2013). Does a shared neurobiology for foods and drugs of abuse contribute to extremes of food ingestion in anorexia and bulimia nervosa? *Biological Psychiatry*, 73(9), 836–842

Le Grange, D., & Lock, J. (2009). *Treating bulimia in adolescents: A family-based approach.* New York, NY: Guilford Press.

Le Grange, D., Lock, J., Agras, W. S., Bryson, S. W., & Jo, B. (2015). Randomized clinical trial of family-based treatment and cognitive-behavioral therapy for adolescent bulimia nervosa. *Journal of the American Academy of Child & Adolescent Psychiatry*, 54(11), 886–894.

Le Grange, D., Lock, J., Loeb, K., & Nicholls, D. (2010). Academy for eating disorders position paper: The role of the family in eating disorders. *International Journal of Eating Disorders*, 43(1), 1–5.

Leen, E., Sorbring, E., Mawer, M., Holdsworth, E., Helsing, B., & Bowen, E. (2013). Prevalence, dynamic risk factors and the efficacy of primary interventions for adolescent dating violence: An international review. *Aggression and Violent Behavior*, 18, 159–174.

Lindgren, B.-M., Enmark, A., Bohman, A., & Lunström, M. (2014). A qualitative study of young women's experiences of recovery from Bulimia Nervosa. *Journal of Advanced Nursing*, 71(4), 860–869.

Linehan, M. (1993). *Skills training manual for treating Borderline Personality Disorder*. New York, NY: Guilford Press.

Linehan, M. (2015) *DBT skills training manual* (2nd ed.). New York, NY: Guilford Press.

Lock, J. (2005) Adjusting cognitive behavior therapy for adolescents with bulimia nervosa: Results of case series. *American Journal of Psychotherapy*, 59(3), 267–281.

Lock, J., & Le Grange, D. (2015). *Treatment manual for anorexia nervosa: A family-based approach*. New York, NY: Guilford Press.

Mehlum, L., Tørmoen, A. J., Ramberg, M., Haga, E., Diep, L. M., Laberg, S., … Grøholt, B. (2014). Dialectical behavior therapy for adolescents with repeated suicidal and self-harming behavior: A randomized trial. *Journal of the American Academy of Child & Adolescent Psychiatry*, 53(10), 1082–1091.

Meyer, D. F. (2001). Help-seeking for eating disorders in female adolescents. *Journal of College Student Psychotherapy*, 15(4), 23–36.

Miller, A. L., Rathus, J. H., & Linehan, M. M. (2007). *Dialectical behavior therapy with suicidal adolescents*. New York, NY: Guilford Press.

Morgan, J. F., Reid, F., & Lacey, J. H. (2000). The SCOFF questionnaire: A new screening tool for eating disorders. *Western Journal of Medicine*, 17(3), 164–165.

Muehlenkamp, J. J., Claes, L., Havertape, L., & Plener, P. L. (2012). International prevalence of adolescent non-suicidal self-injury and deliberate self-harm. *Child and Adolescent Psychiatry and Mental Health*, 6(1), 10–18.

Murray, J. (2000). *But I love him: Protecting your teen daughter from controlling, abusive dating relationships*. New York: NY: HarperCollins.

Myers, T., & Crowther, J. (2009). Social comparison as a predictor of body dissatisfaction: A meta-analytic review. *Journal of Abnormal Psychology*, 118(4), 683–698.

Powell, D. M. (2014). *Do parents use of DBT skills change after a 12 week parent/adolescent DBT skills group?* (Unpublished master's thesis). State University of New York, Brockport.

Rancourt, D., Choukas-Bradley, S., Cohen, G. L., & Prinstein, M. J. (2014). An experimental examination of peers' influence on adolescent girls' intent to engage in maladaptive weight-related behaviors. *International Journal of Eating Disorders*, 47(5), 437–447.

Rathus, J., Campbell, B., Miller, A., & Smith, H. (2015). Treatment acceptability study of walking the middle path: A new DBT skills module for adolescents and their families. *American Journal of Psychotherapy*, 69(2), 163–178.

Reynolds, W. M. (2002). *RADS-2: Reynolds adolescent depression scale* (2nd ed.): Professional manual. Lutz, FL: Psychological Assessment Resources.

Rhind, C., Hibbs, R., Goddard, E., Schmidt, U., Micali, N., Gowers, S., ... Treasure, J. (2014). Experienced Carers Helping Others (ECHO): Protocol for a pilot randomised controlled trial to examine a psycho-educational intervention for adolescents with anorexia nervosa and their carers. *European Eating Disorder Review*, 22(4), 267–277.

Rienecke, R. D., & Richmond, R. L. (2017). Psychopathology and expressed emotion in parents of patients with eating disorders: Relation to patient symptom severity. *Eating Disorders*, 25(4), 318–329.

Roberts, T. A., & Klein, J. (2003). Intimate partner abuse and high-risk behavior in adolescents. *Archives of Pediatrics and Adolescent Medicine*, 157(4), 375–380.

Romito, P., & Grassi, M. (2007). Does violence affect one gender more than the other? The mental health impact of violence among male and female university students. *Social Science and Medicine*, 65(8), 1222–1234.

Schaefer, J. (2003). *Life without Ed: How one woman declared independence from her eating disorder and how you can too.* New York, NY: McGraw-Hill.

Schmidt, U., Lee, S., Beecham, J., Perkins, S., Treasure, J., Yi, I., ... Johnson-Sabine, E. (2007). A randomized controlled trial of family therapy and cognitive behavior therapy guided self-care for adolescents with bulimia nervosa and related disorders. *American Journal of Psychiatry*, 164(4), 591–598.

Sepulveda, A. R., Lopez, C., Todd, G., Whitaker, W., & Treasure, J. (2008). An examination of the impact of "the Maudsley eating disorder collaborative care skills workshops" on the well being of carers. *Social Psychiatry and Psychiatric Epidemiology*, 43(7), 584–591.

Silverman, J. G., Raj, A., Mucci, L. A., & Hathaway, J. E. (2001). Dating violence against adolescent girls and associated substance use, unhealthy weight control, sexual risk behavior, pregnancy, and suicidality. *The Journal of the American Medical Association*, 286(5), 572–579.

Smolak, L. (2011). Body image development in childhood. In T. F. Cash & L. Smolak (Eds.), *Body image: A handbook of science, practice, and prevention* (2nd ed.; pp. 67–75). New York, NY: Guilford.

Swannell, S. V., Martin, G. E., Page, A., Hasking, P., & St. John, N.J. (2014). Prevalence of nonsuicidal self-injury in nonclinical samples: Systematic review, meta-analysis and meta-regression. *Suicide and Life-Threatening Behavior*, 44(3), 273–303.

Treasure, J., & Alexander, J. (2013). *Anorexia nervosa: A recovery guide for sufferers, families and friends.* New York, NY: Routledge.

Treasure, J., & Nazar, B. P. (2016). Interventions for the carers of patients with eating disorders. *Current Psychiatry Reports*, 18(2), 15–21.

Treasure, J., Smith, G., & Crane, A. (2007). *Skills based learning for caring for a loved one with an eating disorder: The new Maudsley Method.* New York, NY: Routledge.

Vagi, K. J., Olsen, E. O. M., Basile, K. C., & Vivolo-Kantor, A. M. (2015). Teen dating violence (physical and sexual) among US high school students: Findings from the 2013 National Youth Risk Behavior Survey. *JAMA Pediatrics*, 169(5), 474–482.

van Furth, E. F., van Strien, D. C., Martina, L. M., van Son, M. J., Hendrickx, J. J., & van Engeland, H. (1996). Expressed emotion and the prediction of outcome in adolescent eating disorders. *International Journal of Eating Disorders*, 20(1), 19–31.

Wade, T. D., & Tiggemann, M. (2013). The role of perfectionism in body dissatisfaction. *Journal of Eating Disorders*, 1(2), 1–6.

Walsh, B. T., Agras, W. S., Devlin, M. J., Fairburn, C. G., Wilson, G. T., Kahn, C., & Chally, M. K. (2000) Fluoxetine for bulimia nervosa following poor response to psychotherapy. *American Journal of Psychiatry*, 157(8), 1332–1334.

Westmoreland, P., Krantz, M. J., & Mehler, P. S. (2016). Medical complications of anorexia nervosa and bulimia. *The American Journal of Medicine*, 129(1), 30–37.

Whitney, J., Murray, J., Todd, G., Whitaker, W., & Treasure, J. (2005). Experience of caring for someone with anorexia nervosa: Qualitative study. *The British Journal of Psychiatry*, 187, 444–449.

Wilks, C. R., Valenstein-Mah, H., Tran, H., King, A. M. M., Lungu, A., & Linehan, M. M. (2016). Dialectical behavior therapy skills for families of individuals with behavioral disorders: Initial feasibility and outcomes. *Cognitive and Behavioral Practice*, 24(3), 288–295.

Wise, R. A. (2004). Dopamine, learning and motivation. *Nature Reviews Neuroscience*, 5(6), 483–494.

Wong, S. P. Y., & Chang, J. C. (2016). Altered eating behaviors in female victims of intimate partner violence. *Journal of Interpersonal Violence*, 31(20), 3490–3505.

6 Emma

The Secret Eater

Emma sat comfortably on the living-room couch, sinking into their end-of-the-day cushions that so often wooed her into a relaxed state. The familiar sounds of her mother busying herself in their post-dinner kitchen were comforting. "Bang-clash-squeak" – the pans clattered as dishes were put away and the dishwasher was unloaded. "Maybe a Netflix movie tonight? No – it was Mom's favorite sitcom night. No problem," thought Emma. "Netflix, maybe, Friday night." She was content. She drifted into a haze of sleepiness while she waited for her family to join her in the living room for a night of TV. Content to be home and comfortable, Emma relaxed after another harrowing school day.

Earlier that afternoon, Emma, age 16, had ridden the school bus home. She hated the bus. Kids grabbed seats, were loud, and acted way too pushy. Emma texted her Mom at lunchtime hoping she would pick her up from school after work. She had anticipated how awful she would feel on the bus. She always did. It was so much easier to just get a ride home. She got teased sometimes. Larger-sized, because of her genetic heritage, Emma was well aware of size prejudice and the sadistic entertainment size-bullying provided some students. At school, within earshot of teachers, people were more careful about what they said. Zero tolerance for bullying was frequently announced at her school. However, the bus was another matter. No aides were around. The bus driver was trying hard to stay focused on safely transporting his cargo. It was a free-for-all when it came to teasing. Bullying went unseen. Or if it was seen, nothing was done. Emma hated running the bus gauntlet every day.

Long accustomed to body teasing, Emma mostly didn't react when two particularly cruel boys on her bus said things like, "How is Miss Ugliness today?" Emma usually pretended she didn't hear. She hoped her embarrassment wouldn't give itself away in the heat rising to her cheeks. The boys laughed at their own jokes, looking for support from other students who might be laughing with them. Other boys usually laughed. Sometimes they stopped when they saw how Emma didn't say anything. They seemed embarrassed for her. Emma didn't know which was worse – pity or humiliation. Even though she didn't respond on the outside, she reacted on the inside. She was always hurt and sad and felt like crawling under the seat. She thought to herself, "When those ridiculously evil kids teased me, everyone looked. Horrifying.

Totally horrifying." When Emma was teased she felt on display – on stage for everyone to see how awful and disgusting she was. If her self-confidence had been stronger, maybe she wouldn't have internalized the hateful indictments.

Emma didn't need the teasing boys on the bus to tell her about weight stigma, or its negative effects. Like most teens, she was well acquainted with weight bias. It came from peers, educators, and her family. A large longitudinal study known as Project EAT (Eisenberg, Neumark-Sztainer, Haines, & Wall, 2006) followed over 2,000 youth through different phases of adolescence. Both boys and girls who were teased about weight earlier in their adolescence were more prone to negative body image, lower self-esteem, and depressive symptoms 5 years later. More recent research has shown overweight children are more prone to depression and body dissatisfaction (Goldschmidt, Wall, Loth, & Neumark-Sztainer, 2015) and unhealthy weight-control behaviors (Madowitz, Knatz, Maginot, Crow, & Boutelle, 2012; Loth, Wall, Larson, & Neumark-Sztainer, 2015). In keeping with this, Emma was embarrassed by her own body. It took up too much space and was clearly unattractive to her peers. Emma's self-loathing was intense, because she longed for acceptance, but instead, experienced rejection.

Being self-consciousness about body appearance is part of the struggle of middle and high school puberty and post-puberty years. However, Emma's level of depression and self-loathing went well beyond anything usual for her self-conscious peer group. Emma wanted to hide herself from the world. She often believed all eyes were on her no matter where she was – except maybe at home. She experienced a notable level of paranoia about being judged for her body size and appearance when she walked down the hallway at school. Riding the bus was excruciating. Except for a few friends she liked seeing every day, her first choice would be to not attend school. Getting out the door in the morning was a chore no one in Emma's house looked forward to. Emma labored with which outfit to wear. She spent as long as possible in the bathroom she shared with Josh, her older brother, so that she could check and re-check herself in the mirror. The dread of school hung over Emma like a dark cloud that never quite gave way to rain and was mostly foreboding, for her and her whole family. They all knew she hated school, but they didn't know she hated her body as much as she did.

Eating in the cafeteria was an especially difficult part of her school day, because, like the bus, it was a free-for-all marked by social chaos. She was anxious about eating in front of others. Also, forbidden "unhealthy" foods were available at school. She sometimes picked a large cookie and milk for lunch rather than the usual cafeteria fare of a salad, pizza bagel, and milk. Cooked on the school premises, these chocolate chip cookies were warm and beyond excellent to Emma. "My mother would NOT approve," she thought. This was followed by another thought, "What did she know about what was eaten at school lunch? … Not much." That was fine with Emma. That is, until she developed a link between eating and guilt.

Emma still loved her cookies at school, but as she became increasingly self-conscious about her larger-sized frame, she began to project onto others her own self-consciousness. If someone saw her eat one of those big school cookies, she was sure they were thinking, "No wonder she's so fat – look at her eat that cookie!" Emma imagined every girl in the cafeteria wondering, "Why is she eating that cookie at her size?" She would rather hide. It was just too uncomfortable to keep eating what she liked in the school cafeteria. On the other hand, Emma had a few friends who were important to her. Friends she ate lunch with every day. Catching up with them was something she looked forward to. Even though the thought had occurred to her to eat alone elsewhere, she didn't want to. Nevertheless, her suspiciousness about what others thought when she ate in front of them grew.

Emma struck a compromise with herself. She would differentiate between public eating and private eating. Public eating would be for those around her. It was socially acceptable, "normal eating." Normal eating included not eating large cookies for lunch. Since many girls in her grade were already skimping on lunches and had their own issues with eating and weight, Emma ate a salad with her friends, or skipped food altogether. Those lunches were not only acceptable, but made it look like she was on a diet, something to be admired. Her friend Brianna noticed the lunch-time change: "Hey Emma – Dude, where's your cookie? That is some good food!" Emma responded with, "Yeah – it has too many calories!" No one in her friend group said anything about Emma's larger-than-average size. It was just understood that weight loss down to at least an average size was desirable, even if it wasn't media-ideal thin.

To put the near-impossible media-ideal thinness into perspective, the average American fashion model weighs 23% less than the average American woman (The Body Project, n.d.). Very few could aspire to those proportions, even the best high school dieters, without developing anorexia nervosa. Emma ate "the rest" of her "not normal" lunch alone in the school library, a much less public place than the cafeteria. Away from evaluating eyes, she guiltily consumed her favorite cafeteria foods.

Emma was subjected to weight bias not only by peers, but also by her parents. Emma's father James was also larger-sized and declared obese by his family doctor. He chronically dieted and struggled with his own self-body-hatred. Although he took medication for high blood pressure, he didn't suffer from the other health-related consequences commonly associated with obesity – problems like diabetes, high total cholesterol, or coronary heart disease. He counted himself lucky and wanted to stave off further problems forecasted by everything he observed or heard in the media. "The costs of obesity rise!" "Obesity causes early death!" The word *obese* is so negative. The headlines were ubiquitous.

One night at dinner, Emma's father declared, "We need lower salt in everything. I'm going to get sick if we don't." And so, depending on what diet he was on, James required various special food restrictions. At one point the whole family was subjected to whole-grain everything – brown rice, nothing but whole-wheat bread, pasta that was brown in color before being boiled. At another point, the supply of any carbohydrates was at an all-time low in Emma's house. During that diet era, very little bread was allowed. A typical dinner included lots of salad with nuts and bad-tasting low fat cheese chunks drowned in lemon juice and olive oil. Food changed like the seasons at Emma's house. Sometimes "white" foods were forbidden, like white-flour pastries. Sometimes there was plenty of low-fat food, or gluten-free food. Always, regardless of the season, there was one goal – lose weight.

It wasn't long before Emma realized that her mother, Carolyn, and father hoped to spare her her father's weight-related, self-loathing. In the guise of everyone getting on board with father's "healthy" diets, they indirectly put her on one form or another of a restrictive diet. Dieting at home was a way of life. The result was that Emma was increasingly vulnerable to secretly eating "unacceptable foods" away from the judgmental eyes of her family.

Unlike her older brother, Emma found herself fielding questions from her mother like, "Are you sure you need that?" or "Just take a few potatoes – you want to be beautiful, right?" Josh was born with his mother's body-type – averaged-sized with broadening shoulders – and these developed as he sailed into his late teens. He didn't get the are-you-sure-you-need-that question. Emma sometimes surreptitiously made herself a cheese sandwich with some of the "normal" cheese and bread in the house. Her mother, with her full-surveillance radar, noticed Emma's eating. Emma felt it coming. "Why don't you try an apple instead?" When Emma heard her mother's question, mid-bite and sandwich in hand, what Emma heard in her head was, "You shouldn't be eating that because you're fat like your father and that is absolutely bad." Little did Emma's parents know, but the seeds of secret overeating followed by restricting intake were being sown. Emma was starting to want to eat when she wasn't hungry. Food became a secret comfort – a way to soothe herself in private. As with Emma, Balantekin, Birch, and Savage (2017) found that eating in the absence of hunger often predicted binge-eating disorder in adolescents.

Recent research revealed that repeated dietary restraint and its resulting weight cycling were prevalent not just among those who were overweight. Women, men, children, teenagers, older and younger adults, certain athletes and performers, and people in all weight categories (overweight, normal weight, and underweight) were commonly concerned with appearance and image and, as a result, prone to dieting and weight cycling (Gillen, Markey, & Markey, 2012; Montani, Schutz, & Dulloo, 2015). It seems that everybody worries that they weigh too much in a culture that ideals the thin image – a value that is communicated and promoted by media, schools, coaches, society at large, and often, unwittingly, parents.

A pattern of dietary restraint has, in turn, been linked to the development of all types of eating disorders (Fairburn, Cooper, Doll, & Davies, 2005; Patton, Selzer, Coffey, Carlin, & Wolfe, 1999; Stice, Davis, Miller, & Marti, 2008). Growing evidence links chronic levels of dieting behavior, in particular, to the development of disordered eating (Patton, Johnson-Sabine, Wood, Mann, & Wakeling, 1990; Polivy & Herman, 2002; Shisslak, Crago, & Estes, 1995;

Stice & Burger, 2015), especially in adolescents (Loth, MacLehose, Bucchianeri, Crow, & Neumark-Sztainer, 2014). As in Emma's family, concern with weight and self-consciousness about body size and shape can lead to frequent weight-control behaviors that can turn into disordered eating. When this occurs, a well-meaning pursuit of wellness becomes a pathological relationship with food. This dangerous road is all the more likely in a culture that accepts weight obsession and chronic dieting as a way of life.

Bish et al. (2005) found that 46% of American women and 33% of American men were trying to lose weight, despite readily available information about the risks of frequent dieting. As people gain more years of education, they are more, not less, likely to try to lose weight (Bish et al., 2005). Slof-Op 't Landt et al. (2017) more recently found increased dieting was associated with being female, having a higher body mass index (BMI), and having a fear of weight gain – all traits of Emma's. Further, past research found that 35–60% of women were chronic dieters (Polivy & Herman, 2007). These findings might suggest teen weight-management behaviors are chronic and common, because body dissatisfaction runs high among adolescents. However, in another sample, Slof-Op 't Landt et al. (2017) found only 2.8% of females in the 13 to 16 age range were *often* or *always* on a diet. According to this data, there was a trend for chronic dieting to be less prevalent in young teens compared to post-adolescent women. This finding suggests Emma's drift into chronic dietary restraint was extreme and unusual for her age range. Emma's mother may have unwittingly played a role in this.

Carolyn was frequently anxious about larger-sized bodies in her family. Her fears were well founded. She had married a larger-sized man and wished he could lose weight. She endured the humiliation of people sometimes staring at his girth. She felt the emotional pain of his body not fitting into airplane seats. She worried about his health. She half expected him to have a heart attack in his sleep, although she would never verbalize such thoughts. When she married him, Carolyn never thought that she would pass on his family genes for larger-sized bodies to her children.

When Emma was born, she was a normal, healthy weight. It was only when she failed to lose her baby-fat as she headed into middle school that Carolyn realized Emma might suffer the way her husband did. Plus, she was a girl. "How would she attract friends and eventually a mate if she were considered fat? … Girls are so mean about weight," she worried. Yet the thought of talking to Emma directly about her size was almost impossible. Weight was a touchy subject with her. Carolyn didn't want to appear critical or judgmental about Emma's size, yet she silently was.

Research, old and new, has shown that girls and women are at a greater risk than men for body dissatisfaction related to the desire to be thinner (Cho & Lee, 2013; Furman, Badmin, & Sneade, 2002). Men, while also prone to body dissatisfaction, may be just as likely to want to increase their size related to muscularity as they are to losing weight. Both men and women are influenced by current cultural ideals about what constitutes an attractive body shape and size. For women, thin and lean is desired, and for men, lean but muscular is desired.

Emma's mother correctly tapped into Emma's risk to suffer from low body esteem and related weight teasing because of her gender. What Carolyn didn't realize was that what is known as *adiposity*, or degree of body fat, is not necessarily a predictor of low body esteem. While high BMI has been shown to be a risk factor for body dissatisfaction and eating disorders in the past (Fan et al., 2010), recent research suggests that it may not be increased body size that puts teen girls at risk for eating disorders. Rather, it is the degree of body dissatisfaction at any size that is the biggest risk factor for later eating pathology (Rohde, Stice, & Marti, 2015). Carolyn's best effort at prevention was misplaced. The focus on changing Emma's body size might be better directed toward body satisfaction, regardless of her size.

Emma cringed when her mother tried to limit her food or question her about it. Even though Emma rarely objected out loud, she clearly flared with defensiveness at any mention of her eating. Emma's facial expression and body language were, without a doubt, saying, "Back off. Leave me alone." The topic of weight was so prickly and sensitive with Emma, it was out of the question to speak to her about it directly. Carolyn hoped Emma's family doctor would say something. Or maybe the school nurse. Yet, when Carolyn took Emma for her physical each year in elementary school, the doctor said nothing except that Emma was on track with her developmental growth history. Carolyn was disappointed by this seeming omission of the obvious, but accepted that Emma might be oddly normal from a medical perspective. Nonetheless, Carolyn and James were so fearful about Emma's future, they both took on the responsibility of preventing any chance of her becoming obese.

Emma's parents, along with so many others in her environment, were guilty of weight bias. Weight bias is "the inclination to form unreasonable judgments based on a person's weight" (Washington, 2011, Weight Bias section, para. 1). These judgments are founded on the mistaken belief that people need to lose weight if they do not meet society's thin standard. Furthermore, weight bias rests on the assumption that if weight is not lost, there has been a failure of willpower and self-discipline. Emma's pediatrician, Dr. Chen, observed Emma's weight and growth history over time and determined that she was in a higher-than-average weight percentile combined with an average height. She was consistently in the same height and weight percentiles throughout her childhood and teen years. Combined with other health data, he determined Emma was in a healthy weight range given her growth history. However, because our culture values thinness, and because our culture supports, or at least overlooks weight bias, Emma's parents were unsatisfied with his failure to suggest Emma lose weight. They wanted Dr. Chen to support their fears for their daughter's future by supporting weight bias.

Neumark-Sztainer (2005) in her classic book for parents, *"I'm, Like, SO Fat": Helping Your Teen Make Healthy Choices about Eating and Exercise in a Weight-Obsessed World*, says:

> parents often encourage their children to diet because of genuine concern for their children. They want their kids to avoid all the physical and psychosocial complications of being obese in our society. The problem is this just doesn't work. Encouraging your children to diet is likely to lead to the use of unhealthy weight control behaviors. Ironically these behaviors can lead to binge eating, which can actually lead to weight gain.
>
> (p. 49)

Emma's parents had every intention of doing what was best for their daughter. But they, like so many advocates for public health, were caught in the blind spot of public efforts to prevent childhood obesity (Austin, 2011). The message of the anti-obesity campaign has long been weight management and related healthy eating for better health. The blind spot is that well-intended, weight-management behaviors, like dieting and restricting food intake, can result in eating disorders. In an effort to prevent Emma from being obese, Emma's parents unwittingly gave her messages that she needed to lose weight to be healthy and, as an added incentive, successful. What they didn't know was that Emma was on her way to a binge-eating disorder (Decaluwé & Braet, 2003).

Emma was already primed to hide eating she thought her parents would disapprove of. Her distress led her to learn the tricks of food stealth, such as getting to the kitchen when her parents were busy in order to hide food. Emma was hungry when she got home from school. She loved to eat. She found that an empty house after school (except for Josh – with ear-buds) was often a perfect time to engage in stealth. Carolyn worked part-time, but was home after school. When Carolyn gave Emma a ride home, she would usually drop her off before running errands. Alternatively, when Emma arrived home post-bus, her mother was usually gone, once again running errands before getting home. Emma generally declined invitations to join her mother on errands, claiming she had homework to do.

Two or three times a week, Emma would hit the kitchen like a concentrated storm. Careful not to empty any containers lest they (and she) be noticed in the aftermath, she would scoop up the cereal, sandwiches, and snack materials needed to provide a hidden stash in her room. Later, after raiding her stash and consuming it all, she hid telltale food wrappers between the mattress and box springs of her bed. If her mother noticed food disappearing, there were plenty of other eaters in the house to account for it. Josh had a voracious appetite and provided an especially good cover.

Emma learned early, through her own love of food, that it could soothe her worst moods. There was something about the yummy taste, even if for only a few seconds, that allowed her to disconnect from her worst feelings, even her guilt about eating. Pearson, Combs, Zapolski, and Smith (2012) examined a large group of 5th-grade children and discovered that the youngsters like Emma, who had a tendency to act impulsively when distressed, were at greater risk for expecting food to reduce their distress, and, therefore, they were more inclined to binge eat. For Emma, the seeds of using food to quell unhappiness and upset or boredom were sown early. Once this practice is started, there is ample evidence that young people, like Emma, who use out-of-control binge eating to regulate their moods, maintain their binge-eating problems vis-à-vis the temporary relief they experience from binge eating (Czaja, Rief, & Hilbert, 2009).

Prone to something called *negative urgency* (Cyders & Smith, 2008), Emma tended to act rashly when she was experiencing negative emotions. For example, on more than one occasion when she had a bad day on the bus, Josh was the object of her displaced wrath. Irritable, she would call him names. "You suck!" she would yell at him if he dared step one foot into her room. Or if her parents commented on her eating, rather than bark at her mother, she would tell Josh, "You have no friends because you're such a dork!" Projection of her own low self-esteem onto Josh was both mean and commonplace for Emma. He was just a teenager so he made a good target.

Especially with the onset of puberty, Emma's negative moods seemed to barrel out of control. Her experience was consistent with neurological evidence that puberty onset is associated with accelerated neuronal growth in the limbic system, the emotional brain center. This occurs without equal levels of increased growth in executive functioning (the frontal cortex area of the brain). Teens are noted for their exaggerated and unwieldy emotional outbursts. Without parallel growth of the frontal-brain regions that are needed to reign in and filter the powerful, intense feelings associated with puberty onset, the adolescent years can feel like a time of decreased emotional control. Emma was at a loss for how to subdue her upsets and resolve her negative moods. She easily turned to the relative pleasure of eating to help her along.

Those with vulnerabilities to dysregulated behavior, poor appetite control, and poor cognitive controls (an impaired executive function) like Emma, seem to be more prone to binge-eating disorder, independent of overweight or obesity (Manasse et al., 2015). Regardless of pre-existing body size, binge-eating issues in youth can put people at greater risk for later increased weight, morbid obesity, and associated health risks (Sonneville et al., 2013; Tanofsky-Kraff et al., 2009). Hopefully, Emma and her family's eventual decision to get professional help for Emma for binge-eating disorder protected her from these untoward health consequences 5 to 10 years into the future.

Meanwhile, Emma was exposed to a number of environmental risk factors, which made her vulnerable to eating-disorder onset. For example, the kind of bullying Emma received on the school bus as a result of weight-related prejudice contributed to Emma's body dissatisfaction. That, in turn, contributed to her frequent attempts to restrict food intake to lose weight. Unfortunately, periods of restriction can easily be followed by uncontrolled eating (Libbey, Story, Neumark-Sztainer, & Boutelle, 2008). As many people who have tried restricting food intake have found, Emma discovered temporary self-starvation led to a stronger craving for foods she loved. Once the cravings were indulged, Emma, like many with body dissatisfaction, experienced guilt and self-loathing. The upshot was a vicious cycle of restricting, binge eating, and guilt, followed by more attempts to restrict. This was the direction in which Emma was moving.

Unfortunately, the teasing Emma experienced at school is common for overweight children (Madowitz et al., 2012). Sometime after the worst of Emma's bus experiences, Emma's teacher paired her with a boy named Max in science lab. She heard Max say to his friend – loud enough for Emma to hear – "I don't want to be with the pig face." On the inside, Emma was embarrassed and angry. No doubt this verbal abuse exacerbated her over-concern with appearance and weight. However, in this instance Emma's embarrassed feelings on the inside did not manifest on the outside. After the bus trouble, Emma had learned to retort. She sternly said to Max, "Stop it! That's not funny!" The more sources of teasing and the more distressed children are as a result of weight teasing, the more they become depressed and engage in unhealthy weight-control behaviors, such as attempting to restrict after guilty eating. Surprisingly, the Madowitz study showed peer teasing, like when Max teased Emma, was particularly damaging, because peer teasing was more likely than familial teasing to result in depression and unhealthy weight-control behaviors in overweight youth.

As if teasing about weight weren't enough of an environmental risk, as well as a maintaining factor for eating disorders, the media gives the distinct impression that weight can be changed via alterations to either diet or exercise, or a combination of both, no matter what the individual circumstances. In truth, weight is under physiological control to the extent that it is determined by medical conditions, a complex set of environmental factors, and complex genetics (e.g., genetic variations in the leptin gene, which helps to register appetite; Erez et al., 2011). Current evidence indicates genetics make complicated contributions to cognitive control, appetite mechanisms, and emotions. Yet the diet industry has long been promising weight-loss results to people by seducing them to engage in one program or another, regardless of their individual biological, psychological, or environmental circumstances.

Weight bias favoring thinness provides fertile marketing ground for selling weight-loss products (e.g., money-back guarantees at fitness centers if weight isn't lost), weight-loss books, and many famous and not-so-famous weight-loss programs. The truth, as reflected in the science of weight control, is that short-term weight loss is often possible – just enough to reward honest efforts. But long-term maintenance of weight loss is more elusive. For example, Curioni and Lourenco (2005) completed a systematic review of long-term weight loss in adults following exercise or dietary-restraint interventions, or a combination of both methods together, and found that almost half of the initial weight lost was regained after one year. Many famous weight-loss programs ignore strong evidence of weight gain after program participation.

Emma had weight-loss programs peddled to her through media advertising like every other teen. "Just eat enough fat-free yogurt and that bathing suit will look great!" "You, too, could control your weight if you just tried hard enough." Her father was a poster child for weight-loss programs. He believed more than any religious follower that weight loss was possible and likely if he just applied his will power to the right places. A failed diet to him was a personal failure. Likewise, through her father's example and repeated media exposure, Emma was indoctrinated into the world of weight loss. In this world, personal success was measured in pounds, or sizes lost.

As might be expected given her exposure to environmental, biological, and individual risk factors, Emma was eventually diagnosed with Binge-Eating Disorder (BED; *Diagnostic and Statistical Manual of Mental Disorders*, *DSM*-5; American Psychiatric Association, 2013) by Dr. Chen. In a review of prospective studies that examined predictive factors for eating disorders, Stice (2016) found that adolescents like Emma who demonstrated the "triple confluence" (p. 367) of being somewhat overweight, overvaluing appearance, and dieting were more likely to develop binge-eating disorder. Further, He, Cai, and Fan (2016) found, in a meta-analytic overview of 36 studies with a cumulative sample size of 9,818 children between the ages of 5 and 21, binge- or loss-of-control eating was a problem for more than one quarter of children like Emma with overweight or obesity. That was regardless of characteristics such as race, gender, or age.

Dr. Chen was familiar with eating disorders. When Emma came in, as she had for years with her parents for her annual physical in the spring of her tenth-grade year, she had already been secretly cycling between restricting and binge eating for over a year. Dr. Chen was acutely aware that Emma's parents were anxious about her larger-sized body. He had tried to reassure them in the past. Having acquired some specialty training in eating disorders, he could see the impact on Emma of her parents' worry about her weight. Steeped in a negative cultural environment that valued thinness, and a home environment that supported the view that Emma overate, or ate the wrong foods, Emma was at risk for damaging body dissatisfaction.

That year, Dr. Chen brought out Emma's pediatric growth charts and showed Carolyn and James how Emma consistently tracked at a higher weight and BMI percentile. The charts indicated Emma continued to grow and gain weight in a manner that was healthy and natural for her genetic body type. Dr. Chen encouraged James and Carolyn to adopt an attitude of body acceptance towards Emma. Speaking about nutrition, Dr. Chen suggested they provide Emma with a wide variety of normally portioned foods spread across three meals a day plus snacks. With regard to dieting, he said, "James and Carolyn, I know you've been worried about Emma's weight for a long time. As I've said in the past, considering Emma's growth history, she's well within the limits of normal. Because she's on track, I want to discourage you from imposing any kind of dietary restraint aimed at weight loss on her. I think she's fine if she eats three well-portioned meals a day with 2 or 3 snacks. This keeps Emma's blood sugar and, thus, energy level even through the day and prevents excessive hunger, which can be a biological trigger for binge eating. We want to help Emma feel like she's nurturing herself with food and not depriving herself." Dr. Chen knew that if Emma dieted or skipped meals and deprived herself, she would expose herself to an emotional trigger for binge eating. As we've seen, Emma's mom wasn't satisfied with this reasoning.

Carolyn thought for minute and responded, "Well, James is on a diet. We try to eat healthy. We don't eat fatty foods. We buy mostly low-fat, and we avoid sugary foods. James sometimes switches diets because he has to monitor his weight for high blood pressure. I'm not sure what we should do about Emma, because she eats what we eat." James nodded in agreement, because it sounded to him like Emma should be left alone regarding his diet programs. Dr. Chen responded, "I would like you to normalize Emma's food as much as possible – regular meals that involve reasonable portions of grains and carbohydrates, protein sources, and fruits and vegetables are best. Eliminating whole categories of foods gives a message that some foods are bad and need to be avoided. If you don't feel confident in preparing Emma's meals, I'll give you the name of a nutrition counselor to consult. I would suggest avoiding diet talk and diet foods at meals. These foods might suggest to Emma that there's something wrong with her body and she needs to be dieting."

Dr. Chen then interviewed Emma alone and discovered she was largely restricting her food intake well into the late afternoon in an attempt to lower her weight. She skimped on or skipped breakfast, snacked in the library after a salad lunch at school, ate dinner with her family, and, in an out-of-control fashion, picked her way through snack foods from the late afternoon into the evening. For example, Emma reported to Dr. Chen she often intended to eat only one bowl of cereal for a snack at night after dinner, but ended up eating half a box. Emma told how in the space of a few hours she made several trips to the kitchen, especially after her parents went upstairs to watch TV. No longer hungry as she continued to eat through the evening, it seemed to Dr. Chen that she ate to the point of being too full in order to soothe boredom and numb angst about the homework she hadn't done.

Dr. Chen kept short surveys available to measure the presence of various types of eating disorders (e.g., the SCOFF; J. Morgan, Reid, & Lacey, 2000) and the Binge-Eating Scale (BES; Celio, Wilfley, Crow, Mitchell, & Walsh, 2004; Gormally, Black, Daston, & Rardin, 1982), a 16-item self-report scale administered to adolescents ages 12–17 that measures both cognitive and behavioral aspects of binge eating, such as guilt related to eating, binge episodes during dieting, poor control over urges to eat, difficulty eating in front of others, and difficulty stopping eating even though full). On the BES, Emma scored at the low end of the clinically severe range for binge-eating symptoms using established criteria (Balantekin et al., 2017; Pasold, McCracken, & Ward-Begnoche, 2014). Based on interview and survey results, Dr. Chen diagnosed Emma with BED.

BED is a relatively new diagnosis – the result of revisions to the *DSM* (the *Diagnostic and Statistical Manual of Psychiatric Disorders*). Although not new to health-care providers or researchers, BED has emerged as a category of symptoms with its own environmental and biological underpinnings (Pope et al., 2006). It tends to be more common in women, but unlike anorexia and bulimia, there is less of a gender gap (*DSM*-5). Average age of onset has been thought to be later than anorexia and bulimia, but research suggests symptoms often occur during adolescence (Hudson, Hiripi, Pope, & Kessler, 2007).

BED is characterized by recurrent binge eating and is distinguished from bulimia by a lack of compensatory behaviors, such as self-induced vomiting, that are done in an attempt to prevent weight gain. Estimates of lifetime full-syndrome BED among adolescents in community samples vary from 1.6% (Swanson, Crow, Le Grange, Swendsen, & Merikangas, 2011) to 2.3% among girls (Smink, van Hoeken, Oldehinkel, & Hoek, 2014) and 0.7% for boys (Smink et al., 2014). Criteria include eating an inordinately large amount of food ("larger than what most people would eat in a similar [discrete] period of time under similar circumstances"; *DSM*-5, p. 350) at least once a week over a 3-month period. Such a specific definition of binge eating helps to distinguish "objective" binges from subjective binges, during which a person believes they have eaten an excessive amount of food that is not truly large and only seems so relative to the desired amount of intake. Subjective binge eating may not technically meet criteria for a BED diagnosis, but it usually occurs in the context of dietary restraint and is also worthy of eating-disorder treatment (Fitzsimmons-Craft et al., 2014). In Emma's case, her binge episodes were objectively large (e.g., half a box of cereal in a 2-hour period of time).

A second criterion required for a diagnosis of BED is a sense of uncontrolled eating during a binge episode. As in Emma's case, this is often accompanied by more pervasive issues of dysregulated thoughts, feeling, or behaviors (Kittel, Brayhardt, & Hilbert, 2015). BED also includes demonstrating a majority of the following behaviors: eating rapidly, eating until feeling uncomfortably full, eating in the absence of physical hunger, solo eating due to embarrassment about binge eating, marked distress related to overeating, and self-loathing or guilt after overeating (*DSM*-5).

For youth who present for BED treatment with out-of-control eating, but do not meet full criteria for BED (Goldschmidt et al., 2008), binge-eating behavior can be a stepping-stone to full-syndrome BED (Stice, Marti, & Rohde, 2013; Stice, Marti, Shaw, & Jaconis, 2009). This is what happened to Emma. Historically, through middle school, Emma secretly ate smuggled snacks and only occasionally binge ate. But the summer before her ninth-grade year, binge-eating behavior stepped up to increasing levels of intensity. Typical for teens with BED, that led to anxiety, depressed moods, and increased body dissatisfaction (Hilbert, Hartmann, Czaja, & Schöbi, 2013; Sonneville et al., 2013), which in turn, precipitated a strong determination to restrict and "diet" during the day. In this way, a cycle of binge eating and daytime restricting tipped Emma into full-syndrome BED.

After Dr. Chen had evaluated Emma alone in her office for BED, she shocked Emma by telling her she was going to invite her parents in. She explained to Emma that she needed to tell them about her food restricting and binge-eating issues so that she could refer them to a specialty-trained psychotherapist and dietitian for Emma's treatment. Emma objected at first, "You can't tell them about my eating food in the library, or about all the food I take from the kitchen at home. They'll freak out!" Emma was immediately worried about her parents finding out her vulnerable secrets and, perhaps, being angry with her for keeping them and being deceptive about disappearing food. Dr. Chen reassured her that she was going to set the stage to lift the burden of blame by pointing out that restricting and binge eating were part of an illness, not a choice, and those behaviors were no one's fault – not theirs, not hers. Further, Dr. Chen told Emma it wasn't important to call the illness "binge-eating disorder" at this point, except in medical records. Emma could choose whatever words she wanted to describe her relationship with food. Dr. Chen asked Emma to participate in the discussion with her parents so there could be a collaborative effort about how to move forward with treatment. Reluctantly, Emma agreed, but asked Dr. Chen to do most of the talking. She still felt anxious and embarrassed.

Together Dr. Chen and Emma's family decided to pursue enhanced cognitive behavior therapy (CBT-E; Fairburn, Cooper & Shafram, 2003; Fairburn, 2008) with a specialty-trained psychotherapist and nutrition counselor at a nearby eating-disorders clinic. So far, there are far more research assessments of effective treatments for adolescent anorexia and bulimia than for BED (Vall & Wade, 2015), and there are no well-established outpatient treatments for adolescents with BED (Lock, 2015). The experimental treatments include enhanced cognitive behavior therapy (CBT-E) dialectical behavior therapy (DBT) used in May's treatment (Linehan, 1993), and interpersonal psychotherapy (IPT) used in Claire's treatment (Klerman & Weissman, 1993).

CBT-E was chosen for Emma because it is well suited to outpatient individual psychotherapy; it can be used for adolescents older than 14 to 15 years (Fairburn, 2008); parents play a major role; and it is manualized for empirically supported, standardized use. Fairburn (2008; Fairburn et al., 2003) developed CBT-E as a transdiagnostic treatment for eating disorders (i.e., treatment applied across eating-disorder diagnoses). It is based on the idea that distorted or inaccurate self-appraisals lead to disordered-eating behaviors (e.g., Emma's thought that her body was too large led her to restrict food intake which, in turn, led to out-of-control episodes of overeating). Emma's CBT-E therapist, Dr. Reagan, helped Emma identify her binge triggers (e.g., being alone in the house after school).

Although Dr. Reagan mainly met with Emma alone for psychotherapy sessions, regular meetings over a 20-week period of treatment were scheduled with James and Carolyn so that they could be kept abreast of Emma's treatment goals and progress. They negotiated support for Emma's treatment during these sessions. For example, it was agreed Carolyn would remove the bathroom scale, and Carolyn and James would help Emma eat a balanced daily breakfast. After meeting with the nutrition counselor, Carolyn and James helped Emma prepare a balanced lunch to take to school each day. Emma was on the honor system to completely consume her lunch. Instead of feeling helpless in the face of the eating disorder, James and Carolyn were able to contribute to their daughter's recovery in significant ways. As part of the treatment plan, Dr. Chen continued as a member of the treatment team (mental health, nutrition, and medical professionals) for purposes of medical management.

In CBT-E Emma also had regular homework. She kept a real-time written record ("monitoring record"; Fairburn, 2008) of estimated amounts of all food and drink consumed, including any unplanned eating. Her eating record included time and place of consumption, indication of excessive food consumed, and any thoughts or feelings that might have influenced each eating episode. Each individual session began with an in-session weight check, followed by a careful review of food records, then a review of Emma's personal "formulation" (Fairburn, 2008), a "big picture" diagram with a visual representation of the process and factors maintaining the eating disorder. The formulation could be added to or altered as the eating disorder's destructive processes became more apparent to Emma.

At first Emma was overwhelmed. She said to Dr. Reagan, "Why should I pay this much attention to what I eat by writing all my food down? I'm already obsessed with eating. This will probably make it worse." Dr. Reagan explained, "You're right that paying attention to all you eat and drink will increase your attention to what you consume. Unlike the eating disorder's preoccupation with food, because of fear of weight gain, this preoccupation is constructive. You're about to become more aware of your behavior in a mindful way. You'll come to understand the thoughts, feelings, and body sensations associated with your behaviors, like when you feel depressed and tired after you compare your body to others. Or like when you feel angry and embarrassed after someone verbally abuses you at school, and then you eat out of control when you get home."

At each session, Emma was encouraged to problem solve and develop homework assignments such as a plan to expose herself to previously avoided foods at breakfast. Dr. Reagan set an agenda for each session. It included a chance for Emma to review previously assigned homework and address any new topics or important items of significance. With time, Emma's adherence to doing her homework paid off. Her self-awareness increased exponentially with CBT-E. She learned to identify five different binge triggers and to make different, constructive coping choices in response to them. For example, when her mother tried to guide her to "healthy foods" (a binge trigger), Emma became angry and wanted to eat in secret to soothe her anger. As an alternative to clandestine eating, Emma took a deep breath, relaxed herself with some slow, even breathing, and reminded her mother not to judge her food choices. She took increasing responsibility for planning her meals and snacks.

Emma also learned to identify the difference between emotional hunger and physical hunger. When she had an urge to respond to a big emotion with binge eating, she redirected her thinking to alternative coping strategies. For example, one way she coped with negative affects was to write down her feelings on her monitoring record. With the help of her nutrition counselor, Emma eventually was able to eat three meals a day with a few snacks in between. To increase her self-awareness and connection to herself, Emma was also advised by Dr. Reagan to build mindfulness skills and begin taking yoga. Emma followed through and experienced her body in a whole new way. Her body began to feel like an integral whole made up of interdependent parts, rather than a disparate collection of good and bad fragments. She was able to redefine her appraisal of her body weight and shape in a more positive way by re-focusing on body function, rather than on body appearance. CBT-E helped Emma in innumerable ways. When she ended her psychotherapy and nutrition counseling, Emma was binge eating once a month and was increasingly able to inhibit both restricting and binge-eating behavior.

As Emma became more connected with her genuine feelings, as well as her bodily and emotional needs, it sometimes created challenges for her parents. It wasn't all smooth sailing for the family when navigating Emma's recovery. For example, Emma set some limits with Carolyn: "Mom, I know you're trying to help, but what would be best for me is if you wouldn't make judgmental comments about my food choices." This hurt Carolyn's feelings. However, Carolyn was able to connect with other parents in an online eating-disorder support community (e.g., F.E.A.S.T., n.d.), and she found ways to cope with moments like those. Carolyn was tempted to become defensive with Emma more than once, but she learned to check in with online friends first. Rather than get defensive, she would say nothing when she felt the urge to express opinions about Emma's food selections. For Carolyn, the process of retreating to gentle guidance without taking over Emma's recovery was a challenge that was ultimately worth the frustration.

At first Emma's family was a little dumbfounded by Emma's treatment for an eating disorder. They thought she loved to snack and in that way was a pretty normal kid. They didn't know much about binge-eating disorder in contrast to anorexia and bulimia. They learned how serious a disorder it was for Emma and ended up, during the treatment process, understanding and connecting with Emma and with each other in ways they had not previously. Looking back, Emma said, "My parents had no idea I had a secret life with food and I hated my body. I couldn't imagine telling them, but I did and it was okay."

Question

Binge-eating disorder in teens gets less attention than anorexia and bulimia. I know it's more common. Is it as serious?

Answer

Yes! Binge-eating disorder in adolescents is very serious. It has been under-diagnosed and under-treated by health-care professionals. In adults, lifetime prevalence data indicated 2% of males and 3.5% of females met full criteria for BED, compared to 0.5% of males and 1.5% for females with bulimia nervosa and 0.3% of males and 0.9% of females with anorexia nervosa (Hudson et al., 2007). Other adult sample data from the WHO World Mental Health Surveys indicated a lifetime prevalence rate of 1.4% (Kessler et al., 2013). An adolescent sample found a lifetime prevalence rate by age 20 of 3% (Stice et al., 2013). The revised-frequency criteria for binge-eating episodes in the *DSM*-5 from an average of two binge-eating episodes per week to one episode, has likely expanded these numbers (Wilfley, Citrome, & Herman, 2016).

Medical and mental health co-morbidities of BED impair quality of life. BED predicts function-impairing chronic back and neck pain, chronic headaches, and other chronic pain conditions and hypertension (Kessler et al., 2013). Other data indicates higher risk for glucose dysregulation, diabetes, and gastro-intestinal disorders (Mitchell, 2016; Wilfley et al., 2016), and, among children with loss-of-control eating, future metabolic syndrome and weight gain (Tanofsky-Kraff et al., 2009, 2012). Grilo, White, Barnes, and Masheb (2013) found that 37% of individuals with BED had at least one current psychiatric disorder, the most common being anxiety (27%), and a mood disorder (17%). Those with psychiatric co-morbidities showed poorer overall functioning.

As stated earlier, binge-eating disorder appears to begin in childhood or adolescence with a sub-syndromal presentation. Stice et al. (2013) found that among adolescent girls, progression from sub-threshold BED to threshold BED was 28%. Tanofsky-Kraff et al. (2013) reported that BED "typically manifests in adolescence or adulthood. However, retrospective data from adult samples and prospective studies in young children suggest that risk for BED may be present well before the manifestation of the disorder or even symptoms of the disorder" (p. 196).

Evidence of BED among youth is strong. C. Morgan et al. (2002) examined binge eating in 112 overweight 6 to 10 year olds and found that one-third of them experienced loss-of-control eating along with higher weights, while 5.3% met questionnaire criteria for BED along with having higher levels of anxiety, body dissatisfaction, and depression symptoms. Johnson, Rohan, and Kirk (2002) examined 822 adolescents (grades 6 through 12) of different races in the US and found a lower prevalence rate for BED (1% for the full-syndrome), but found 26% of African American boys, 18.3% of white boys, 16.7% of African American girls, and 17.8% of white girls met questionnaire criteria for binge eating (i.e., binge-eating syndrome and episodic overeating). In the past, research suggested onset of BED occurred at a significantly older age than anorexia or bulimia (e.g., 25.4 years in one study [Miller & McManus, 2016] and 15.5 to 27.2 years in another [Kessler et al., 2013]). However, Swanson et al. (2011) examined a large nationally representative sample of adolescents in the US and found median ages of onset for anorexia, bulimia, and binge-eating disorder were 12.3 years, 12.4 years, and 12.6 years, respectively. These numbers being medians indicates BED often started earlier in childhood.

BED also tends to be persistent and chronic in terms of severity and duration. Kessler et al. (2013) reviewed international data from community surveys and found a median duration of BED to be 4.3 years. Yet despite the seriousness and prevalence of BED among youth, treatment for BED may be rare. Of those with BED in Swanson et al.'s (2011) large sample of adolescents, almost 73% had received some kind of treatment for emotional or behavioral problems, but only 11.4% had sought treatment specifically for weight or eating problems. That suggests a significant number of teens who struggle with BED are not receiving much-needed eating-disorder treatment.

Treatment professionals should increase screening for binge-eating disorder even when binge eating is not a presenting complaint. Besides using an assessment survey for BED like Dr. Chen used with Emma, Wilfley et al. (2016) suggest assessing for BED whenever there is obesity, over a 5% weight gain (beyond developmental expectations), a family history of BED, or known psychiatric co-morbidities (e.g., mood disorders).

Question

Do most people with obesity have binge-eating disorder?

Answer

No. The *DSM*-5 distinguishes BED from clinical obesity. Wilfley et al. (2016) overviewed a large number of publications concerning the diagnosis of BED and found it was present in people across a spectrum of BMIs. However, in individuals with obesity, between 36.2% and 42.4% have BED. Wilfley et al. found a number of studies indicating that BED is a genetically determined phenotype that congregates in families, independent of the presence of obesity. Further those authors report, "Obese individuals with BED have poorer psychological functioning (e.g., higher depression, lower self-esteem, and more emotional eating and shape and weight concerns) than obese individuals without BED" (p. 2217). This would indicate that those with obesity without BED are quite distinct from those with BED.

Question

My 14-year-old son overeats when he's stressed. I would like to help him stop his emotional eating. I'm hesitant to say anything because he's sensitive to my judging his eating habits.

Answer

Seeing a child consistently use food to soothe feelings as opposed to using food to fuel the body is cause for concern, but it is important to recognize that everyone eats in response to emotional hunger and not physical hunger sometimes. Eating a yummy dessert for pleasure after finishing a filling dinner is a good example. That aside, too much eating in response to negative or positive emotional states can lead to health problems. More importantly, it is an unsatisfying way to cope with emotions. Once the temporary pleasure of eating has subsided, the feelings return.

Research supports the idea that those with eating disorders, including those with BED, often have emotional-regulation difficulties, alexithymia, or difficulty identifying and expressing emotions (Kittel et al., 2015). Difficulty understanding and coping with emotions makes those with BED vulnerable to using food as a self-harm coping strategy. Kittel et al. (2015) completed a systematic review of research examining cognitive and emotional functioning in those with BED. The brain-imaging studies showed a particular sensitivity to the brain reward (dopamine release) associated with food and food-related stimuli. Along with demonstrated difficulties with delayed gratification and inhibition (Kittel et al., 2015), a high degree of sensitivity to food rewards in those with BED suggests how difficult it is for them to resist the draw of food in order to deal with difficult-to-cope-with emotions.

Your son may be at risk for binge-eating problems, because he uses food to soothe feelings when he's not physically hungry. He may have found powerful solace in eating as a response to difficult emotions. In addressing this with him, it may be tempting to express worry about his weight or size as a feared negative consequence of overeating. It is best not to do this. Here's why. Wansink, Latimer, and Pope (2016) showed that comments about a child's weight can have a lasting negative impact on body satisfaction and lead to unhealthy weight-control behavior and binge eating – just the things you are trying to prevent.

However, parents can safely address healthy eating. Researchers found parents' comments about healthy-eating behaviors (not weight) could be helpful (Berge et al., 2013; Wansink et al., 2016). Berge et al. (2013) concluded that parent conversations with their teens about weight and size put them at high risk for eating disorders, while conversations about healthful eating protected them from eating disorders.

Specifically for girls, Dr. Puhl, deputy director at the Rudd Center for Food Policy and Obesity at the University of Connecticut, stated in a recent *New York Times* article, "Parents who have a child who's identified as having obesity may be worried, but the way those concerns are discussed and communicated can be really damaging" (Rabin, 2016, para. 5), because "girls are exposed to so many messages about thinness and body weight, and oftentimes women's value is closely linked to their appearance. If parents don't challenge those messages, they can be internalized" (para. 7). She goes on to say that when children get the message that there is something wrong with their weight, their worth as a person can be perceived as discounted.

Parents are encouraged to role model and talk about healthful eating behaviors. There is a caveat, though. Neumark-Sztainer (2005) pointed out in her seminal book *I'm, Like, SO Fat*, "it is often best to say less and do more when it comes to conversation about healthy eating." Here are some "do" strategies for parents:

1 Provide healthful family meals. Role model by serving nutritionally healthful portions, variety, and balance. Celebrate the opportunity to share

food combined with social-emotional connection. Keep conversation positive and turn off distracting digital entertainment devices.
2 Select family mealtimes that can be counted on by your child. With busy schedules (e.g., sports practices), teens often get the message that healthful meals are inconsequential and an afterthought. The result is "eating on the run," little meal planning, and snacking instead of eating a meal.
3 Avoid communicating your own self-vigilance about weight, size, or intake of foods, such as fats, carbohydrates, or dessert foods. These foods may be seen as "bad" and encourage your child to restrict them.
4 Keep a ready supply of a variety of nutritious foods around the house. Encourage your child to eat three discrete meals a day, no more than 4 to 5 hours apart. Encourage well-timed snacks in between meals. Letting too much time elapse between meals encourages binge eating as a response to intense hunger.
5 Encourage family physical activity (e.g., take a walk) in order to balance out teens' tendency to settle into sedentary, digital screen time.
6 Steer away from role modeling or using food as a reward or a way to soothe emotions.

Here are some ideas for alternative (to emotional eating) coping strategies:

1 Stop and ask, "Am I physically or emotionally hungry?" Learn to tell the difference.
2 If you are trying to cope with stress or big emotions, call or text a friend instead of eating.
3 Be careful not to use eating to procrastinate (e.g., doing homework).
4 Start a mood-food journal. Learn which feelings trigger emotional eating so that in the future choices other than eating can be made.
5 Avoid comfort eating when coming home at the end of a hard day.
6 When emotional eating is tempting or likely, try to put a little space and time between the urge to eat and the actual eating. Even a few minutes delay will help break eating routines and promote self-reflection.

While the coping strategies enumerated above can be helpful, there is no substitute for a professional evaluation by a specialty-trained (in eating disorders) health-care professional. If your child is exhibiting or experiencing one or more of the following eating patterns, it may be time to seek professional guidance: out-of-control eating, guilt and distress after eating, eating an excessive amount of food in discreet periods of time, engaging in secret eating, eating when not physically hungry, or eating too rapidly.

References

American Psychiatric Association. (2013). *Diagnostic and statistical manual of mental disorders* (5th ed.). Arlington, VA: Author.

Austin, S. B. (2011). The blind spot in the drive for childhood obesity prevention: Bringing eating disorders prevention into focus as a public health priority. *American Journal of Public Health*, 101(6), e1–e4.
Balantekin, K. N., Birch, L. L., & Savage, J. S. (2017). Eating in the absence of hunger during childhood predicts self-reported binge eating in adolescence. *Eating Behaviors*, 24, 7–10.
Berge, J. M., MacLehose, R., Loth, K. A., Eisenberg, M., Bucchianeri, M. M., & Neumark-Sztainer, D. (2013). Parent conversations about healthful eating and weight: Associations with adolescent disordered eating behaviors. *JAMA Pediatrics*, 167(8), 746–753.
Bish, C., Blanck, H., Serdula, M., Marcus, M., Kohl, H., III, & Kahn, L. K. (2005). Diet and physical activity behaviors among Americans trying to lose weight: 2000 Behavioral Risk Factor Surveillance System. *Obesity Research*, 13(3), 596–607.
The Body Project. (n.d.). Facilitator Fact Sheet. Retrieved from www.bodyprojectsupport.org/assets/pdf/materials/facilitator_fact_sheet.pdf
Celio, A. A., Wilfley, D. E., Crow, S. J., Mitchell, J., & Walsh, B. T. (2004). A comparison of the binge eating scale, questionnaire for eating and weight patterns-revised, and eating disorder examination questionnaire with instructions with the eating disorder examination in the assessment of binge eating disorder and its symptoms. *International Journal of Eating Disorders*, 36(4), 434–444.
Cho, A., & Lee, J.-H., (2013). Body dissatisfaction levels and gender differences in attentional biases toward idealized bodies. *Body Image*, 10(1), 95–102.
Curioni, C. C., & Lourenco, P. M. (2005). Long-term weight loss after diet and exercise: A systematic review. *International Journal of Obesity*, 29(10), 1168–1174.
Cyders, M. A., & Smith, G. T. (2008). Emotion-based dispositions to rash action: Positive and negative urgency. *Psychological Bulletin*, 134(6), 807–828.
Czaja, J., Rief, W., & Hilbert, A. (2009). Emotion regulation and binge eating in children. *International Journal of Eating Disorders*, 42(4), 356–362.
Decaluwé, V., & Braet, C. (2003). Prevalence of binge-eating disorder in obese children and adolescents seeking weight-loss treatment. *International Journal of Obesity and Related Metabolic Disorders*, 27(3), 404–409.
Eisenberg, M. T., Neumark-Sztainer, D., Haines, J., & Wall, M. (2006). Weight-teasing and emotional well-being in adolescents: Longitudinal findings from Project EAT. *Journal of Adolescent Health*, 38(6), 675–683.
Erez, G., Tirosh, G. A., Rudich, A., Meiner, V., Schwarzfuchs, D., Sharon, N., … Shai, I. (2011). Phenotypic and genetic variation in leptin as determinants of weight regain. *International Journal of Obesity*, 35(6), 785–792.
Fairburn, C. G. (2008). *Cognitive behavior therapy and eating disorders.* New York, NY: Guilford.
Fairburn, C., Cooper, Z., Doll, H., & Davies, B. (2005). Identifying dieters who will develop an eating disorder: A prospective, population-based study. *American Journal of Psychiatry*, 162(12), 2249–2255.
Fairburn, C. G., Cooper, Z., & Shafran, R. (2003). Cognitive behavior therapy for eating disorders: A "transdiagnostic" theory and treatment. *Behavior Research and Therapy*, 41, 509–528.
Fan, Y., Li, Y., Liu, A., Hu, X., Ma, G., & Xu, G. (2010). Associations between body mass index, weight control concerns and behaviors, and eating disorder symptoms among non-clinical Chinese adolescents. *BMC Public Health*, 10, 314–325.
F.E.A.S.T. (n.d.) Families empowered and supporting treatment of eating disorders. Retrieved from www.feast-ed.org

Fitzsimmons-Craft, E. E., Ciao, A. C., Accurso, E. C., Pisetsky, E. M., Peterson, C. B., Byrne, C. E., … Le Grange, D. (2014). Subjective and objective binge eating in relation to eating disorder symptomatology, depressive symptoms, and self-esteem among treatment-seeking adolescents with bulimia nervosa. *European Eating Disorders Review*, 22(4), 230–236.

Furman, A., Badmin, N., & Sneade, I. (2002). Body image dissatisfaction: Gender differences in eating attitudes, self-esteem, and reasons for exercise. *The Journal of Psychology*, 136(6), 581–596.

Gillen, M., Markey, C., & Markey, P. (2012). An examination of dieting behaviors among adults: Links with depression. *Eating Behaviors*, 13(2), 88–93.

Goldschmidt, A. B., Jones, M., Manwaring, J. L., Luce, K. H., Osborne, M. I., Cunning, D., … Taylor, C. B. (2008). The clinical significance of loss of control over eating in overweight adolescents. *International Journal of Eating Disorders*, 41(2), 153–158.

Goldschmidt, A. B., Wall, M. M., Loth, K. A., & Neumark-Sztainer, D. (2015). Risk factors for disordered eating in overweight adolescents and young adults. *Journal of Pediatric Psychology*, 40(10), 1048–1055.

Gormally, J., Black, S., Daston, S., & Rardin, D. (1982). The assessment of binge eating severity among obese persons. *Addictive Behaviors*, 7(1), 47–55.

Grilo, C. M., White, M. A., Barnes, R. D., & Masheb, R. M. (2013). Psychiatric disorder co-morbidity and correlates in an ethnically diverse sample of obese patients with binge eating disorder in primary care settings. *Comprehensive Psychiatry*, 54, 209–216.

He, J., Cai, Z., & Fan, X. (2016). Prevalence of binge and loss of control eating among children and adolescents with overweight and obesity: An exploratory meta-analysis. *International Journal of Eating Disorders*, 50(2), 91–103.

Hilbert, A., Hartmann, A. S., Czaja, J., & Schöbi, D. (2013). Natural course of pre-adolescent loss of control eating. *Journal Abnormal Psychology*, 122(3), 684–693.

Hudson, J. I., Hiripi, E., Pope, H. G., Jr., & Kessler, R. C. (2007). The prevalence and correlates of eating disorders in the national comorbidity survey replication. *Biological Psychiatry*, 61(3), 348–358.

Johnson, W. G., Rohan, K. J., & Kirk, A. A. (2002). Prevalence and correlates of binge eating in white and African American adolescents. *Eating Behaviors*, 3(2), 179–189.

Kessler, R. C., Berglund, P. A., Chiu, W. T., Deitz, A. C., Hudson, J. I., Shahly, V., … Xavier, M. (2013). The prevalence and correlates of binge eating disorder in the World Health Organization World Mental Health Surveys. *Biological Psychiatry*, 73 (9), 904–914.

Kittel, R., Brauhardt, A., & Hilbert, A. (2015). Cognitive and emotional functioning in binge-eating disorder: A systematic review. *International Journal of Eating Disorders*, 48(6), 535–554.

Klerman, G. L., & Weissman, M. M. (Eds.). (1993). *New applications of interpersonal psychotherapy*. Washington, DC: American Psychiatric Press.

Libbey, H. P., Story, M. T., Neumark-Sztainer, D. R., & Boutelle, K. N. (2008). Teasing, disordered eating behaviors, and psychological morbidities among overweight adolescents. *Obesity*, 16(Suppl. 2), S24–29.

Linehan, M. (1993). *Skills training manual for treating Borderline Personality Disorder*. New York, NY: Guilford.

Lock, J. (2015). An update on evidence-based psychosocial treatments for eating disorders in children and adolescents. *Journal of Clinical Child & Adolescent Psychology*, 44(5), 707–721.

Loth, K. A., MacLehose, R., Bucchianeri, M., Crow, S., & Neumark-Sztainer, D. (2014). Predictors of dieting and disordered eating behaviors from adolescence to young adulthood. *Journal of Adolescent Health*, 55(5), 705–712.

Loth, K., Wall, M., Larson, N., & Neumark-Sztainer, D. (2015). Disordered eating and psychological well-being in overweight and nonoverweight adolescents: Secular trends from 1999 to 2010. *International Journal of Eating Disorders*, 48(3), 323–327.

Madowitz, J., Knatz, S., Maginot, T., Crow, S. J., & Boutelle, K. N. (2012). Teasing, depression and unhealthy weight control behaviour in obese children. *Pediatric Obesity*, 7(6), 446–452.

Manasse, S., Espel, H., Forman, E., Ruocco, A., Juarascio, A., Butryn, M., ... Lowe, M. (2015). The independent and interacting effects of hedonic hunger and executive function on binge eating. *Appetite*, 89(1), 16–21.

Miller, R. M., & McManus, J. D. (2016). Binge-eating disorder: A primer for professional counselors. *Journal of Professional Counseling, Practice, Theory, & Research*, 43(1), 2–16.

Mitchell, J. E. (2016). Medical comorbidity and medical complications associated with binge-eating disorder. *International Journal of Eating Disorders*, 49(3), 319–323.

Montani, J., Schutz, Y., & Dulloo, A. G. (2015). Dieting and weight cycling as risk factors for cardiometabolic diseases: Who is really at risk? *Obesity Reviews*, 16(Suppl. 1), 7–18.

Morgan, C. M., Yanovski, S. Z., Nguyen, T. T., McDuffie, J., Sebring, N. G., Jorge, M. R., ... Yanovski, J. A. (2002). Loss of control over eating, adiposity, and psychopathology in overweight children. *International Journal of Eating Disorders*, 31(4), 430–441.

Morgan, J. F., Reid, F., & Lacey, J. H. (2000). The SCOFF questionnaire: A new screening tool for eating disorders. *Western Journal of Medicine*, 172(3), 164–165.

Neumark-Sztainer, D. (2005). *"I'm, like, SO fat!": Helping your teen make healthy choices about eating and exercise in a weight-obsessed world.* New York, NY: Guilford.

Pasold, T. L., McCracken, A., & Ward-Begnoche, W. L. (2014). Binge eating in obese adolescents: Emotional and behavioral characteristics and impact on health-related quality of life. *Clinical Child Psychology and Psychiatry*, 19(2), 299–312.

Patton, G. C., Johnson-Sabine, E., Wood, K., Mann, A. H., & Wakeling, A. (1990). Abnormal eating attitudes in London schoolgirls: A prospective epidemiological study: Outcome at twelve month follow-up. *Psychological Medicine*, 20(2), 383–394.

Patton, G., Selzer, R., Coffey, C., Carlin, J., & Wolfe, R. (1999). Onset of adolescent eating disorders: Population based cohort study over 3 years. *British Medicine Journal*, 318(7186), 765–778.

Pearson, C. M., Combs, J. L., Zapolski, T. C. B., & Smith, G. T. (2012). A longitudinal transactional risk model for early eating disorder onset. *Journal of Abnormal Psychology*, 121(3), 707–718.

Polivy, J., & Herman, C. P. (2002). Causes of eating disorders. *Annual Review of Psychology*, 53(1), 187–213.

Polivy, J., & Herman, C. P. (2007). Is the body the self? Women and body image. *Collegium Antropologicum*, 31(1), 63–67.

Pope, H. G., Jr., Lalonde, J. K., Pindyck, L. J., Walsh, T., Bulik, C. M., Crow, S. J., ... Hudson, J. I. (2006). Binge eating disorder: A stable syndrome. *American Journal of Psychiatry*, 163(12), 2181–2183.

Rabin, R. C. (2016). Parents should avoid comments on a child's weight. *The New York Times*, June 16. Retrieved from https://well.blogs.nytimes.com/2016/06/16/parents-should-avoid-comments-on-a-childs-weight/?_r=0

Rohde, P., Stice, E., & Marti, C. N. (2015). Development and predictive effects of eating disorder risk factors during adolescence: Implications for prevention efforts. *International Journal of Eating Disorders*, 48(2), 187–198.

Shisslak, C. M., Crago, M., & Estes, L. S. (1995). The spectrum of eating disturbances. *International Journal of Eating Disorders*, 18(3), 209–219.

Slof-Op 't Landt, M. C., van Furth, E. F., van Beijsterveldt, C. E., Bartels, M., Willemsen, G., de Geus, E. J., ... Boomsma, D. I. (2017). Prevalence of dieting and fear of weight gain across ages: A community sample from adolescents to the elderly. *International Journal of Public Health*. Advance online publication. doi:10.1007/s000380017-0948-7

Smink, F. R. E., van Hoeken, D., Oldehinkel, A. J., & Hoek, H. W. (2014). Prevalence and severity of *DSM*-5 eating disorders in a community cohort of adolescents. *International Journal of Eating Disorders*, 47(6), 610–619.

Sonneville, K. R., Horton, N. J., Micali, N., Crosby, R. D., Swanson, S. A., Solmi, F., & Field, A. E. (2013). Longitudinal associations between binge eating and overeating and adverse outcomes among adolescents and young adults: Does loss of control matter? *The Journal of the American Medical Association Pediatrics*, 167, 149–155.

Stice, E. (2016). Interactive and mediational etiologic models of eating disorder onset: Evidence from prospective studies. *Annual Review of Clinical Psychology*, 12, 359–381.

Stice, E., & Burger, K. (2015). Dieting as a risk factor for eating disorders. In L. Smolak & M. P. Levine (Eds.), *The Wiley handbook of eating disorders* (Vol. 1; pp. 312–323). New York, NY: John Wiley.

Stice, E., Davis, K., Miller, N. P., & Marti, C. N. (2008). Fasting increases risk for onset of binge eating and bulimic pathology: A 5-year prospective study. *Journal of Abnormal Psychology*, 117, 941–946.

Stice, E., Marti, C. N., & Rohde, P. (2013). Prevalence, incidence, impairment, and course of the proposed *DSM*-5 eating disorder diagnoses in an 8-year prospective community study of young women. *Journal of Abnormal Psychology*, 122(2), 445–457.

Stice, E., Marti, C. N., Shaw, H., & Jaconis, M. (2009). An 8-year longitudinal study of the natural history of threshold, subthreshold, and partial eating disorders from a community sample of adolescents. *Journal of Abnormal Psychology*, 118(3), 587–597.

Swanson, S. A., Crow, S. J., Le Grange, D., Swendsen, J., & Merikangas, K. R. (2011). Prevalence and correlates of eating disorders in adolescents: Results from the national comorbidity survey replication adolescent supplement. *Archives of General Psychiatry*, 68(7), 714–723.

Tanofsky-Kraff, M., Bulik, C. M., Marcus, M. D., Striegel, R. H., Wilfley, D. E., Wonderlich, S. A., ... Hudson, J. I. (2013). Binge eating disorder: The next generation of research. *International Journal of Eating Disorders*, 46(3), 193–207.

Tanofsky-Kraff, M., Shomaker, L. B., Stern, E. A., Miller, R., Sebring, N., DellaValle, D., ... Yanovski, J. A. (2012). Children's binge eating and development of metabolic syndrome. *International Journal of Obesity*, 36(7), 956–962.

Tanofsky-Kraff, M., Yanovski, S. Z., Schvey, N. A., Olsen, C. H., Gustafson, J., & Yanovski, J. A. (2009). A prospective study of loss of control eating for body weight gain in children at high risk for adult obesity. *International Journal of Eating Disorders*, 42(1), 26–30.

Vall, E., & Wade, T. D. (2015). Predictors of treatment outcome in individuals with eating disorders: A systematic review and meta-analysis. *International Journal of Eating Disorders*, 48(7), 946–971.

Wansink, B., Latimer, L. A., & Pope, L. (2016). "Don't eat so much": How parent comments relate to female weight satisfaction. *Eating and Weight Disorders*. Advance online publication. doi:10.1007/s40519-016-0292-6

Washington, R. (2011). Childhood obesity: Issues of weight bias. *Preventing Chronic Disease*, 8(5), A94.

Wilfley, D. E., Citrome, L., & Herman, B. K. (2016). Characteristics of binge eating disorder in relation to diagnostic criteria. *Neuropsychiatric Disease and Treatment*, 12, 2213–2223.

7 Maeve

Like Mother, Like Daughter

Sadly for Maeve, when she was 5 years old, the summer before she started kindergarten, she and her mother Ellen left California. Her parents had separated. At the time, Maeve had been hoping that it wouldn't happen. She knew something between her parents wasn't right even though they never fought – at least she hadn't ever heard them arguing. But here it was. Her mother and father sat her down and nicely explained how they were going to live in separate places. Maeve was devastated. She later recalled that she cried and exclaimed, "You can't do that to me!" They told her she was too young to understand everything, but they had decided they could no longer be married. They would be happier apart. They had tried to find a way to stay together, but they just couldn't. Not only did they decide to live separately, but Maeve and her mother were also moving to Massachusetts where her mom's parents lived. Maeve would be with her father during summer visits, and he would come to Massachusetts every month to see her. That was the plan.

That was 6 years ago. Maeve remembered that, at the time, she couldn't believe what was happening to her world. Now 11 years old, she had finished fifth grade in a small city outside of Boston, life had moved on, and Maeve's mother had remained single. Maeve's father visited every month, and Maeve loved to see him. They did lots of fun things in Boston, and she went to California for 3 weeks every summer. In lots of ways, Maeve seemed well adjusted. Her parents enrolled her in a private school from the beginning of kindergarten. There she had lots of friends and learned to play the clarinet, perform modern dance, and act in school plays. She was, however, increasingly anxious about her appearance in ways that troubled Ellen.

Maeve, like most fifth graders, was hyper-aware of the size of her stomach. She heard other girls complain about being "fat," and she was clear that she didn't want that, whatever it meant. To her, it meant that her stomach stuck out past her hipbones. Staring at herself in the full-length mirror in her room, Maeve was vigilant about whether or not her hipbones were more prominent as she scanned the front of her body. Maeve was, of course, very careful about what she wore, but the state of her stomach could not be hidden. The reigning fashion required short shirts (crop tops) that just met the top of the waistband of low-riding pants. Any movement allowed anyone who cared to look to see one's stomach.

On a typical morning before school, Maeve's mom could be heard saying, usually in exasperation, "Hurry up! You're going to be late!" Maeve would be stuck in front of her mirror, body checking and surveying her clothes: Turn to the side. Suck in the stomach. Hip bones out. Turn to the back – squeeze in the buttocks. Make sure the pants were holding the thighs in. Maeve had already weighed herself – after peeing, of course – to make sure she was at her least noxious weight. Her morning routine of checking and re-checking took half an hour and seemed to be increasing in its complexity.

More importantly, Maeve's daily agenda was all about the relative projection of her stomach to her hipbones. As long as the hipbones won out, she was happy at the end of the day. It was a precarious problem to keep the size of her belly under control and no surprise that this was how Maeve's eating disorder started. At 11 years old, Maeve was already limiting her food intake to manage the size of her stomach. She wanted to skimp on breakfast and ate small lunches at school. Research has shown that children at Maeve's age begin to develop eating habits that can trend into a disordered relationship with food and their own body that lasts for years (Combs, Pearson, Zapolski, & Smith, 2013; Kotler, Cohen, Davies, Pine, & Walsh, 2001). Maeve was moving in that direction.

Unbeknownst to Maeve, Ellen had developed an eating disorder when she was an older teenager. Ellen struggled with anorexia for the first 2 years of college and, on her own, recovered enough weight to fly below the radar for being recognized as having a serious illness. Barely. Her college friends noticed that she ran too much around campus, and, at one point, grew so painfully thin that they began to comment. Usually it was with a jealous, "How did you lose all that weight?" Later, it was with an, "I'm concerned. You're kinda thin." That was caution enough for Ellen to watch her food intake even more carefully so she could be thin in order to be attractive, but not so thin that her dieting efforts were noticed. She didn't want to be discovered under-eating. It was okay to be thin, but not okay to have an illness to get there.

Ellen always controlled her food intake. Persistently. Rigidly. She never got over that. Later in life when she became a mother, she continued to eat less than 1000 kcal a day. She had long ago eliminated red meat and mayonnaise-based salad dressings from her palate. She avoided dessert food (unless to do so would offend the host of a party). Virtually all her behaviors around food were easy enough to pass off as socially acceptable in a society that positively sanctioned exactly those behaviors in the name of good health. Obesity avoidance and illness prevention dictated the advantages of Ellen's food choices. It was commonly accepted that regular mayonnaise had too much fat, and dessert foods were not only unnecessary, but also full of "toxic sugar." Dessert foods were not only considered junk food by Ellen, but also empty or wasted calories.

Ellen's long-time friend Laurie had learned over the years to tolerate Ellen's peculiar habits around food. Ellen was not obviously ill, so Laurie thought she was okay – just a little too thin, too fussy about food, and very sensitive about her body size. However, Laurie was concerned enough about the impact of

Ellen's restrictive eating habits on her daughter that she had once tried to say something. "Ellen – I don't mean to overstep my bounds, and it's hard for me to bring this up, but I worry that your careful approach to food might make Maeve a little nervous about following your eating guidelines. I know you're an expert on this, but I am worried." Ellen's response was, "I know you mean well, but I know how to feed my daughter. We eat healthy, and we are healthy. I hope you can get over your worries." That was the last time Laurie raised the issue.

Maeve, meanwhile, seemed to have inherited some of her mother's desire to have the perfect body. It is likely some of her shared concern about weight, shape, and dietary restraint was due to inherited characteristics. There is a large body of scientific evidence showing that eating disorders run in families. That is, there is a genetic vulnerability for developing an eating disorder that is passed from generation to generation (Bulik, 2004, 2005; Klump, Kaye, & Strober, 2001; Pinheiro, Root, & Bulik, 2009). First-degree relatives of people who have had an eating disorder (like Maeve is to her mom) are 10 times more likely to have an eating disorder themselves than those without relatives with an eating disorder (Bulik, Reba, Siega-Riz, & Reichborn-Kjennerud, 2005; Bulik et al., 2006; Lilenfeld et al., 1998; Strober, Freeman, Lampert, Diamond, & Kaye, 2000; Strober, Freeman, Lampert, Diamond, & Kaye, 2001).

Research bears out that anorexia nervosa, a disorder characterized by a fear of becoming bigger, more weighty, fat, or more curvy, aggregates in families "largely due to the effect of genes" (Pinheiro et al., 2009, "Future Directions," para. 3). Additive genetic factors probably contribute to familial aggregation of eating disorders. The results of twin studies that compared eating disorders in identical versus fraternal twins showed identical twins (fundamentally genetically identical) were more likely than fraternal twins (who share only 50% of their genomes) to suffer similar eating-disorder illnesses. Yet there is no one gene or gene variant that directly predicts anorexia or other types of eating disorders.

It is believed that several genes, perhaps hundreds, may be driving some of the behaviors responsible for the development of an eating disorder (Pinheiro et al., 2009).

For example, heritable characteristics that are associated with disordered eating are: obsessionality, earlier age at menarche, anxiety, body-mass obsession, concern over mistakes, food-related obsessions, drive for thinness, and impaired satiety (Kaye, 2007). Further, gene-carried problems with the neurotransmitter serotonin (Bergen et al., 2003), the neurotransmitter dopamine (Bachner-Melman et al., 2007), and brain-derived neurotropic factor, a protein that supports neuronal growth (Ribasés et al., 2006) may be implicated in inherited transmission of psychiatric disorders in general – including anorexia nervosa. In summary, research suggests what is inherited may be a complex set of gene combinations linked to certain characteristics that put some individuals like Maeve at higher risk for eating disorders.

Two heritable characteristics shared by Ellen and Maeve were anxiety and perfectionism. For example, Ellen was perfectionistic about her body size and shape. She had little tolerance for anything less than a muscular, flat, movie-star stomach and, unbeknownst to her, neither did her young, preteen daughter. For her part, Maeve noticed that the thin girls were the popular ones. Thinness was also a dominate attribute of the actors on the Nickelodeon TV shows she liked to watch, such as Miranda Cosgrove as Carly in the sitcom *iCarly* (Schneider & Hoefer, 2007–2012). Miranda was thin. Research has born out that the above-average-weight characters on children's TV often suffer social marginality, whereas popular characters like Carly are thinner (Herbozo, Tantleff-Dunn, Gokee-Larose, & Thompson, 2004; Robinson, Callister, & Jankoski, 2008). Both Ellen and Maeve were acutely tuned into media-ideal body types for girls and women. Combined with their genetic loading for anxiety and perfectionism, they were hyper-aware of how they appeared, what size their body was, how it compared to those around them, and, in general, how they were judged by others in social interactions.

Watching Internet shows and television together, Ellen would comment to Maeve how beautiful some woman or girl was, and Maeve would likewise identify or flag thin, attractive women and girls in the media. It was a kind of entertainment for Ellen and Maeve to sit in front of their digital screen together and pick out and admire women and girls who met a certain beauty standard. They liked their clothes, their hair, their style, and their "amazing bodies." Later, by contrast, when Ellen was trying to support Maeve's eating-disorder recovery, Ellen learned to point out non-appearance-based attributes in people.

Like her mother, Maeve seemed prone to social anxiety and perfectionism long before she became abnormally self-conscious about her body. She often felt shy in new situations, like at the beginning of a school year in new classes. After she talked with friends at school, she would labor over whether or not she had said the right thing at the right time and what she thought those friends thought she looked like. She often worried that she had said something offensive, or that her outfit was inadequate.

In fifth grade, a major anxiety for Maeve was the importance of wearing different outfits each day. She was afraid someone would notice she wore the same thing she had worn before. A different T-shirt with the same jeans was okay, just not the same T-shirt. Also, the same T-shirt with the same jeans within the same month was not acceptable. The worst for Maeve was the fear that an outfit made her stomach or thighs look large. This sometimes led her to change clothes in the morning before school two or three times before she could settle on an outfit that made her look thin enough. Ellen noticed Maeve's pokiness in the morning, but thought that it was normal, 11-year-old, emerging-adolescent self-consciousness.

Reflecting on both Maeve and Ellen – their anxious self-consciousness combined with their poor body images and propensity to restrict balanced food intake is similar to as many as two-thirds of teens and adults with eating disorders who also struggle with some type of anxiety disorder. What is particularly remarkable is that anxiety usually precedes the occurrence of an eating disorder, is often an obstacle during recovery, and often remains after recovery

(Kaye et al., 2004). Researchers Watson, Hoiles, Egan, and Limburg (2014) found the degree of anxiety in a large sample of teens with eating disorders was significantly higher than normative levels of anxiety in the adolescent community at large. It is likely that anxiety and eating disorders interact synergistically to enhance each other during the course of an eating-disorder illness. Over time an eating disorder can leave an individual focusing predominantly on worries about their body size and shape, disconnecting them from other worries (e.g., social) that fuel the focus on appearance.

The study of epigenetics addresses the ways in which environmental factors like school-yard bullying and familial abuse (Pallister & Waller, 2008) can have an impact on genes in such a way that heritable illnesses like eating disorders are more likely to be expressed. Maeve's genetic proclivities for both anxiety and disordered eating may have been enhanced by exposure to multiple environmental factors (e.g., television body ideals and bullying). Maeve was steeped in a culture that promoted thin idealization, and she grew up in the environment of Ellen's restrictive eating. Although she appeared to have emerged intact after the breach in her family, we can't know how Maeve would have fared if she had continued to live with both her parents. It wouldn't have changed the fact that Maeve became a prime target for bullying at school because of her hyper-sensitivity to body criticisms and a long history of social anxiety.

For example, once when Maeve was in the cafeteria, a boy she liked, in the awkward manner of a fifth grader, said, "You wanna go on a date? Wait, you aren't that sexy." Maeve was stunned by his attention and barely responded with, "What do you mean?" The boy just laughed and walked away. Maeve rarely thought about sex or looking sexy or even dating. But she did know this boy was popular and for him to be paying attention to her raised intense emotions. She was excited when she saw him. But she was embarrassed and anxious when he spoke to her. Mostly she felt humiliated by his comment that she wasn't "that sexy." She didn't understand that he was messing with her for the sake of his male buddies, and that the whole encounter was a joke for him. She immediately took his comment to mean she was ugly and unattractive and "not cool" or datable. This, in turn, led to thoughts of needing a better body – a thinner body – with more beautiful hair. Then she might be sexy enough for the popular boy. She didn't even realize he had been intentionally mean to her when he criticized her looks. She was much more focused on taking his criticism seriously and trying to fix her flaws. Maeve's focus on her perceived physical flaws allowed her to ignore the emotional pain associated with the bullying.

In addition to the impact of bullying at age 11 Maeve's issues were exacerbated by an unhelpful social environment that featured *fat talk*, conversations and comments that encourage fifth graders like Maeve to struggle with a negative body image. Fat talk among girls is altogether common and starts young (Nichter, 2000). It refers to people speaking about their bodies in a disparaging way. Fat talk has become an almost normative form of communication among girls and women (Barwick, Bazzini, Martz, Rocheleau, & Curtin,

2012). For example, a common conversation during lunchtime between Maeve and her friend Bryn went like this: "My stomach sticks out so much in this shirt – I don't like it." Bryn responded, "I wish I had your stomach – you don't have one. I'm dieting starting today." Bryn was, of course, trying to make Maeve feel better, as well as establish a bond with Maeve. It is a strange but common language between friends in which one friend complains about being fat and the other reassures her and supplicates herself by declaring she's the one who's "fat." To show how common fat talk is, a recent study found that by the time women were in college, 93% were engaging in it (Salk & Engeln-Maddox, 2011).

A meta-analysis of 24 studies showed a clear connection between fat talk and negative body image (Sharpe, Naumann, Treasure, & Schmidt, 2013). As it turns out, being in a social environment where fat talk is the norm, even if one doesn't participate, has a negative impact. In other words, someone like Maeve just has to be listening to be negatively influenced. Cruwys, Leverington, and Sheldon (2016) found a causal link between listening to friends engage in fat talk and thoughts and urges associated with eating disorders (e.g., thin idealization, body dissatisfaction, and intention to diet). Their evidence supported the view that fat talk is culturally normative. That is, in many social groups it is expected and helps to build cohesion among friends. As a young girl, to express something positive about your body risks appearing either conceited, or at least un-empathetic to girlfriends. On the other hand, a friend who discloses something negative about her body is expressing vulnerability. Girls are supposed to engage in fat talk in response. As with Maeve and her friend Bryn, putting one's body down calls for both reassurance from a friend, as well as mutual disclosure of that friend's own body dissatisfaction.

It is important to point out that the vast majority of girls Maeve's age are *afraid* of being fat (National Eating Disorders Association [NEDA], 2016). Both the media and young people's social environments promote thin idealization, dietary restraint, and weight and shape consciousness. Therefore, thin internalization and body dissatisfaction are the byproducts of simply marinating in American culture. Parents and schools can ameliorate this impact by giving attention to prevention practices (NEDA, n.d.).

As noted earlier, a source of thin internalization for Maeve was television. She probably watched the same amount as any American kid. She had her favorite shows and saw maybe a few hours a day when she had done all her chores and finished her homework. She was used to seeing most of the characters portrayed in the children's sitcoms she viewed as either average weight (47%), or below-average weight (38%), with only 15% of the characters above average in weight (Robinson et al., 2008). For her, that was just how it was. As for the many viewers of social media Internet sites that promote the thin ideal, it was normal, and Maeve didn't question the ratios. It didn't occur to her that the world wasn't really like that. Instead, just like most American kids, she compared her body size to what she saw, and, unfortunately for her sense of esteem, she came up *wrong* most of the time.

Despite living in an environment that idealized thinness and stigmatized obesity, Maeve was lucky that she was fairly athletic. She initially took in an adequate amount of nutrient energy to participate in sports and enjoyed being active and physically strong. Sports also were a great way to manage anxiety. She swam in the summer, sledded and skied in the winter, and had fun with all the ball games during school recess. She also liked to dance and had been taking tap dancing lessons for 2 years at her private school. Her sports activities were a positive for Maeve. They put her in touch with her body in ways other than worrying about how it looked.

While sports can be protective with regard to girls' self and body esteem, females who are vulnerable to eating disorders can engage in social comparison and experience negative body image, which can eventually lead to unhealthy weight control practices. During dance classes starting at age 10, Maeve's mind drifted to thoughts of body size. She was dancing, sure, but she was also carefully watching herself and everyone else in the mirrors. She wanted to look like "a thin girl." She especially wanted a flat stomach. One way to tell how flat her stomach was was to compare herself to the other girls in the mirrors on the walls of the studio. On the one hand, Maeve liked having the opportunity to stand side by side with other girls to see how she "sized-up." On the other hand, like most girls and women, the act of socially comparing body size almost always ended in Maeve feeling like she was too fat. For Maeve, body comparing happened so quickly in dance class it had become a mental habit she engaged in each time she entered the studio.

Recent research studies have shown that young people's body comparisons to others, whether face-to-face or via Internet social media sites (e.g., Facebook), are associated with body dissatisfaction, negative attitudes toward themselves, and a propensity to gravitate toward unhealthy weight-management behaviors (Mabe, Forney, & Keel, 2014; Myers & Crowther, 2009; Smith, Hames, & Joiner, 2013; Tiggemann & Slater, 2014). It was troubling to Maeve if her friend Sophia, who was taller and particularly thin, was standing near her in dance class. Even at 10 years old, that specific comparison made her feel so ugly and unhappy with herself that she went home more inspired to eat less food that night than usual, all in order to be thinner. She sometimes felt the same way after watching Carly on television. If only she could be thinner.

While taking in the messages from the broader culture that placed a premium on thinness, at home Maeve also experienced an atmosphere around food that contributed to disordered eating. Research has shown that mothers like Ellen, who have untreated eating disorders, often have trouble nurturing their children around feeding, growth, and development. Maternal eating disorders are known risk factors for feeding problems in young children and for eating-disorder symptoms like restriction and eating to soothe emotions in older children (Allen, Gibson, McLean, Davis, & Byrne, 2014; Hoffman et al., 2014; Micali, De Stavola, Ploubidis, Simonoff, & Treasure, 2013; Micali, Simonoff, Stahl, & Treasure, 2011; Runfola et al., 2014; van Wezel-Meijler & Wit, 1989). It's no wonder Maeve developed problems in these areas. Like Ellen, mothers with prior histories are almost always well intended as they provide a healthy food environment for their children. However, if they still have an eating-disorder mindset, like Ellen, it is a struggle for them not to unwittingly impose their own biased standards for eating, appearance, and exercise onto their children.

While Ellen was totally committed to fostering Maeve's nutritional health, she was unaware of how her eating disorder influenced meal times and obstructed her feeding efforts. Looking back to when Maeve was an infant, Ellen was very uncomfortable with how eagerly her little girl ate. It made her anxious that Maeve might grow up to be out of control around food. When Maeve would grasp food with her tiny hands and push it into her mouth, Ellen felt disgusted. When Maeve whimpered if she wanted more food and eagerly responded to second helpings, Ellen panicked. She projected her own fears of binge eating onto Maeve and worried Maeve was turning into a glutton. She was also on guard against chubbiness, something that infants need to be for healthy development. In other words, Maeve experienced a great degree of tension around food, eating, and body size as she grew and developed under her mother's watchful eye, because of her mother's lingering fears and attitudes toward food and body size (Agras, Hammer, & McNicholas, 1999; Evans & Le Grange, 1995; Hoffman et al., 2014; Johnson & Birch, 1994; Lacey & Smith, 1987; Russell, Treasure, & Eisler, 1998; Stein & Woolley, 1996; Waugh & Bulik, 1999).

Ellen's friend, Laurie, also witnessed the tensions associated with meal times. When Maeve was a baby, Laurie visited Ellen for a few weeks. She recounted she was worried about Ellen's mounting anxiety over feeding Maeve. It was as if Ellen was obsessed. Laurie saw Maeve's eager attitude toward food as healthy. She was surprised by Ellen's obvious response to Maeve's eating behaviors. Ellen tried to disguise her disgust when Maeve would grab food, stuff it in her mouth, get it all over her face, and generally make a mess. She recoiled when Maeve wanted more food than Ellen gave her.

Part of the problem was Ellen lacked full self-awareness of her own negative body image and her own restrictive eating. Laurie tried to help Ellen relax, but Ellen's attitude was that Laurie didn't see the problem with Maeve's robust (and quite normal) appetite. For example, once when Laurie cared for Maeve so that Ellen and her then-husband could have a night to themselves, Ellen seemed afraid Laurie would over-feed Maeve and (projecting her own fears) turn her into an overweight child. This anxious possessiveness around feeding Maeve created tension in their close friendship. Laurie was faced with Ellen's skewed perspective, and she knew it was spilling over onto Maeve.

Mothers with eating disorders can become so preoccupied with their children's weight that they may inadvertently place their children at risk by over-emphasizing concerns with their shape or size, even when they are within normal range. These mothers also often have a distorted or naive idea of how fast or slow food should be eaten, or what overeating actually looks like in a young child (Evans & Le Grange, 1995). They may encourage their normal-size, normal-weight children to diet in order to lose or control their weight. As noted by researchers, "Mothers' satisfaction with their children's size is negatively associated with the severity of their own ED [eating disorder] symptomatology" (Mazzeo, Zucker, Gerke, Mitchell, & Bulik, 2005, p. S78). When this happens, mothers may role model unhealthy eating even though their well-meaning intent is the opposite.

Researchers have also found that fewer positive comments and more negative comments are made during mealtimes than at other times by individuals with eating disorders (Stein, Woolley, Cooper, & Fairburn, 1994). Maeve once heard Ellen say, "I think this quiche was made with too much cheese – we should only eat a little if we want to stay healthy and thin." She also grew up with her mother teaching that the right to eat food was contingent on whether or not compensatory exercise took place. For example, Ellen sometimes said things like, "I didn't go to Yoga today so I can't eat dessert." Further, Ellen placed value judgments on food (e.g., "healthy (good) food" versus "junk (bad) food"), which encouraged guilt in Maeve for indulging in "bad food" (e.g., chips, chocolate, and cheese curls). Children learn how to behave from their parents. After experiencing the way her mother was around food for years and years, Maeve, as an 11-year-old, began to actively emulate and imitate Ellen's restricting behavior, as well as her concern about body size and shape (Russell et al., 1998).

Despite Ellen's attempts to carefully hide her restriction and exercise from her first and only child, mealtimes remained a challenge for her. She knew she should be sharing food with her daughter in the form of family meals because they are a protective factor against dieting and unhealthy weight-control behaviors (Loth et al., 2015). Yet mealtimes were often problematic. Many of the wide variety of foods Ellen thought she should be giving her daughter, she avoided because of their weight-gain potential. While Ellen was among the 28% of parents who regularly served leafy green salads, she was not among the 21% of parents who served fast food a few times a week (Neumark-Sztainer et al., 2014). She was extreme in her choices of what she considered healthy. Always olive oil instead of butter. No pastries around the house. Food rules abounded.

Ellen was left juggling the eating disorder and her better judgments about parenting. On a positive note, raising Maeve turned out to be a challenge that inspired her own continued recovery. For example, when Ellen was caught up in her concerns for healthy eating, she sometimes heard herself say things to Maeve she knew she needed to change. One time she said to 2-year-old Maeve, "you sweet thing – you can't have that cookie because you want keep your cute body." Ellen heard herself promote restrictive eating almost as fast as she said that and vowed to work hard to not place her internalized preference for thin on Maeve.

Ellen wanted to be responsive to Maeve's nutritional needs, but her eating disorder often got in the way. Parents, and especially mothers, have been noted to fit into five major feeding styles: *indulgent* (those who limit neither the quantity nor the quality of the food their children consume), *responsive* (mothers and fathers who monitor the quality of their children's diets and attend closely to their hunger and satiety cues), *restrictive* (place limits on the quantity of food their children eat and restrict their intake to strictly healthy foods), *pressuring* (parents who use food as comfort for their children and pressure them to eat more), and *laissez-faire* (those who do not control intake in quantity or quality and have a hands-off approach to feeding; Thompson et al., 2009). Maeve's mother would likely be classified as restrictive.

One time when Ellen was serving rice for dinner during Maeve's younger years, Maeve said she wanted more. Ellen responded, "I think you've had enough, don't you?" Maeve remembers feeling annoyed and a little humiliated for asking. It was like she had done something wrong by asking for more rice. In fact, once again, Ellen, trying not to voice her worries, was concerned that Maeve might eat too much. "Too much for what?" you might ask. For Ellen. Maeve's body might become too large if she ate too many carbohydrates and then she would be unattractive and suffer social marginalization.

Maeve was all too aware that her mother was worried about her eating too much. In fact, Maeve, at 7 years old, was well aware from media, friends, and her community that a thin body – not a stuffed body – was best. But at 7 Maeve was still a hearty eater who, like many children, loved pasta and rice dishes. Her love of such things started to become "not okay." As stated earlier, Ellen's worries about her own body were projected onto Maeve's. As when Maeve was an infant, Ellen's fear of fat and a larger-sized body became Ellen's fear for Maeve's body in her older childhood years. Ellen had often imagined her body as the object of others' gazes and others' judgments. In order to be successful and popular and valuable, she – as the object of an imagined audience – needed to have the right, "healthy" look. And so, eventually, did Maeve.

Put simply, the main peril for the offspring of women with eating disorders, anorexia nervosa especially, is the risk for developing eating disorders themselves. Even though those with eating disorders are very focused on their children's well-being, they are at risk for indirectly influencing their children's development of the same illness. It isn't that they are bad mothers. On the contrary, they are good, concerned mothers. They are involved with their children, and they care. Nevertheless mothers with eating disorders can have an approach to feeding, nutrition, and body weight – starting with their pregnancy – that can put their genetically vulnerable offspring at risk for perinatal mortality, premature birth, low birth weight, birth defects, feeding problems, and nonorganic failure to thrive (Mazzeo et al., 2005).

Ellen developed disordered eating in her late teens during college at a time when her brain had almost fully developed. Maeve, on the other hand, was much younger and at higher risk because her brain was rapidly developing and changing. When a young person like Maeve stops eating enough for growth requirements, the restriction in nutrition can lead to dramatic changes in the brain. Then the race is on to catch and reverse the impact of undereating. "Because of the unique way a person's brain and body respond to limited nutrition, the longer they are malnourished, the harder it becomes to eat normally again" (Kaye et al., 2012, p. 2), or to think normally again (Castro-Fornieles et al., 2009; Fintrop et al., 2017). Fortunately, evidence suggests that loss of gray and white matter in the brain related to malnourishment is largely reversible with restored nutrition (Wagner et al., 2006). In Maeve's case, Ellen became aware of Maeve's eating and body-image problems when she was still young. This likely protected Maeve from early damage to her brain from undereating.

Ellen eventually learned she had even more work to do to change the atmosphere of eating around her home so that Maeve and she could beat their unhealthy, disordered-eating behaviors. Among other things, Ellen had many habits that revealed her own intense anxiety about weight gain, body image, and eating. For example, she was prone to disparage her own body with offhand comments to Maeve like, "Don't you worry about your stomach. You will never have to struggle to keep the weight off like I do." Later on when Maeve started receiving professional help for her negative body image and her restrictive, disordered eating, Ellen learned not to discount her body in front of Maeve, especially when she was tempted to do so after eating a meal that Ellen felt "guilty" about. Later, Ellen also learned to avoid classifying foods as "healthy" or "junk" so that Maeve wouldn't do the same. She did her best to appear pleasant when Maeve asked for previously forbidden foods, like desserts. "So many things to change," Ellen lamented.

A monumental change for Ellen was serving previously condemned foods, like French fries or full-fat yogurt. Eating-disorder-treatment professionals treating Maeve later told Ellen not to worry about unhelpful behaviors toward Maeve she may have engaged in during the past, such as avoiding full-fat foods. Ellen and everyone who knew her were aware she had the best of intentions for Maeve – always. It was the eating disorder Ellen struggled with in her own partial recovery that continued to exert its influence in subtle ways. Ellen learned that whatever had happened in the past, it was best to move on and look with hope to the future. Even though eating habits are established at home in children as young as 2 years old (Runfola et al., 2014), and it is easier to instill healthy eating habits early on (Dattilo et al., 2012), it is always possible to adopt a more helpful pattern of eating behaviors and attitudes down the road.

Fortunately for Maeve, Ellen was consistent in taking her for annual checkups to the same pediatrician, who kept good records. Her doctor, Dr. Mackey, noticed Maeve at 11 years old had fallen off her growth trajectory – the curve indicating a person's physical advancement in terms of weight and height. In a healthy, young individual, those curves rise consistently until adult maturity, when they flatten out. In Maeve's case, the weight and height trajectories always tracked at a consistent 40 to 45 percentile – a little lower than average despite her mother's fears. Up until age 10, the weight trajectory had steadily followed a normal upward trajectory. So when it failed to rise at 10 and fell below the 40th percentile at age 11, her doctor knew something was wrong. She told Maeve's mother that, for the sake of her daughter's health, Maeve needed to eat more – she needed to pick up some weight. Maeve was diagnosed with Other Specified Feeding or Eating Disorder (OSFED; *Diagnostic and Statistical Manual of Mental Disorders; DSM*-5; American Psychiatric Association, 2013). It was not a full-blown case of anorexia nervosa. However,

Maeve was undereating in order to manage weight and was actively trying to prevent normal weight gain. Ellen, faced with the doctor's authority, decided to comply. She determined within herself she would help Maeve treat her body with more care by eating more and gaining weight.

Dr. Mackey referred Maeve for nutrition counseling and brief psychotherapy with the hope that Maeve's emerging eating disorder could be prevented from becoming more severe and debilitating. Partial-syndrome eating disorders like Maeve's have been known to resolve spontaneously without evolving into full-syndrome eating disorders during mid-teen years. However, Maeve was a high risk for developing a full-blown eating disorder. First, upon questioning by Dr. Mackey, Maeve reported at least some concern with body image and dietary restraint since early elementary school. Second, when asked about family history, Ellen disclosed an eating-disorder history. She was embarrassed to admit her secret to Dr. Mackey, but she found it hard to suppress the information in light of Maeve's illness. Dr. Mackey pointed out the heritability of eating disorders and the extra risk factor for Maeve.

Ellen was accustomed to being ashamed and trying to hide any trace of disordered eating. She didn't realize it at the time, but admitting her history to Dr. Mackey was an important step in moving forward. Ellen blamed herself for the eating disorder and was at risk for passing on an attitude of self-blame to Maeve. Dr. Mackey was not judgmental and clearly stated to Ellen that the past eating disorder was not her fault any more than it was Maeve's fault for her problems with eating. Besides, Dr. Mackey was aware that parental self-blame has a negative impact on the outcome of parent refeeding efforts (Stillar et al., 2016), something he knew Ellen was about to embark on with Maeve. Dr. Mackey explained that untreated mild eating disorders can easily grow during mid-teen years and may develop into full-syndrome eating disorders like anorexia nervosa during adolescence and early adulthood.

After Maeve's doctor told her to help Maeve gain weight and improve her nutrition, Ellen became more of a responsive feeder of her daughter. Before treatment, Ellen thought Maeve's pursuit of "clean, healthy" foods and her reduction of portions of denser, thicker foods like lasagna were a sign of her growing maturity about health. It cheered her when Maeve said, "Mom, could you just buy me zero fat yogurt this week?" or "I don't like soda anymore. Don't get me any." Partly because of Ellen's own biases, she easily missed Maeve's slow, almost imperceptible failure to gain weight and the rigidity that Maeve began to show around her shrinking repertoire of foods. It was the annual visit to the pediatrician's office and the stark reality of seeing how Maeve had failed to grow that eventually raised Ellen's anxiety about Maeve's increasingly troubled attitude toward food. Ellen was motivated to make changes in Maeve's behavior even if she was less able to make changes in her own.

Dr. Mackey referred Ellen and Maeve to a family therapist, Jerry, who gave Ellen full responsibility to oversee Maeve's nutrition restoration and to interrupt any eating-disorder behaviors. This was consistent with best practices for treating eating disorders (anorexia nervosa and bulimia nervosa) in children

(Lamb & Scholey, 2013; Lock & Le Grange, 2015). Although Maeve did not meet full criteria for anorexia nervosa, Family Based Treatment (Lock & Le Grange, 2015) is useful for normalizing eating in restrictive-eating disorders. Jerry discovered through a family-history interview and in talking to Dr. Mackey that Ellen had disordered-eating issues. He was instrumental in helping her address those issues while she tended to Maeve.

Because of her own long-term biased practices with food, Ellen needed initial direction from a nutrition counselor to make sure she was choosing well-balanced and adequately portioned meals and snacks for Maeve. Her mother's intuition for how to feed Maeve had been scarred by an eating disorder. Like Jerry, the nutrition counselor, Hannah, specialized in eating-disorders treatment, an important factor for optimal outcomes when treating eating disorders (Grumet, 2014). Both Jerry and Hannah found Ellen easy to work with because she was motivated to change and she was confident she could be effective. As it turns out, self-efficacy in parents like Ellen is an important mediating factor in the success of Family Based Treatment (Robinson, Strahan, Girz, Wilson, & Boachie, 2013).

It was slow work. Ellen's encouragement of her daughter to eat more and gain weight went against how she'd lived the majority of her life. That was very painful. Nevertheless, for Maeve's sake, she stuck to her agreement with the pediatrician. She was grateful Maeve was only in fifth grade. She naturally had more interaction and oversight of Maeve's eating than if she were older, more independent, and around the house less.

In the first 2 months of treatment, Maeve was resistant to Ellen's doctor- and therapist-directed interventions. She told her mother, "I don't want to eat so much food." She said she was full and her stomach hurt from "all that food." She argued with her mother, "This isn't fair. How come I have to eat all this food and you don't?" Jerry was helpful in normalizing Maeve's complaints for Ellen so that she didn't lose momentum or become too discouraged. Maeve's resistance to eating gradually decreased as she saw her mother maintain a persistent, unrelenting stance against the eating disorder.

When Maeve complained to Ellen that she served her more food than she (Ellen) fed herself, Ellen had to admit to Maeve sometimes it was true. First, Ellen explained to Maeve that Maeve was recovering from an illness and needed much more food than she was accustomed to. Second, Ellen discouraged Maeve from comparing their different food amounts, because each ate according to her own personal need. And third, Ellen shared that she had her own history of dietary restraint and disordered eating and was trying to adjust her nutrition intake to match her body's needs. With Jerry's help, Ellen realized early on she would need to separate her food issues from Maeve's. One day in a family therapy session in the first month of treatment, Ellen said to her daughter, "I'm concerned that you haven't been eating enough. I have different needs than you do. I'm going to ask you not to compare your food to my food. You need the food I'm giving you. I'm sorry if I've made you think about food as too much, or too sweet, or too unhealthy. I'm doing my best to help you see that all foods can be good in the right balance, and enough food is important for you to grow in a healthy way." Somehow, from Maeve's perspective, bonding with her mother over improved nutrition seemed important, and it felt good.

They were forging a better relationship than they had in years. Maeve was partly happy to see her mother not make such a big deal over what kind of food she was eating. They were trying different foods at dinner and breakfast, and that was sometimes fun. Gradually, Maeve learned to trust her mother about two things. First, Ellen was intent on making sure she ate more, even if she objected. And, second, Ellen was happy about her weight gain, even if that meant her body grew in size. By the fourth month of treatment Maeve began to spontaneously fix her own adequate snacks under the watchful eye of her mother. Family meals became a priority and happened at regular times. They replaced previously strained, now-and-then meals that had often been interrupted by busy schedules.

Although not addressed in treatment until later, Jerry was also helpful in diagnosing Ellen and Maeve with Social Anxiety Disorder (*DSM*-5), pointing out the ways social anxieties help maintain an eating disorder. Using cognitive behavior therapy (CBT) in a family therapy context, Jerry helped Ellen come to terms with her internalized thin bias and her distorted thinking about whether or not foods were healthy. Jerry knew if Ellen believed what she was teaching Maeve, she would be a stronger positive influence than if she were simply saying the right thing without personal conviction. Jerry's work to restructure Ellen's thoughts and Ellen's strong alliance with him allowed her to eventually pursue CBT with an individual therapist.

A few of Ellen's mistaken ideas (cognitive distortions) about nutrition were co-addressed by Hannah and Jerry, each weaving in brief cognitive-behavior-therapy interventions. These included the examples shown in Table 7.1.

After 6 months of Family Based Treatment, Maeve started to recover and develop a maturing body. Even though she still struggled with body image as her stomach went beyond the bounds of her hips, she steadily increased her ability to eat. Gradually for Maeve, eating felt good. On occasion, she found herself actually enjoying previously avoided foods. Ellen tried to make eating a positive experience rather than a tense, guilt-ridden one. Once in a while when Maeve ate too fast, or seemed to enjoy her food too robustly, it reminded Ellen of Maeve as a baby, when she was a tiny, enthusiastic eater. It raised old fears of unrestrictive eating turning into binge eating – a projection of Ellen's own fears for herself. However, Ellen was afraid if she said anything to Maeve about eating too fast or too much or the wrong thing, Maeve would interpret this as, "You think I'm fat." She was probably right. So she carefully reframed her anxious thoughts before saying anything. Later in the recovery process, on the rare occasion when Maeve filled her mouth to the brim with food in front of Ellen, Ellen would gently say, "You'll enjoy the food so much more if you eat smaller bites and taste how good it is before you take the next bite."

Table 7.1

Cognitive distortion	*Type of distortion*	*Therapy correction*
"There are good foods and bad foods."	Black and white thinking/ overgeneralization.	"The truth is, all palatable food is fuel for the body, and it is too little or too much of particular foods that can lead to poor nutrition."
"Fats should be avoided because they will cause weight gain and lead to illness."	Black and white thinking/ catastrophic thinking Thought-shape fusion (TSF; Shafran, Teachman, Kerry, & Rachman, 1999).	"Unless someone has a medical condition for which avoiding certain kinds of fats is indicated, fats are an essential part of nutritional balance and need to be consumed in moderation and in combination with other nutrients in order to maximize health."
"If I think about eating too many fats and carbohydrates, I might as well have eaten them, and thinking about them too much makes me feel fat."	Thought-shape fusion (TSF; Shafran et al., 1999).	"I have lived so long believing I should avoid fats and carbohydrates, I started to believe I'd done something wrong if I ate more than a little of them. I am not wrong to eat those foods. Thinking about those foods is unrelated to weight gain, and fat is not a feeling."

And so it was that Maeve learned lessons that were especially hard for her mom to teach. Ellen realized that after 20 years of restrictive eating, she was limited in her ability to role model for her daughter from her own relationship with food. It was often difficult to set boundaries between her occasional fussy eating and Maeve's new, open relationship with food, especially since Ellen bore most of the responsibility for setting those boundaries. Ellen was successful in presenting a wider range of foods and a more positive attitude about eating all kinds. She was careful to never, never comment on Maeve's body size.

Meanwhile, Ellen continued coming to terms with her own eating and body-image issues. Over the years, Ellen never exhibited seriously life-threatening behaviors around food. Instead, she had largely stayed beneath the scrutiny of her family and friends (under their radar) while also holding fast to the wish that she were thinner. For her, restriction was the proper way to approach life. The limited nutrition she allowed herself kept her going, but she never thrived. She had never been the best at anything except staying as thin as she dared. When Ellen began to examine her own patterns in the wake of Maeve's issues, she realized she clung to the pursuit of thinness as one of the only things she was good at. Who was she without this? The question troubled her and she later pursued it in her own individual psychotherapy. Yet the thought of making serious changes in her eating habits, even for Maeve's sake, was troubling.

What Ellen could not always do was reign in her own proclivities to restrict, although she was making slow and steady progress. Twenty years is a long history to overcome. The eating disorder, for Ellen, was a well-entrenched and formidable force against which she labored. Eventually, she worked with her own separate psychotherapist and nutrition counselor. Her anxiety was high. However, admitting to Maeve that this was an issue for her helped create an accepting atmosphere of patience for changes in their home. Ellen knew that no matter what happened to her, Maeve needed to be well. She wanted Maeve to avoid the pitfalls Ellen realized she, herself, had fallen into. Sometimes, "Do as I say and not as I do when it comes to eating," was understood between them. Ellen admitted to her old friend Laurie and to Maeve that she had previously minimized, even denied, her own issues. This was no longer the case.

Even though Ellen was not free from thoughts and urges to engage in disordered eating, and she didn't know if she ever would be, she felt more motivated and committed to recovery steps. Ellen rested in a firm understanding that her own restrictive-eating behaviors and related anxieties had been part of a longstanding, chronic illness – one to which she did not want Maeve to succumb. She firmly placed her hopes on her daughter living a life without disordered eating.

Again, Ellen was a good mother. She knew she might not have the best mothering skills, but she was dedicated to Maeve's well-being. Early on she often didn't know how to alter her behavior so it would benefit Maeve. Ever since Maeve was an infant, Ellen had worried that she might be overfeeding her. When her daughter was older, Ellen promoted Maeve's interest in healthy physical exercise, even though for her, secretly, promoting exercise was closely linked to weight and size management. She tried hard to help Maeve be healthy. She had always felt ill-prepared to raise her daughter by herself with confidence, but she was finally getting some guidance and confidence about how much and what to feed her from Maeve's and her own treatment teams. Ellen now knew she could not depend on her own skewed perceptions about eating, body image, and body size to guide her with Maeve. Her distortions got sorted out with her own specialty-trained treatment professionals so she could help Maeve develop a more positive, flexible relationship with her body and with food.

Question

My daughter has been diagnosed with an eating disorder and she doesn't know I have the same history. Should I tell her?

Answer

Because eating disorders are heritable, a specialty-trained treatment professional will likely ask parents, perhaps in the presence of the young person struggling with an eating disorder, about any family history of eating disorders. This is often a good time to tell your child about your history if you have not already. Pointing out the heritability of eating disorders helps relieve both parental and patient self-blame. After all, no one is to blame for their genes. Further, discussing your history of an eating disorder reduces the chances your child will feel ashamed. If parents are matter-of-fact about genetic risk factors and their own eating-disorder history, then offspring will be likely to follow suit. Stigmatizing attitudes towards those with eating disorders are well documented (Griffiths, Mond, Murray, & Touyz, 2015; Makowski, Mnich, Angermeyer, Löwe, & von dem Knesebeck, 2015) with people commonly blaming sufferers for their condition (Ebneter & Latner, 2013). Feeling stigmatized and ashamed not only has a negative impact on general mental health, but also impedes recovery. Parents who speak openly about their history help their child reduce her or his fear of stigmatization.

Perhaps one of the greatest advantages of a parent or guardian sharing their eating-disorder story with a child with an eating disorder is it gives them the support of a knowledgeable parent who has "been there" and "gets it." Eating disorders are not intuitively understood (e.g., the myth that if patients "just ate" they would recover). A parent who has struggled with an eating disorder has a unique understanding that affords a greater level of empathy and support for a child with an eating disorder.

Question

I want to shield my children and partner from my eating-disorder behaviors (restricting, binge eating, and self-induced vomiting). However, I am having difficulty hiding behaviors from my family. What is recommended?

Answer

In many ways eating disorders are illnesses like any other. It is best to talk about them with trusted family members. Keeping an illness a secret may suggest there is something to be ashamed of (e.g., if a person has an eating disorder they must have caused it or failed to control it). If eating disorders are openly discussed like any other illness might, there is a better chance of receiving helpful support from loved ones. It is especially important that trusted partners know about eating-disorder behaviors. Eating disorders are diseases of disconnection and isolation (Tantillo, Sanftner, & Hauenstein, 2013; Tantillo & Sanftner, 2010). Building connection with a trusted partner by allowing him or her to be aware of the illness can facilitate recovery. Partners can be the most supportive and helpful by being patient, compassionate, willing to learn, willing to ask questions, willing to listen, and willing to be guided by their recovering partner.

Schmidt and Treasure (2006) summarized important research that showed many psychiatric disorders are influenced by the emotional responses of close others. In fact, eating disorders often feed on something called high expressed emotion (EE). Expressed emotion "reflects the amount of criticism, hostility, and emotional over-involvement expressed by relatives of psychiatric patients towards them" (Schmidt & Treasure, 2006, p. 354). The more intense or higher the expressed emotion on the part of family members toward the person with the illness, the more recovery is negatively impacted. Relatives are encouraged to not judge or criticize and to remain positive, patient, flexible, steady, and dependable. Two of Treasure's animal metaphors for carer styles, the St. Bernard (steady, calm, and dependable) and the dolphin (swimming alongside, encouraging, and nudging without controlling), represent the ideal stance of supportive loved ones (Treasure, Smith, & Crane, 2007).

Here is another way partners can be helpful. Parent-based programs have been developed to support mothers with eating disorders in order to minimize negative outcomes in their offspring. In these programs partners provide both emotional and behavioral support to mothers in order to facilitate change away from damaging parent practices (e.g., negative perceptions of children, restricting children's food, over-monitoring children's eating, and excessive pressure on children to eat). For example, Sedah-Sharvit, Zubery, Mankovski, Steiner, and Lock (2016) developed Parent-Based Prevention (PBP) for children (aged 5 or under) of mothers with eating disorders. That program requires full disclosure, positive communication, and trust between mothers with eating disorders and their spouses. Collaborative co-feeding of children by parents is central to participation. The authors also hope to adapt their PBP program to fathers with eating disorders.

Telling children about a parent's eating disorder can prevent tension created by the shame and secrecy of not telling. As with a partner, presenting an eating disorder as one would any other serious illness makes the most sense. Depending on the age of the child or children, the amount and type of information may vary. Language used should be developmentally adapted to the child's age. It is important that parents identify any unusual behaviors a child might observe that are part of the illness so that they are not frightened or anxious by what they see. Imagine a father telling his son about a few unusual but difficult OCD rituals. A father might say, "I have an illness called Obsessive Compulsive Disorder or OCD. Sometimes when you see me washing my hands after I touch the floor or a doorknob it is because the OCD is the kind of illness that makes me want to do that. In the future, I might not always wash after touching things. A little at a time, I am working on not washing so much. There is nothing you can do to help me with this illness except to be patient and understand the illness is nobody's fault and it will likely get better with time." Similarly, with regard to an eating disorder, a mother might say to her daughter, "I have an illness called Bulimia Nervosa. When you see me eating lots of food or just a little food, it's because the illness makes me want to do that. I might not always be eating especially large or small amounts of food. A little at a time I'm working at having just the right amount of food for meals and snacks. There's nothing you can do to help me with this illness except be patient and understand this is nobody's fault and it will likely get better with time." Finally, offer children the opportunity to ask any questions they might have.

Question

My daughter and I both have eating disorders and are in recovery in separate programs. Her eating-disorder recovery inspired me to seek treatment so I could better support her. What are helpful and unhelpful communications I need to observe when talking to my daughter?

Answer

Maor and Cwikel (2016) found the following communication strategies from mothers to daughters to be the most helpful:

1 Be cautious and filter any message that has to do with body image (e.g., mothers be very careful not to criticize their own bodies in front of their daughters)
2 Transmitting information about the dangers of dieting and eating disorders
3 Speaking positively about body acceptance
4 Teaching daughters to engage in critical thinking about popular media ideals such as media promoting thin idealization (e.g., teach children to think about the meaning conveyed by television commercials)
5 Emphasize taking pleasure in food rather than promoting guilt and negative feeling about unhealthy eating (e.g., eat what feels and tastes good and promote a wide variety of foods rather than talk about foods that are "too fattening" or "too processed")

Arroyo, Segrin, and Andersen (2017) looked at intergenerational transmission of disordered eating. They examined daughters' perceptions of direct and indirect communications from their mothers that may have influenced their disordered eating. In keeping with previous research, they found the following communications from mother to daughter were unhelpful:

1 Any comments about weight and size
2 Criticizing daughter's weight
3 Teasing about daughter's weight
4 Positive comments about daughter's body (the authors explain any judgmental body comment, even a positive one, objectifies a woman's body and can lead to over-valuation of appearance and imply a comparison to an ideal-body standard)
5 Mothers commenting on their own weight
6 Mothers worrying about their own weight

By practicing helpful communications and avoiding unhelpful communications, mothers can promote resilience in the face of body dissatisfaction and eating disorders.

References

Agras, S., Hammer, L., & McNicholas, F. (1999). A prospective study of the influence of eating-disordered mothers on their children. *International Journal of Eating Disorders*, 25, 253–262.

Allen, K., Gibson, L., McLean, N., Davis, E., & Byrne, S. (2014). Maternal and family factors and child eating pathology: Risk and protective relationships. *Journal of Eating Disorders*, 2(1), 11.

American Psychiatric Association. (2013). *Diagnostic and statistical manual of mental disorders* (5th ed.). Arlington, VA: Author.

Arroyo, A., Segrin, C., & Andersen, K. K. (2017). Intergenerational transmission of disordered eating: Direct and indirect maternal communication among grandmothers, mothers, and daughters. *Body Image*, 20, 107–115.

Bachner-Melman, R., Lerer, E., Zohar, A. H., Kremer, I., Elizur, Y., Nemanov, L., ... Ebstein, R. P. (2007). Anorexia nervosa, perfectionism, and dopamine D4 receptor (DRD4). *American Journal of Medical Genetics Part B: Neuropsychiatric Genetics*, 144B(6), 748–756.

Barwick, A., Bazzini, D., Martz, D., Rocheleau, C., & Curtin, L. (2012). Testing the norm to fat talk for women of varying size: What's weight got to do with it? *Body Image*, 9(1), 176–179.

Bergen, A. W., van den Bree, M. B., Yeager, M., Welch, R., Ganjei, J. K., Haque, K., ... Kaye, W. H. (2003). Candidate genes for anorexia nervosa in the 1p33–36 linkage region: Serotonin 1D and delta opioid receptor loci exhibit significant association to anorexia nervosa. *Molecular Psychiatry*, 8(4), 397–406.

Bulik, C. M. (2004). Genetic and biological risk factors for eating disorders. In J. Thompson (Ed.), *Handbook of eating disorders and obesity*, pp. 3–16. New York, NY: Wiley.

Bulik, C. M. (2005). Exploring the gene-environment nexus in eating disorders. *Journal of Psychiatry and Neuroscience*, 30(5), 335–339.

Bulik, C. M., Reba, L., Siega-Riz, A. M., & Reichborn-Kjennerud, T. (2005). Anorexia nervosa: Definition, epidemiology, and cycle of risk. *International Journal of Eating Disorders*, 37(S1), S2–S9.

Bulik, C. M., Sullivan, P., Tozzi, F., Furberg, H., Lichtenstein, P., & Pedersen, N. (2006). Prevalence, heritability, and prospective risk factors for anorexia nervosa. *Archives of General Psychiatry*, 63, 305–312.

Castro-Fornieles, J., Deulofeu, R., Martínez-Mallen, E., Baeza, I., Fernández, L., Lázaro, L., ... Bernardo, M. (2009). Plasma homovanillic acid in adolescents with bulimia nervosa. *Psychiatry Research*, 170(2–3), 241–244.

Combs, J. L., Pearson, C. M., Zapolski, T. C. B., & Smith, G. T. (2013). Preadolescent disordered eating predicts subsequent eating dysfunction. *Journal of Pediatric Psychology*, 38(1), 41–49.

Cruwys, T., Leverington, C. T., & Sheldon, A. M. (2016). An experimental investigation of the consequences and social functions of fat talk in friendship groups. *International Journal of Eating Disorders*, 49(1), 84–91.

Dattilo, A. M., Birch, L., Krebs, N. F., Lake, A., Taveras, E. M., & Saavedra, J. M. (2012). Need for early interventions in the prevention of pediatric overweight: A review and upcoming directions. *Journal of Obesity*, 2012.

Ebneter, D. S., & Latner, J. D. (2013). Stigmatizing attitudes differ across mental health disorders: A comparison of stigma across eating disorders, obesity, and major depressive disorder. *The Journal of Nervous and Mental Disease*, 201(4), 281–285.

Evans, J., & Le Grange, D. (1995). Body size and parenting in eating disorders: A comparative study of the attitudes of mothers towards their children. *International Journal of Eating Disorders*, 18, 39–48.

Fintrop, L., Liesbrock, J., Paulukat, L., Johann, S. Kas, M. J., Tolba, R., … Seitz, J. (2017). Reduced astrocyte density underlying brain volume reduction in activity-based anorexia rats. *The World Journal of Biological Psychiatry*, 1–11.

Griffiths, S., Mond, J. M., Murray, S. B., & Touyz, S. (2015). The prevalence and adverse associations of stigmatization in people with eating disorders. *International Journal of Eating Disorders*, 48(6), 767–774.

Grumet, K. K. (2014). The role of the registered dietitian/nutritionist on the eating disorder team. *Gürze-Salucore Eating Disorders Resource Catalogue*, June 05. Retrieved from www.edcatalogue.com

Herbozo, S., Tantleff-Dunn, S., Gokee-Larose, J., & Thompson, J. K. (2004). Beauty and thinness messages in children's media: A content analysis. *Eating Disorders: The Journal of Treatment &Prevention*, 12, 21–34.

Hoffman, E. R., Bentley, M. E., Hamer, R. M., Hodges, E. A., Ward, D. S., & Bulik, C. M. (2014). A comparison of infant and toddler feeding practices of mothers with and without histories of eating disorders. *Maternal & Child Nutrition*, 10(3), 360–372.

Johnson, S., & Birch, L. (1994). Parents' and children's adiposity and eating style. *Pediatrics*, 94(5), 653–661.

Kaye, W. (2007). Neurobiology of anorexia and bulimia nervosa. *Physiology and Behavior*, 94(1), 121–135.

Kaye, W. H., Bulik, C., Thornton, L., Barbarich, B. S., Masters, K., & Group, P.F.C. (2004). Comorbidity of anxiety with anorexia and bulimia nervosa. *American Journal of Psychiatry*, 161(112), 2215–2221.

Kaye, W. H., Lyster-Mensh, L. D., Klump, K. L., Kreipe, R. E., Madden, S., Mitchell, J. E., Treasure, J. (Eds.). (2012). *Puzzling symptoms: Eating disorders and the brain: A family guide to the neurobiology of eating disorders.* Warrenton, VA: Families Empowered and Supporting Treatment of Eating Disorders (F.E.A.S.T.).

Klump, K. L., Kaye, W. H., & Strober, M. (2001). The evolving genetic foundations of eating disorders. *Psychiatric Clinics of North America*, 24(2), 215–225.

Kotler, L. A., Cohen, P., Davies, M., Pine, D. S., & Walsh, B. T. (2001). Longitudinal relationships between childhood, adolescent, and adult eating disorders. *Journal of the American Academy of Child Psychiatry*, 40(12), 1434–1440.

Lacey, J., & Smith, G. (1987). Bulimia nervosa: The impact of pregnancy on mother and baby. *The British Journal of Psychiatry*, 150, 777–781.

Lamb, K., & Scholey, S. (2013). Establishing consistency and best practice in the care of children and adolescents with eating disorders: Developments at the Mater Children's Hospital (MCH) and Mater Child and Youth Mental Health Service (CYMHS). *Journal of Eating Disorders*, 1(Suppl 1), O61.

Lilenfeld, L. R., Kaye, W. H., Greeno, C. G., Merikangas, K. P., Plotnicov, K., & Pollice, C., … Nagy, L. (1998). A controlled family study of anorexia nervosa and bulimia nervosa: Psychiatric disorders in first-degree relatives and effects of proband comorbidity. *Archives of General Psychiatry*, 55, 603–610

Lock, J., & Le Grange, D. (2015). *Treatment manual for anorexia nervosa: A family-based approach*. New York, NY: Guilford.

Loth, K., Wall, M., Choi, C. W., Bucchianeri, M., Quick, V., Larson, N., & Neumark-Sztainer, D. (2015). Family meals and disordered eating in adolescents: Are the benefits the same for everyone? *International Journal of Eating Disorders*, 48(1), 100–110.

Mabe, A. G., Forney, K. J., & Keel, P. K. (2014). Do you "like" my photo? Facebook use maintains eating disorder risk. *International Journal of Eating Disorders*, 47(5), 516–523.

Makowski, A. C., Mnich, E. E., Angermeyer, M. C., Löwe, B., & von dem Knesebeck, O. (2015). Sex differences in attitudes towards females with eating disorders. *Eating Behaviors*, 16, 78–83.

Maor, M., & Cwikel, J. (2016). Mothers' strategies to strengthen their daughters to strengthen. *Feminism & Psychology*, 26, 11–29.

Mazzeo, S. E., Zucker, N. L., Gerke, C. K., Mitchell, K. S., & Bulik, C. M. (2005). Parenting concerns of women with histories of eating disorders. *International Journal of Eating Disorders*, 37, S77–S79.

Micali, N., De Stavola, B., Ploubidis, G. B., Simonoff, E., & Treasure, J. (2013). The effects of maternal eating disorders on offspring childhood and early adolescent psychiatric disorders. *International Journal of Eating Disorders*, 47(4), 385–393.

Micali, N., Simonoff, E., Stahl, D., & Treasure, J. (2011). Maternal eating disorders and infant feeding difficulties: Maternal and child mediators in a longitudinal general population study. *Journal of Child Psychology and Psychiatry*, 52(7), 800–807.

Myers, T. A., & Crowther, J. H. (2009). Social comparison as a predictor of body dissatisfaction: A meta-analytic review. *Journal of Abnormal Psychology*, 118(4), 683–698.

National Eating Disorders Association. (n.d.). Parent toolkit. Retrieved from www.nationaleatingdisorders.org/sites/default/files/Toolkits/ParentToolkit.pdf

National Eating Disorders Association. (2016). Dieting and the drive for thinness. Retrieved from www.nationaleatingdisorders.org/get-facts-eating-disorders

Neumark-Sztainer, D., MacLehose, R., Loth, K., Fulkerson, J. A., Eisenberg, M. E., & Berge, J. (2014). What's for dinner? Types of food served at family dinner differ across parent and family characteristics. *Public Health Nutrition*, 17(1), 145–155.

Nichter, M. (2000). *Fat talk: What girls and their parents say about dieting*. Cambridge, MA: Harvard University Press.

Pallister, E., & Waller, G. (2008). Anxiety in the eating disorders: Understanding the overlap. *Clinical Psychology Review*, 28(3), 266–386.

Pinheiro, A. P., Root, T., & Bulik, C. M. (2009). The genetics of anorexia nervosa: Current findings and future perspectives. *International Journal of Child and Adolescent Health*, 2(2), 153–164.

Ribasés, M., Gratacòs, M., Fernández-Aranda, F., Bellodi, L., Boni, C., Anderluh, M., … Estivill, X. (2006). Association of BDNF with restricting anorexia nervosa and minimum body mass index: A family-based association study of eight European populations. *European Journal of Human Genetics*, 13(4), 428–434.

Robinson, R., Callister, M., & Jankoski, T. (2008). Portrayal of body weight on children's television sitcoms: A content analysis. *Body Image*, 5(2), 141–151.

Robinson, A. L., Strahan, E., Girz, L., Wilson, A., & Boachie, A. (2013). "I know I can help you": Parental self-efficacy predicts adolescent outcomes in family-based therapy for eating disorders. *European Eating Disorders Review*, 21(2), 108–114.

Runfola, C. D., Zucker, N. L., Von Holle, A., Mazzeo, S., Hodges, E. A., Perrin, E. M., ... Bulik, C. M. (2014). NURTURE: Development and pilot testing of a novel parenting intervention for mothers with histories of an eating disorder. *International Journal of Eating Disorders*, 47(1), 1–12.

Russell, G. F., Treasure, J., & Eisler, I. (1998). Mothers with anorexia who underfeed their children: Their recognition and management. *Psychological Medicine*, 28, 93–108.

Salk, R. H., & Engeln-Maddox, R. (2011). "If you're fat, then I'm humongous!": Frequency, content, and impact of fat talk among college women. *Psychology of Women Quarterly*, 35(1), 18–28.

Schmidt, U., & Treasure, J. (2006). Anorexia nervosa: Valued and visible. A cognitive-interpersonal maintenance model and its implications for research and practice. *British Journal of Clinical Psychology*, 45(Pt 3), 343–366.

Schneider, D. (Producer), & Hoefer, S. (Director). (2007–2012). *iCarly* [Television series]. Los Angeles, CA: Nickelodeon.

Sedah-Sharvit, S., Zubery, E., Mankovski, E., Steiner, E., & Lock, J. D. (2016). Parent-based prevention program for the children of mothers with eating disorders. *Eating Disorders*, 24(4), 312–325.

Shafran, R., Teachman, B. A., Kerry, S., & Rachman, S. (1999). A cognitive distortion associated with eating disorders: Thought-shape fusion. *British Journal of Clinical Psychology*, 38(2), 167–179.

Sharpe, H., Naumann, U., Treasure, J., & Schmidt, U. (2013). Is fat talking a causal risk factor for body dissatisfaction? A systematic review and meta-analysis. *International Journal of Eating Disorders*. 46(7), 643–652.

Smith, A. R., Hames, J. L., & Joiner, T. E., Jr. (2013). Status update: Maladaptive Facebook usage predicts increases in body dissatisfaction and bulimic symptoms. *Journal of Affective Disorders*, 149(1–3), 235–240.

Stein, A., & Woolley, H. (1996). The influence of parental eating disorders on young children: Implications of recent research for some clinical interventions. *Eating Disorders: The Journal of Treatment and Prevention*, 4(20), 139–146.

Stein, A., Woolley, H., Cooper, S., & Fairburn, C. G. (1994). An observational study of mothers with eating disorders and their infants. *Journal of Child Psychology and Psychiatry*, 35(4), 733–748.

Stillar, A., Strahan, E., Nash, P., Files, N., Scarborough, J., Mayman, S., ... Marchand, P. (2016). The influence of carer fear and self-blame when supporting a loved one with an eating disorder. *Eating Disorders*, 24(2), 173–185.

Strober, M., Freeman, R., Lampert, C., Diamond, J., & Kaye, W. (2000). Controlled family study of anorexia and bulimia nervosa: Evidence of shared liability and transmission of partial syndromes. *American Journal of Psychiatry*, 157, 393–401.

Strober, M., Freeman, R., Lampert, C., Diamond, J., & Kaye, W. (2001). Males with anorexia nervosa: A controlled study of eating disorders in first-degree relatives. *International Journal of Eating Disorders*, 29(3), 263–269.

Tantillo, M., & Sanftner, J. L. (2010). Mutuality and motivation: Connecting with patients and families for change in the treatment of eating disorders. In M. Maine, D. Bunnell, & B. McGilley (Eds.), *Treatment of eating disorders: Bridging the gap between research and practice* (pp. 319–334). London, UK: Elsevier.

Tantillo, M., Sanftner, J., & Hauenstein, E. (2013). Restoring connection in the face of disconnection: An integrative approach to understanding and treating Anorexia Nervosa. *Advances in Eating Disorders: Theory, Research and Practice*, 1(1), 21–38.

Thompson, A. L., Mendez, M. A., Borja, J. B., Adair, L. S., Zimmer, C. R., & Bentley, M. E. (2009). Development and validation of the Infant Feeding Style Questionnaire. *Appetite*, 53(2), 210–221.

Tiggemann, M., & Slater, A. (2014). NetTweens: The Internet and body image concerns in preteenage girls. *The Journal of Early Adolescence*, 34(5), 606–620.

Treasure, J., Smith, G., & Crane, A. (2007). *Skills-based learning for caring for a loved one with an eating disorder: The New Maudsley Model*. East Sussex, UK: Routledge.

van Wezel-Meijler, G., & Wit, J. M. (1989). The offspring of mothers with anorexia nervosa: A high-risk group for undernutrition and stunting? *European Journal of Pediatrics*, 149(2), 130–135.

Wagner, A., Greer, P., Bailer, U. F., Frank, G. K., Henry, S. E., Putnam, K., ... McConaha, C. (2006). Normal brain tissue volumes after long-term recovery in anorexia and bulimia nervosa. *Biological Psychiatry*, 59(3), 291–293.

Watson, H. J., Hoiles, K. J., Egan, S. J., & Limburg, K. (2014). Normative data for female adolescents with eating disorders on the Multidimensional Anxiety Scale for Children. *International Journal of Eating Disorders*, 47(5), 471–474.

Waugh, E., & Bulik, C. M. (1999). Offspring of women with eating disorders. *International Journal of Eating Disorders*, 25(2), 123–133.

8 Preventing Eating Disorders

Adolescents and young adults are particularly vulnerable to eating disorders. Studies have shown the median age range for the onset of anorexia nervosa is 16 to 22 years (Hudson, Hiripi, Pope, & Kessler, 2007). For bulimia nervosa, it's 14 to 22 years (Hudson et al., 2007), and for binge eating disorder (BED), 18 to 22 years (Stice, Marti, & Rohde, 2013). A cross-cultural study showed that approximately 13.1% of young women struggle with a full-blown or sub-clinical eating or feeding disorder (Stice, Marti, & Rohde, 2013). Furthermore, the prevalence of eating disorders rises from 8.5% to 15.1%, in young women ages 14 to 20 and from 1.2% up to 2.9% for similar-aged young men (Allen, Oddy, Byrne, & Crosby, 2013). Studies made in other countries have found similar eating-disorder prevalence rates in adolescents: 14.1% for female adolescent students and 2.9% for male adolescent students (Rutsztein, Murawski, Elizathe, & Scappatura, 2010). The number of adolescents and young adults with eating disorders is alarming because eating disorders can lead to serious medical problems, and they have the highest fatality rate of any psychiatric disorder (Fichter & Quadflieg, 2016; Franko et al., 2013). Eating disorders are often enduring, can become disabling and costly (Striegel-Moore, Leslie, Petrill, Garvin, & Rosenheck, 2000), and place a high burden of care on families and health-care systems (Martin et al., 2015; Treasure et al., 2001).

Eating disorders (i.e., anorexia and bulimia) are the world's 12th leading cause of mental and physical health-related burdens as measured by premature-death rates combined with years lived with a disability due to illness (Erskine, Whiteford, & Pike, 2016). The health burden of eating disorders tends to be higher in youth and in high-income countries (Erskine et al., 2016). However, as low- and middle-income countries are influenced by the culture in higher-income countries, the global burden of eating disorders will likely rise and expand. How much of this burden can be avoided and relieved by effective prevention interventions? It is difficult to say.

In the past few decades, the field of eating-disorder prevention has expanded and become increasingly evidence-based. Prevention programs are intended to reduce eating-disorder behaviors, as well as reduce or stabilize the risk factors known to be associated with eating disorders. Common evidence-based risk factors for eating disorders include body satisfaction, negative affect, weight and shape concerns, obesity, depression, anxiety, self-esteem, body acceptance, drive for thinness, internalization of the thin ideal, disordered-eating behaviors, dieting, feelings of ineffectiveness, dietary inhibition, and perfectionism. Among these risk factors, body dissatisfaction is noted to be the most consistent and robust predictor of eating disorders (Neumark-Sztainer, Wall, Story, & Sherwood, 2009; Rohde, Stice, & Marti, 2015; Stice, Marti, & Durant, 2011). Most prevention interventions target multiple eating-disorder risks and maintaining factors in order to boost their overall effectiveness.

The current focus on risk-factor reduction remains popular because direct assessment of the impact of prevention programs on the development of full-blown eating disorders is cumbersome. Eating disorders develop over time in a small percentage of a much larger population potentially exposed to prevention programs. Investigations of new-onset cases require longitudinal follow-up of a large number of prevention-program participants, as well as their matched controls in order to have sufficient statistical power. Actual diagnosed cases are low in prevalence. It is for this reason that only a small percentage of randomized control trials have examined the impact of prevention programs on the onset of new eating disorders. Rather, the focus has most often been on more prevalent eating-disorder risk factors and eating-disorder behaviors (Le, Barendregt, Hay, & Mihalopoulos, 2017).

Prevention interventions, by today's standards, cannot be based on intuition about what would prevent eating disorders. Rather, systematic empirical investigation is needed to sort out effective from ineffective strategies. Meta-analyses by Stice and Shaw (2004), Stice, Shaw, and Marti (2007), Le et al. (2017), Watson et al. (2016), and others have focused on the efficacy of prevention programs for reducing eating-disorder risk factors and eating disorders. Interventions can be grouped into three major categories, as identified by Mrazek and Haggerty (1994): those that target general populations (*universal prevention programs*; Le et al., 2017; Levine, 2016; Watson et al., 2016), those that target selected at-risk populations (*selective prevention*; Le et al., 2017; Watson et al., 2016), and those that target populations already at high risk because they demonstrate eating-disorder behavior (*indicated prevention*; Le et al., 2017; Watson et al., 2016). It is simpler to study the impact of prevention programs on this last category of program participants, because the target population is already at risk for eating disorders and is therefore smaller and easier to follow over time (Cuijpers, 2003). On the other hand, the general problem remains that it is difficult to demonstrate when prevention programs prevent new cases of eating disorders. Theoretically, this remains the goal.

Watson et al. (2016) found about one-quarter of the prevention programs in the universal intervention category were directed toward teachers and health-care professionals. Fewer were directed toward college students, and the vast majority targeted school-age children – mostly those in middle school. Media literacy programs like MediaSmart (Wilksch & Wade, 2009a) were the most promising of these strategies (Le et al., 2017; Watson et al., 2016). Positive outcomes for mixed-sex adolescents have been found for shape and weight concern, body dissatisfaction, feeling ineffective, and depression (Wilksch & Wade, 2009b). Le et al. also determined that for universal interventions, media literacy programs were the most efficacious for reducing eating-disorder risk factors such as weight and shape concerns.

Stice et al. (2011) found, "Body dissatisfaction was the strongest predictor of risk for onset of any eating disorder; 24% of adolescent girls in the upper 24% of body dissatisfaction showed onset of any eating disorder versus 6% of those with less body dissatisfaction" (p. 625). Since body dissatisfaction is considered the major risk factor for eating disorders, it is a well-deserved target for prevention programs (Stice, 2002).

Body dissatisfaction is an especially important risk factor because we have known for some time in the US that this experience increases steadily with age. Look at the following statistics about girls in various age groups as reported in a press release by the National Eating Disorder Association (NEDA, 2013):

- 42% of 1st–3rd grade girls want to be thinner.
- 81% of 10-year-olds are afraid of being fat.
- 46% of 9- to 11-year-olds are "sometimes" or "very often" on diets and 82% of their families are "sometimes" or "very often" on diets.
- Over one-half of teenage girls and nearly one-third of teenage boys use unhealthy weight control behaviors such as skipping meals, fasting, smoking cigarettes, vomiting, and taking laxatives.
- 35–57% of adolescent girls engage in crash dieting, fasting, self-induced vomiting, diet pills, or laxatives.
- Overweight girls are more likely than normal-weight girls to engage in such extreme dieting.
- Even among clearly non-overweight girls, over one-third report dieting.
- 35% of "normal dieters" progress to pathological dieting. Of those, 20–25% progress to partial or full-syndrome eating disorders (para. 6).

As if these statistics about girls weren't enough to raise concerns, a recent study by Runfola et al. (2013) showed the ubiquitous presence of body dissatisfaction in older adult populations. Body dissatisfaction was measured by looking at the discrepancy between current and preferred body size. In a large sample of American women, 88–93% of women between the ages of 25 and 74 were dissatisfied with their current body size. It is no wonder that we are increasingly identifying eating disorders in mid-life and older men and woman (Bulik, 2013; Maine, Samuels, & Tantillo, 2015; Reas, & Stedal, 2015).

Popular media promotes discontent with current body size in favor of an ideal body size. Teaching media literacy is a useful way to reduce susceptibility to body dissatisfaction. McLean, Paxton, and Wertheim (2016b) describe aspects of teaching media literacy. For example, it trains young people how to process media presentations by showing them how to be skeptical about what the media presents, how to notice the positive and negative messages that come across, and how to discern the motives behind the ads. Further, young people can be taught not to identify with the ideal characters of advertising (e.g., models, singing stars) and to view their desirability with skepticism. They can learn critical-thinking skills, which allow them to step back and understand the purpose of media presentations so they can form their own independent thoughts and opinions. For example, it is known that in the advertising world, pictures of models are photoshopped to make their teeth whiter, their waists thinner, their muscles bigger (for men), their hair blonder, their hips smaller, and more. The marketing intent is to influence people to be dissatisfied with their own appearance and to aspire to what is presented in media. Teaching young people that media images are intended to sell and are often fake or unrealistic potentially reduces the credibility and influence of media messages. Parents and schools in particular are in a good position with children to debunk media influences, like thin idealization or muscle idealization.

The purpose of raising media literacy IQ in young people is to reduce media's negative influence on self-esteem and body esteem and to lower the pressure to conform to media ideals. This is done, in part, by attempting to reduce an internalization of media ideals. The reason prevention programs often target younger people is because fantasies like the thin or muscled ideal take root early and become accepted as a young person's personal standard. This in turn can lead to body dissatisfaction, excessive and competitive comparison with others' appearance, low self-esteem, and, ultimately, eating disorders. Although the influence of media-literacy interventions may not always directly reduce eating disorders, a systematic review of the impact of media literacy-based interventions (McLean, Paxton, & Wertheim, 2016a) has shown significant positive effects on skepticism about truth in media, media influence, awareness of advertising profit motives in media, and improvements in body-related variables such as drive for thinness in girls and boys (Golan, Hagay, & Tamir, 2013), thin-ideal internalization in girls (Richardson, Paxton, & Thomson, 2009), body size acceptance in girls (Neumark-Sztainer, Sherwood, Coller, & Hannan, 2000), and body satisfaction (Richardson et al., 2009).

Here are some tips for increasing media literacy:

1 Raise consciousness about size and weight prejudice. The message that thin or muscular (for boys), or both, is better, is ever-present in the media. Furthermore, body fat, in contrast to body thinness, is frequently associated with being lazy, undisciplined, and out of control. Researchers have shown that exposure to media ideals and size prejudice can increase body dissatisfaction (Rodgers, McLean, & Paxton, 2015), which can lead to eating disorders.
2 Talk about for-profit motives in the media. Expose marketing that encourages dissatisfaction with the self in order to promote deficit repair through advertised products (e.g., thin models advertising fashion that will slenderize the appearance of the body).
3 Promote skepticism about media realism (e.g., models are not, in reality, what they appear). Identify offensive media messages and complain to those who posted them.

4 Keep media ideals "externalized," or outside of the self. Think critically about media images and recognize that internalization of media ideals can be prevented. The internalization of socioculturally defined ideal-body types (thin or muscular) increases the risk of disordered eating by increasing the likelihood of low self-esteem, body dissatisfaction, and dieting. Champion media messages that promote body acceptance and realistic portrayals of body diversity, as well as media that promotes body functionality versus physical appearance. Our bodies are more than ornaments. Our arms allow us to hug those we love, and our hands allow us to help others.
5 Take responsibility for what you post online. Everyone who shares online can promote responsible media messages. For example, vow to not retouch photos of yourself to enhance your appearance (National Eating Disorders Association [NEDA], 2017).
6 Use the many digital and media-literacy resources available to the public. Several of these are referenced by NEDA at www.nationaleatingdisorders.org/sites/default/files/Toolkits/GetRealToolkit.pdf.

Weight-control behavior (e.g., dieting) is another important eating-disorder risk factor often targeted by prevention interventions. Dieting has long been found to be a risk factor for disordered eating. Neumark-Sztainer, Wall, Larson, Eisenberg, and Loth (2011) followed a large sample of adolescents into young adulthood and found dieting and disordered eating during teen years predicted the same behavior 10 years later. Goldschmidt, Wall, Choo, Becker, and Neumark-Sztainer (2016) found that dieting and body dissatisfaction were potent risk factors for disordered eating, as well as for becoming overweight and depressed. The researchers addressed the best ways to prevent dieting.

Le et al. (2017) found that multisession cognitive behavioral therapy (CBT) interventions targeting a selective audience of at-risk individuals (e.g., athletes, or those with some disordered-eating behaviors) had a positive effect on dieting outcome. CBT-informed prevention strategies seek to change eating-disorder related knowledge, attitudes, and behaviors. Unhelpful-thinking errors are identified, challenged, and changed. For example, the belief that "diet products are effective or they wouldn't be on the market" is a thinking error. A correction might be, "It is moderate exercise and balanced eating, not diet products, that lead to stable, healthy weight. Diet products can sometimes be harmful to health." Here are some tips for altering beliefs and attitudes about dieting borrowed from selective prevention programs:

1 Most who diet tend to regain their weight. First, diets, by definition, are temporary. Second, restricting intake results in the body compensating by slowing metabolism to conserve energy. Lower metabolism slows weight loss. Third, deprivation diets can lead to cycles of restricting, binge eating, guilt, and restricting again. Once a food is restricted because it is deemed fattening or unhealthy, the more likely it is that a craving for that food will develop.

2 Fad diets (e.g., low-carbohydrate, or high-protein diets) can lead to nutrient-intake imbalance and medical problems.
3 People who diet in the presence of other risk factors (i.e., genetic and psychosocial vulnerabilities) may be more likely to develop an eating disorder (Stice, Gau, Rohde, & Shaw, 2017), especially anorexia nervosa (Hilbert et al., 2014).
4 Intuitive eating, not dieting, is the most healthful approach to eating. It is the anti-diet approach. It is based on connecting to natural, internal body cues for eating – internal cues like hunger and satiety, taste, texture, sight, and smell. Dieting, on the other hand, is based on external cues for how and what to eat. These cues are frequently dictated by fad and weight-loss programs. It is important to note that individuals diagnosed with eating disorders may initially have difficulty with intuitive eating if they have lost a sense of satiety and hunger cues. The use of meal planning with an emphasis on renourishment versus a "diet" that deprives the body of nutrition is emphasized.
5 Help teens base self-esteem and esteem of others on factors other than body size, appearance, and shape in order to reduce their incentive to diet. Teens talk openly and enthusiastically about body shape and size. They are steeped in an Internet culture that promotes the thin ideal with pro-thin and pro-dieting images, blogs, chats, and websites. They associate a thin body with status, attractiveness, and popularity. As a result, valuation of self and others can be based primarily on weight and body size. This can lead to body teasing and bullying about shape and size. Bullying and teasing about appearance are known risk factors for teens to go on to develop unhealthy weight-control behaviors (Gonsalves, Hawk, & Goodenow, 2014; UConn Rudd Center for Food Policy & Obesity, 2017) and eating psychopathology (Matos, Ferreira, Duarte, & Pinto-Gouveia, 2015). In the face of weight prejudice, dieting becomes a justified and respected method of achieving an ideal body. Prevention programs are designed to reduce thin idealization, weight-related bullying and teasing, over-valuation of shape and weight, and dieting.
6 Parents and other adult role models can cultivate a positive body image in children to protect them from the desire to diet and the use of unhealthy weight-control behaviors such as fasting, vomiting, laxative use, and over-exercise. They are role models for children's relationships to their own bodies.

Parents and teachers can work hard to:

a Smile at themselves when they look in the mirror
b Point out ways in which their own bodies are strong and functional
c Talk openly about and celebrate their own intuitive eating
d Honor body diversity and body acceptance
e Have zero tolerance for weight prejudice.

Parents and other adult role models can work to *not*:

a Complain about their own bodies
b Talk about their own desires to diet
c Express prejudices against others who do not have a culturally determined ideal body type
d Divide foods into good and bad foods and complain that junk foods or bad foods will cause harmful weight gain and require self-punishment
e Communicate that a particular sport or activity should be avoided because a person's body doesn't look good enough or doesn't fit a certain profile.

Watson et al. (2016) found that for selective prevention programs (targeting higher-risk populations) there was strong evidence for the efficacy of dissonance-based interventions (DBI). His meta-analysis showed post-intervention outcomes lasting up to 12 months. Like CBT, this approach involves engaging participants in counter-attitudinal behavior exercises to reduce eating-disorder risk. For example, the Body Project, designed by Stice (Stice, Becker, & Yokum, 2013; Stice & Presnell, 2009; Stice, Rohde, & Shaw, 2013), is an empirically supported dissonance-based intervention designed to target thin-ideal internalization in young women. Interactive and presented over four one-hour sessions, it teaches participants to question media and popular thin-ideal messages. It engages them in verbal and behavioral exercises during which participants voluntarily and publicly express anti-thin-ideal views. Following known principles of social psychology, participants experience inner conflict and psychological discomfort when their inner beliefs supporting thin ideals are pitted against their public argument against those beliefs. This leads participants to change their beliefs in order to align with their public statements. An example of a dissonance-based exercise in the Body Project is writing a letter to an adolescent girl explaining why she should not pursue the thin ideal. Regarding the efficacy of the Body Project, Stice, Becker, and Yokum (2013) reported:

> At this point, it appears that the Body Project is the only eating-disorder prevention program that warrants the APA's designation as an efficacious intervention, which means that it (a) has been shown to produce statistically significant and clinically meaningful effects when recruitment and delivery are conducted by natural providers (e.g., teachers, counselors, peer leaders, etc.), as opposed to professional researchers, (b) has been found to significantly outperform active alternative prevention programs in multiple trials, and (c) has yielded positive effects for independent researchers.
>
> (p. 481)

Similarly, Becker, MacKenzie, and Stewart (2015) reported, "In summary, no other program has garnered more empirical support in reducing ED risk factors in both high- and mixed-risk adolescents and young adults than the Body Project" (p. 601).

In addition to the Body Project, media-literacy programs draw on dissonance-based interventions along, as previously noted, with CBT interventions. In sum, DBIs such as the Body Project have been shown to reduce thin-ideal internalization and related eating-disorder risk factors (e.g., body dissatisfaction, dieting, and eating-disorder symptoms; McMillan, Stice, & Rohde, 2011).

Communities are encouraged to host prevention programs like the Body Project (www.bodyprojectsupport.org). Combined evidence shows targeting high-risk populations, like young women and athletes, helps prevent dieting, body dissatisfaction, thin idealization, and eating-disorder behaviors such as fasting, unhealthy weight gain, and compensating for food indulgences with vomiting, laxative use, enemas, or over-exercise. Stice, Rohde, Durant, and Shaw (2012) and Stice, Durant, Rohde, and Shaw (2014) developed a prototype for an Internet-based dissonance-based program which, along with other Internet-based programs (e.g., the 8-week StudentBodies™ program; Beitner, Jacobi, & Taylor, 2012; Jacobi, Völker, Trockel, & Taylor, 2012) are easy-access tools for bringing empirically based prevention programs to groups, schools, and communities at a lower cost.

For those at higher risk for eating disorders, Watson et al. (2016) and Le et al. (2017) found that Healthy Weight programs also reduced eating-disorder risk factors. These selective prevention programs commonly target those with risk factors or sub-syndromal symptoms of eating disorders. Healthy Weight programs (e.g., Healthy Weight Intervention; Stice, Rohde, Shaw, & Marti, 2012; Stice, Shaw, Burton, & Wade, 2006) use the principles of behavior modification and teach participants about biological determinants of weight and body size (Stice et al., 2006). Originally conceived by Stice and colleagues as a control for the Body Project (Stice, Chase, Stormer, & Appel, 2001), Healthy Weight programs have been found to prevent eating disorders and lower risk factors (e.g., thin-ideal internalization, body dissatisfaction, and negative affect), binge eating, and unhealthy weight gain. They encourage long-term lifestyle changes based on balanced nutrition and exercise. For example, a Healthy Weight program might include information about the importance of managing hunger, satiety, and energy levels by eating a healthy combination of nutrients in three well-spaced, daily meals and snacks. Motivational interviewing is used in Healthy Weight programs to promote commitment to a healthy ideal (e.g., how will pursuing the healthy ideal help you achieve your personal life goals?). Participants are encouraged to problem solve and develop personalized plans about how they will achieve healthy eating and exercise.

The efficacy of Healthy Weight programs is consistent with findings by Haltom and associates (Haltom, Kaiser, & Osgood, 2016). In a sample of 324 college students, they found a significant negative correlation for females, but not for males, between exposure to media and education about healthy eating *and* body dissatisfaction and bulimic symptoms, as measured by the Eating Disorder Inventory-3 (EDI-3; Body Dissatisfaction and Bulimia subscales; Garner, 2004). In other words, the more education about healthy eating in college, the less likely students were to report negative body image and bulimic symptoms such as uncontrolled eating.

Haltom et al.'s (2016) data were also consistent with another finding reported in the meta-analyses of prevention research efficacy. For the purpose of eating-disorder prevention, education about healthy eating was superior to education about eating disorders. A first generation of eating-disorder prevention programs was largely psychoeducational (Pearson, Goldklang, & Striegel-Moore, 2002) and not efficacious in reducing eating-disorder risk factors, eating-disorder symptoms, or post-intervention eating disorders. A second generation of educational programs was successful in reducing risk factors, but not eating disorders. The third, current, generation of programs is characteristically multisession, interactive, nondidactic, and participant-driven, and they often include information about healthy eating. Third-generation prevention programs have been effective in reducing empirically validated risk factors, as well as eating-disorder onset. Unpublished data (Haltom et al., 2016) showed that among both male and female college students, exposure to education about eating disorders showed no association with a reduced drive for thinness, body dissatisfaction, or bulimia as measured by the EDI-3. However, as already noted, there was a significant negative relationship between education about healthy eating *and* body dissatisfaction and bulimia behaviors as measured on the EDI-3.

Here are some tips for prevention adapted from healthy weight programs:

1. See food as enjoyable. It is to be tasted, savored, and enjoyed. It is not the enemy. Don't let it produce guilt based on do's and don'ts related to weight management.
2. Avoid seeing food as good or bad, healthy or unhealthy. Allow a wide variety of foods into your home. Make, serve, and ingest a wide and balanced variety of foods, eating them in moderation.
3. Avoid using food to reward or punish. Food can take on positive or negative associations unrelated to natural body cues. This can interfere with eating in response to natural sensory cues.
4. Instead of seeking an ideal body weight, live without pursuit of weight. Natural weight is a range largely determined by genetics. Accepting a genetically determined body means letting go of trying to manipulate its size and shape.
5. Eat breakfast followed by lunch and dinner at regular intervals during the day. Include intermittent snacks. The right balance of fats, carbohydrates, and protein at each meal will keep energy levels elevated evenly across the day. Skipping meals and restricting intake lowers metabolic rate, which decreases energy and causes weight gain. Restricting intake can also lead to excessive hunger and over-consumption of food later on.
6. Eat in response to natural body cues for hunger and fullness. Unless you are on a prescribed diet for medical reasons, allow hunger and satiety cues to guide when, where, and what to eat. Eat when you are hungry and stop

when you are full. Eat for pleasure and comfort sometimes, but be careful not to develop a pattern of using food to avoid, mute, or numb emotional states. Claire's story exemplifies regularly eating to cope with feelings of being overwhelmed and anxious related to a difficult adjustment to freshman year in college. Claire was self-medicating and self-regulating with food. During recovery, she learned alternate strategies for coping with negative emotions.

Le et al. (2017) found no indicated prevention programs (programs geared specifically to those with eating-disorder symptoms) to be effective in reducing eating-disorder risk factors. However, Watson et al. (2016) reported indicated prevention programs based on CBT, DBI, media literacy, mirror exposure, and at least one other program, albeit based on a limited numbers of trials, were at least somewhat effective in reducing risk factors. It stands to reason that sick populations might receive the same prevention interventions as populations receiving universal, selective, and indicated interventions, because they are at risk for succumbing to eating-disorder maintenance and relapse factors. For example, in her recovery, May learned skills to tolerate "big emotions" and distresses without vomiting. Nick learned that the eating disorder had him believing in the thin ideal. Maeve and her mother came to understand the impact of their poor body image and restrictive eating. All of these gains made in recovery can be toppled by exposure to risk factors – like negative affect for Tara, media exposure to the thin ideal for Nick, and temptation to restrict to feel good for Maeve and her mother. Learning prevention messages about media literacy, body acceptance, healthy eating, and healthy weight improves the chances of recognizing and ameliorating the impact of relapse triggers. While further research is needed to determine if prevention programs reduce the onset of new eating disorders, more research is also needed to determine the impact of various prevention interventions on the course of eating-disorder treatment and recovery.

All in all, prevention interventions have evolved in the past few decades into increasingly effective, targeted programs for a continuum of populations ranging from those in the general population to those already demonstrating eating-disorder symptoms. As Levine (2015) noted, "Since 2000 there has been significant progress in understanding the components of eating disorders (EDs) prevention: clarification of risk factors → design innovation → field research → program dissemination (Becker, Stice, Shaw, & Woda, 2009; Wilksch, 2014)" (p. 2). Meta-analyses have helped clinicians, planners, and policy makers pinpoint prevention programs that have the strongest research support and thus should be disseminated for reduction of eating-disorder risk factors and new-onset cases. Efforts to boost the prevention power of established interventions is ongoing. Meanwhile, as promising research continues, the public-health burden for eating disorders is still high. We remain hopeful for improved, evidence-based prevention interventions that are directed toward a wide variety of populations and community environments. We join those advocating for programs that target multiple, empirically identified, eating-disorder risk factors, as well as eating-disorder symptoms.

References

Allen, K. L., Oddy, W. H., Byrne, S. M., & Crosby, R. D. (2013). DSM-IV-TR and *DSM*-5 eating disorders in adolescents: Prevalence, stability, and psychosocial correlates in a population-based sample of male and female adolescents. *Journal of Abnormal Psychology*, 122(3), 720–732.

Becker, C., MacKenzie, K., & Stewart, T. (2015). Cognitive and behavioral approaches to the prevention of eating disorders. In L. Smolak & M. P. Levine (Eds.), *The Wiley handbook of eating disorders* (pp. 597–609). Hoboken, NJ: John Wiley.

Becker, C. B., Stice, E., Shaw, H., & Woda, S. (2009). Use of empirically supported interventions for psychopathology: Can the participatory approach move us beyond the research-to-practice gap? *Behaviour Research and Therapy*, 47(4), 265–274.

Beintner, I., Jacobi, C., & Taylor, C. B. (2012). Effects of an Internet-based prevention programme for eating disorders in the USA and Germany: A meta-analytic review. *European Eating Disorders Review*, 20(1), 1–8.

Bulik, C. M. (2013). *Midlife eating disorders.* New York, NY: Walker.

Cuijpers, P. (2003). Examining the effects of prevention programs on the incidence of new cases of mental disorders: The lack of statistical power. *American Journal of Psychiatry*, 160(8), 1385–1391.

Erskine, H. E., Whiteford, H. A., & Pike, K. M. (2016). The global burden of eating disorders. *Current Opinion in Psychiatry*, 29(6), 346–353.

Fichter, M. M., & Quadflieg, N. (2016). Mortality in eating disorders: Results of a large prospective clinical longitudinal study. *International Journal of Eating Disorders*, 49(4), 391–401.

Franko, D. L., Keshaviah, A., Eddy, K. T., Krishna, M., Davis, M. C., Keel, P. K., & Herzog, D. B. (2013). A longitudinal investigation of mortality in anorexia nervosa and bulimia nervosa. *American Journal of Psychiatry*, 170(8), 917–925.

Garner, D. M. (2004). *Eating disorder inventory-3 (EDI-3). Professional manual.* Odessa, FL: Psychological Assessment Resources.

Golan, M., Hagay, N., & Tamir, S. (2013). The effect of "In favor of myself": Preventive program to enhance positive self and body image among adolescents. *PLoS ONE*, 8(11), e78223.

Goldschmidt, A. B., Wall, M., Choo, T.-H. J., Becker, C., & Neumark-Sztainer, D. (2016). Shared risk factors for mood-, eating-, and weight-related health outcomes. *Health Psychology*, 35(3), 245–252.

Gonsalves, D., Hawk, H., & Goodenow, C. (2014). Unhealthy weight control behaviors and related risk factors in Massachusetts middle and high school students. *Maternal and Child Health Journal*, 18(8), 1803–1813.

Haltom, C., Kaiser, E., & Osgood, L. (2016). Relationship between college lifestyle variables and drive for thinness, bulimia, and body dissatisfaction as measured by the Eating Disorder Inventory-3. Unpublished raw data.

Hilbert, A., Pike, K., Goldschmidt, A., Wilfley, D., Fairburn, C., Dohm, F.-A., … Weissman, R. S. (2014). Risk factors across the eating disorders. *Psychiatry Research*, 220(1–2), 500–506.

Hudson, J. I., Hiripi, E., Pope, H. G., & Kessler, R. C. (2007). The prevalence and correlates of eating disorders in the national comorbidity survey replication. *Biological Psychiatry*, 61, 348–358.

Jacobi, C., Völker, U., Trockel, M. T., & Taylor, C. B. (2012). Effects of an Internet-based intervention for subthreshold eating disorders: A randomized controlled trial. *Behaviour Research and Therapy*, 50(2), 93–99.

Le, L. K. D., Barendregt, J. J., Hay, P., & Mihalopoulos, C. (2017). Prevention of eating disorders: A systematic review and meta-analysis. *Clinical Psychology Review*, 53, 46–58.

Levine, M. P. (2015). Current status of eating disorder prevention research. In T. D. Wade (Ed.), *Encyclopedia of feeding and eating disorders* (pp. 1–6). Sydney, Australia: Springer.

Levine, M. P. (2016). Universal prevention of eating disorders: A concept analysis. *Eating Behaviors*, 25, 4–8.

Maine, M. D., Samuels, K. L., & Tantillo, M. (2015). Eating disorders in adult women: Biopsychosocial, developmental, and clinical considerations. *Advances in Eating Disorders: Theory, Research and Practice*, 3(2), 133–143.

Martín, J., Padierna, A., van Wijngaarden, B., Aguirre, U., Anton, A., Muñoz, P., & Quintana, J. M. (2015). Caregivers consequences of care among patients with eating disorders, depression or schizophrenia. *BMC Psychiatry*, 15, 124.

Matos, M., Ferreira, C., Duarte, C., & Pinto-Gouveia, J. (2015). Eating disorders: When social rank perceptions are shaped by early shame experiences. *Psychology and Psychotherapy: Theory, Research and Practice*, 88(1), 38–53.

McLean, S. A., Paxton, S. J., & Wertheim, E. H. (2016a). The measurement of media literacy in eating disorder risk factor research: Psychometric properties of six measures. *Journal of Eating Disorders*, 4(1), 30.

McLean, S. A., Paxton, S. J., & Wertheim, E. H. (2016b). The role of media literacy in body dissatisfaction and disordered eating: A systematic review. *Body Image*, 19, 9–23.

McMillan, W., Stice, E., & Rohde, P. (2011). High- and low-level dissonance-based eating disorder prevention programs with young women with body image concerns: An experimental trial. *Journal of Consulting and Clinical Psychology*, 79(1), 129–134.

Mrazek, P. J., & Haggerty, R. J. (Eds.). (1994). *Reducing risks for mental disorders: Frontiers for preventive intervention research*. Washington, DC: National Academy Press.

National Eating Disorders Association. (2013). NEDA applauds Massachusetts for discontinuing controversial 'Fat Letters': At least 19 states currently send home BMI reports. Retrieved from www.nationaleatingdisorders.org/neda-applauds-massachusetts-discontinuing-controversial-'fat-letters'

National Eating Disorders Association. (2017). Get REAL! about media and body image. Northridge: California State University. Retrieved from www.nationaleatingdisorders.org/sites/default/files/Toolkits/GetRealToolkit.pdf

Neumark-Sztainer, D., Sherwood, N., Coller, T., & Hannan, P. J. (2000). Primary prevention of disordered eating among preadolescent girls: Feasibility and short-term effect of a community-based intervention. *Journal of the American Dietetic Association*, 100(12), 1466–1473

Neumark-Sztainer, D., Wall, M., Larson, N. I., Eisenberg, M. E., & Loth, K. (2011). Dieting and disordered eating behaviors from adolescence to young adulthood: Findings from a 10-year longitudinal study. *Journal of the American Dietetic Association*, 111(7), 1004–1011.

Neumark-Sztainer, D., Wall, M., Story, M., & Sherwood, N. E. (2009). Five-year longitudinal predictive factors for disordered eating in a population-based sample of overweight adolescents: Implications for prevention and treatment. *International Journal of Eating Disorders*, 42(7), 664–672.

Pearson, J., Goldklang, D., & Striegel-Moore, R. H. (2002). Prevention of eating disorders: Challenges and opportunities. *International Journal of Eating Disorders*, 31(3), 233–239.

Reas, D. L., & Stedal, K. (2015). Eating disorders in men aged midlife and beyond. *Maturitas*, 81(2), 248–255.

Richardson, S. M., Paxton, S. J., & Thomson, J. (2009). Is BodyThink an efficacious body image and self-esteem program? A controlled evaluation with adolescents. *Body Image*, 6(2), 75–82.

Rodgers, R. F., McLean, S. A., & Paxton, S. J. (2015). Longitudinal relationships among internalization of the media ideal, peer social comparison, and body dissatisfaction: Implications for the tripartite influence model. *Developmental Psychology*, 51(5), 706–713.

Rohde, P., Stice, E., & Marti, C. N. (2015). Development and predictive effects of eating disorder risk factors during adolescence: Implications for prevention efforts. *International Journal of Eating Disorders*, 48(2), 187–198.

Runfola, C. D., Von Holle, A., Trace, S. E., Brownley, K. A., Hofmeier, S. M., Gagne, D. A., & Bulik, C. M. (2013), Body dissatisfaction in women across the lifespan: Results of the UNC-SELF and Gender and Body Image (GABI) studies. *European Eating Disorders Review*, 21(1), 52–59.

Rutsztein, G., Murawski, B., Elizathe, L., & Scappatura, M. L. (2010). Trastornos alimentarios: Detección en adolescents mujeres y varones de Buenos Aires. Un studio de doble fase [Eating disorders: Detection in female and male adolescents in Buenos Aires. A two-stage study]. *Mexican Journal of Eating Disorders*, 1, 48–61.

Stice, E. (2002). Risk and maintenance factors for eating pathology: A meta-analytic review. *Psychological Bulletin*, 128(5), 825–848.

Stice, E., & Shaw, H. (2004). Eating disorder prevention programs: A meta-analytic review. *Psychological Bulletin*, 130(2), 206–227.

Stice, E., & Presnell, K. (2009). *The body project: Promoting body acceptance and preventing eating disorders: Facilitator guide.* New York, NY: Oxford University Press.

Stice, E., Becker, C. B., & Yokum, S. (2013). Eating disorder prevention: Current evidence-base and future directions. *International Journal of Eating Disorders*, 46(5), 478–485.

Stice, E., Chase, A., Stormer, S., & Appel, A. (2001). A randomized trial of a dissonance-based eating disorder prevention program. *International Journal of Eating Disorders*, 29(3), 247–262.

Stice, E., Durant, S., Rohde, P., & Shaw, H. (2014). Effects of a prototype Internet dissonance-based eating disorder prevention program at 1- and 2-year follow-up. *Health Psychology*, 33(12), 1558–1567.

Stice, E., Gau, J. M., Rohde, P., & Shaw, H. (2017). Risk factors that predict future onset of each *DSM*-5 eating disorder: Predictive specificity in high-risk adolescent females. *Journal of Abnormal Psychology*, 126(1), 38. doi:10.1037/abn0000219

Stice, E., Marti, C. N., & Durant, S. (2011). Risk factors for onset of eating disorders: Evidence of multiple risk pathways from an 8-year prospective study. *Behaviour Research and Therapy*, 49(10), 622–627.

Stice, E., Marti, C. N., & Rohde, P. (2013). Prevalence, incidence, impairment, and course of the proposed *DSM*-5 eating disorder diagnoses in an 8-year prospective community study of young women. *Journal of Abnormal Psychology*, 122(2), 445–457.

Stice, E., Rohde, P., Durant, S., & Shaw, H. (2012). A preliminary trial of a prototype Internet dissonance-based eating disorder prevention program for young women with body image concerns. *Journal of Consulting and Clinical Psychology*, 80(5), 907–916.

Stice, E., Rohde, P., & Shaw, H. (2013). *The Body Project: A dissonance-based eating disorder prevention intervention*. Oxford, UK: Oxford University Press.

Stice, E., Rohde, P., Shaw, H., & Marti, N. (2012). Efficacy trial of a selected prevention program targeting both eating disorder symptoms and unhealthy weight gain among female college students. *Journal of Consulting and Clinical Psychology*, 80(1), 164–170.

Stice, E., Shaw, H., Burton, E., & Wade, E. (2006). Dissonance and healthy weight eating disorder prevention programs: A randomized efficacy trial. *Journal of Consulting and Clinical Psychology*, 74(2), 263–275.

Stice, E., Shaw, H., & Marti, C. N. (2007). A meta-analytic review of eating disorder prevention programs: Encouraging findings. *Annual Review of Clinical Psychology*, 3(1), 207–231.

Striegel-Moore, R. H., Leslie, D., Petrill, S. A., Garvin, V., & Rosenheck, R. A. (2000). One-year use and cost of inpatient and outpatient services among female and male patients with an eating disorder: Evidence from a national database of health insurance claims. *International Journal of Eating Disorders*, 27(4), 381–389.

Treasure, J., Murphy, T., Szmukler, G., Todd, G., Gavan, K., & Joyce, J. (2001). The experience of caregiving for severe mental illness: A comparison between anorexia nervosa and psychosis. *Social Psychiatry Psychiatric Epidemiology*, 36, 343–347.

UConn Rudd Center for Food Policy & Obesity. (2017). Weight bias & stigma > weight stigmatization in youth. Retrieved from www.uconnruddcenter.org/weight-bias-stigma-weight-stigmatization-in-youth

Watson, H. J., Joyce, T., French, E., Willan, V., Kane, R. T., Tanner-Smith, E. E., … Egan, S. J. (2016). Prevention of eating disorders: A systematic review of randomized, controlled trials. *International Journal of Eating Disorders*, 49(9), 833–862.

Wilksch, S. M. (2014). Where did universal eating disorder prevention go? *Eating Disorders: The Journal of Treatment & Prevention*, 22(2), 184–192.

Wilksch, S. M., & Wade, T. D. (2009a). *MediaSmart*. Adelaide, Australia: Flinders University.

Wilksch, S. M., & Wade, T. D.(2009b). Reduction of shape and weight concern in young adolescents: A 30-month controlled evaluation of a media literacy program. *Journal of the American Academy of Child and Adolescent Psychiatry*, 48(6), 652–661.

Index

abusive dating relationships (or intimate partner abuse/violence) x, 97, 98, 113, 114
Academy for Eating Disorders 86
Acute Stress Disorder 106
adolescent social anxiety 101
alcohol abuse: and anxiety 37–38; College Alcohol Problem Scale – Revised 38; and cyber-addiction 37
Alcohol Use Disorder, Mild viii, 39
alexithymia 8, 139
Ali, K. 116
American College of Sports Medicine, Female Athlete Triad 22
American Psychiatric Association, *Diagnostic and statistical manual of mental disorders* (5th ed.) *see DSM*-5 (American Psychiatric Association)
Andersen, K. K. 164
animal metaphors (for carer styles) 19, 108–109, 115, 163
Anna: case study overview ix; characteristics of Anna's story 71–72; FBT (Family Based Treatment), advantages and overview 72–73, 79; FBT, Phase I 80–86; FBT, Phase II 86–87, 89, 91, 92; FBT, Phase III 87–88; FBT and parental control of adolescent eating (question and answer 2) 90–91; FBT and return of eating-disorder symptoms (question and answer 3) 91–92; FBT and role of pediatrician (question and answer 1) 88–90; healthy-weight range arguments 85–86; laxative abuse and self-induced vomiting 73–74; parents' reaction and role 71–73, 77–80, 81–83, 84, 85, 86–87, 88; perfectionism and practicing being imperfect 87–88; perfectionism and pursuit of ideal body 74–75; refeeding syndrome 80–81; resistance to treatment 78–79; sister's reaction and role 80, 83–84; stimulant laxatives 76, 78; strategies to restrict food and exercise 75–76
anorexia nervosa: and alexithymia 8; and anxiety 56; and caregiver skills 18–20; and cognitive functioning 65; and cognitive-interpersonal maintenance model 18; and emotions 7–8, 20–21; and FBT treatment success rate 89; and fear of meals 13; and food avoidance as way to reduce anxiety 4; and gastroparesis 16; and genes 148; and increased sensitivity to criticism 4; inpatient care treatment 14; of mothers and impact on children 155; and Multi-Family Group Therapy 50; and neural networks 78; onset median age range 170; and perfectionism 3–5, 108; prevalence data vii, 137; seeking treatment vii
Anorexia Nervosa: Binge Eating/Purging Type viii, ix, 56, 78
Anorexia Nervosa, Restricting type viii, 11–12
antidepressant medication 18, 37, 38; fluoxetine (Prozac) 18, 112
anxiety: and alcohol abuse 37–38; anxiety-reducing medication 18; and ARFID/anorexia nervosa 56; and binge eating 37; and eating disorders vii, 149–150; felt by parents 19; and FOMO (fear of missing out) 32; and Interpersonal Psychotherapy (IPT) 39; and perfectionism 148–149; sports and anxiety management 152; and

starvation 4, 16; *see also* social anxiety; Social Anxiety Disorder
ARFID (Avoidant/Restrictive Food Intake Disorder) viii, 56
Arroyo, A. 164
athletes *see* coaches; sports
Attachment-Based Family Therapy (ABFT) 92
Avoidant/Restrictive Food Intake Disorder (ARFID) viii, 56
Avrin, Judy, *Someday Melissa* (documentary film) 73

Bailer, U. F. 4, 78
Balantekin, K. N. 125
Barnes, R. D. 137
Beck Depression Inventory-II (BDI-II) 35, 36–37
Becker, C. B. 174, 176
Berge, J. M. 139
Bhatnagar, K. 92
binge eating: and anxiety 37; and emotional dysregulation 46–47; health risks 23; how to avoid in college 46–47; and mood regulation 128–129; *see also* Anorexia Nervosa: Binge Eating/Purging Type; Binge Eating Disorder (BED); binge eating disorders; bulimia nervosa; Bulimia Nervosa, Moderate; emotional eating; self-induced vomiting
Binge Eating Disorder (BED) x, 46, 131, 132–133, 136–138, 139, 170
binge eating disorders: and obesity 138; prevalence rates among college students 46; prevalence rates for adolescents vii; seeking treatment vii; seriousness of compared to anorexia and bulimia 136–138
Binge-Eating Scale (BES) 132
Birch, L. L. 125
Bish, C. 126
blind weights 37
body dissatisfaction: body checking behaviors 74; from childhood into young adulthood 98; and college lifestyles 39–41; and communication between mothers and daughters 164–165; and fat prejudice 100; and fat talk 9–11, 150–151; and gender 126–127; and media ideals 173–174; NEDA statistics re. body dissatisfaction among girls 172; and objectification of body/idealized model of beauty 98–100, 103; in older adult populations 172; and perfectionism 74–75, 107–108; as predictor of eating disorders 171, 172; and self-starvation/binge eating cycle 129–130; and weight bias/stigma 123, 127–128; *see also* thin idealization; thinspirational images; weight; weight-management behaviors
The Body Project 124, 176–177
Brown, H. 4, 78
Bulik, C. M. 154
bulimia nervosa: and cardiovascular risk 23; and Cognitive Behavior Therapy (CBT-A) x, 110–111, 113; and college lifestyles 39–41; and diuretic abuse 32–33; and family involvement in treatment 111; and food intake control 112; and Interpersonal Psychotherapy (IPT) 39, 41–43; and laxative abuse 32, 33, 37, 41–43, 44, 73–74; medical sequelae of 105; onset median age range 170; and perfectionism 3; prevalence data vii, 136; and Prozac (fluoxetine) 112; seeking treatment vii; and sports practice 21; stable health diagnosis and withdrawal from sports participation 22–23
Bulimia Nervosa, Moderate viii, x, 34, 37, 39, 105
bullying 55, 122, 129, 150, 175

Cai, Z. 131
CAPS (Counseling and Psychological Services) viii, 35–36
cardiovascular risk, and bulimia nervosa 23
care *see* caregiver skills; treatment
caregiver skills: animal metaphors for carer styles 19, 108–109, 115, 163; and anorexia nervosa 18–20; and Dialectical Behavior Therapy 109–110; and emotional eating 138–140; Experienced Carers Helping Others (ECHO) 115–116; and Multi-Family Group Therapy 61, 67–68; and need to restrain from expressing anger/frustration 114–116; *see also* parents
case studies: aim and methodology vii; *see also* Anna; Claire; Emma; Julie; Maeve; May; Nick
CBT *see* Cognitive Behavior Therapy (CBT)

Chang, J. C. 114
Choo, T.-H. J. 174
Claire: case study overview viii; characteristics of Claire's story 28–32; college lifestyles and bulimia 39–41; comfort food, diuretic/laxative abuse and bulimia nervosa 32–33; depression and Beck Depression Inventory-II (BDI-II) 35, 36–37; depression and counseling 34–37; depression and drinking problem 37–38; diagnosis Alcohol Use Disorder, Mild 39; diagnosis Bulimia Nervosa, Moderate 34, 37, 39; diagnosis Major Depressive Episode, Moderate 34, 37, 39; FOMO (fear of missing out) 32; Interpersonal Psychotherapy 39, 41–43; Motivational Interviewing 36, 39, 41; online thinspiration activity 40; question and answer 1: sustaining eating disorder recovery and independence in college 44–45; question and answer 2: avoiding freshman weight gain 45–46; question and answer 3: avoiding binge eating 46–47; recovery 43–44; relationship with mother 42, 43; SCOFF questionnaire 35–36; secret life of weight management 33–34
Clausen, L. 68
Coach & Athletic Trainer Toolkit (National Eating Disorder Association) 11
coaches: coach-athlete conflict and eating disorders 24; influence of and body dissatisfaction 9–10, 11; ways of helping athletes with eating disorders 23; *see also* sports
Cognitive Behavior Therapy (CBT): CBT skills and binge eating 47; CBT-A for adolescents with bulimia x, 110–111, 113; CBT-Enhanced for eating disorders (CBT-E) x, 39, 134–136; for correction of nutrition misconceptions 159, 160; and indicated prevention programs 179; for social anxiety treatment 159; for weight-control behavior correction 174–176; *see also* dissonance-based interventions (DBI)
cognitive functioning, and anorexia nervosa 65
cognitive-interpersonal maintenance model, and anorexia nervosa 18
College Alcohol Problem Scale – Revised 38
college students: avoiding binge eating 46–47; avoiding freshman weight gain (Freshman 15) 45–46; binge-eating disorder prevalence rates 46; college lifestyle and drive for thinness/bulimia/body dissatisfaction 39–41; eating disorder prevalence rates 37; Freshman 15 fears 32, 35; sustaining eating disorder recovery and independence in college 44–45
Combs, J. L. 128
comfort food 32, 114, 140, 179; *see also* emotional eating
co-morbidity, between eating and other psychiatric disorders vii
compulsive exercise: Compulsive Exercise Test 22; and risk of eating disorder 21–22; *see also* sports
continuum of care 15, 17
Costin, C. 100
Counseling and Psychological Services (CAPS) viii, 35–36
cross-country culture 9–10
Cruwys, T. 151
Curioni, C. C. 130
cutting 102–103, 113; *see also* self-harm behaviors
Cwikel, J. 164
cyber-addiction: and eating disorders 37, 40; *see also* Internet

dating, abusive dating relationships (or intimate partner abuse/violence) x, 97, 98, 113, 114
depression: Beck Depression Inventory-II (BDI-II) 35, 36–37; and cyber-addiction 37; and drinking problem 38; and Interpersonal Psychotherapy 39; and intimate partner abuse 97; Reynolds Adolescent Depression Inventory-2 (RADS-2) 106; *see also* Major Depressive Disorder, Moderate; Major Depressive Disorder, Single Episode, Moderate With Anxious Distress
Dialectical Behavior Therapy (DBT) x, 47, 92, 109–110
Diamond, G. S. 92
Dias, K. 100
diet industry: and weight bias/stigma 130–131; *see also* weight-management behaviors

dissonance-based interventions (DBI) 176–177, 179
diuretics, abuse of and bulimia nervosa 32–33
dopamine system 4, 97, 139, 148
drinking *see* alcohol abuse; Alcohol Use Disorder
DSM-5 (American Psychiatric Association): Acute Stress Disorder 106; Alcohol Use Disorder, Mild viii, 39; Anorexia Nervosa: Binge Eating/Purging Type viii, ix, 56, 78; Anorexia Nervosa, Restricting type viii, 11–12; Avoidant/Restrictive Food Intake Disorder (ARFID) viii, 56; Binge Eating Disorder (BED) x, 46, 131, 132–133, 136–138, 139, 170; Bulimia Nervosa, Moderate viii, x, 34, 37, 39, 105; Major Depressive Disorder, Moderate viii, 34, 37, 39; Major Depressive Disorder, Single Episode, Moderate With Anxious Distress x, 106; Nonsuicidal Self-Injury Disorder (NSSID) 102–103; Obsessive Compulsive Disorder 53, 56, 57, 58; Other Specified Feeding or Eating Disorder (OSFED) xi, 156–157; Posttraumatic Stress Disorder 106; Social Anxiety Disorder 159
Durant, S. 177

Eating Disorder Inventory-3 (EDI-3) 39–40, 105, 177, 178
eating disorders: and alexithymia 8, 139; and anxiety vii, 149–150; causes and functions of 100; and coach-athlete conflict 24; and Cognitive Behavior Therapy (CBT-E) x, 39, 134–136; co-morbidity with other psychiatric disorders vii; and cyber-addiction 37, 40; and dietary restraint 125–126, 131–132; diseases of disconnection and isolation 162; and environmental factors 150; and expressed emotion (EE) 163; and gender 59–60, 132–133, 170; and genes 148, 150, 161–162; and intimate partner abuse/violence 114; and laboratory test stable health indicators 22–23; maternal eating disorders 147–149, 152–156, 163; and perfectionism 3–5, 107–108; prevalence rates among college students 37; prevalence rates for adolescents vii, 170; recovery from and independence in college 44–45; risk factors 170–171; risk of and sports practice 21–22; stigmatization of 162; unmet treatment needs among teens vii, 116; and vegetarianism 6; *see also* caregiver skills; preventing eating disorders; treatment
ECHO (Experienced Carers Helping Others) 115–116
Egan, S. J. 150
Eisenberg, D. 37
Eisenberg, M. E. 174
Eisler, I. 68
electrolyte imbalance 23, 33, 37, 73, 106
emetaphobia 32
Emma: case study overview x; characteristics of Emma's story 122–124; Cognitive Behavior Therapy-Enhanced for eating disorders (CBT-E) 134–136; diagnosis Binge-Eating Disorder (BED) 131, 132–133; dietary restraint and eating disorders 125–126, 131–132; gender and body dissatisfaction 126–127; mood regulation and binge eating 128–129; negative urgency and negative emotions 129; parents' reaction and role 124–125, 126–128, 130–132, 133–135, 136; question and answer 1: seriousness of binge eating compared to anorexia and bulimia 136–138; question and answer 2: relationship between obesity and binge eating disorder 138; question and answer 3: emotional eating coping strategies 138–140; self-starvation/binge-eating cycle and body dissatisfaction 129–130; weight bias and body dissatisfaction 123, 127–128; weight bias and diet industry 130–131; weight teasing 130
emotional eating 138–140, 179
emotions: alexithymia 8, 139; and anorexia 7–8, 20–21; emotional dysregulation and binge-eating problems 46–47; emotion-numbing and weight-management behaviors 43; expressed emotion (EE) 163; and human energy 10; negative urgency and negative emotions 129
energy, and emotions 10

environmental factors 150
epigenetics 150
Experienced Carers Helping Others (ECHO) 115–116
expressed emotion (EE) 163

Fairburn, C. G. 134
Families Empowered and Supporting Treatment of Eating Disorders (F.E. A.S.T.) 43, 88, 136
Family Based Treatment (FBT): advantages of 72–73; compared with CBT-A 111; Family Meal goals 82; limitations of approach 15; Phase I 80–86; Phase II 86–87, 89, 91, 92; Phase III 87–88; rate of success with anorexia nervosa 89; and restrictive-eating disorders 158; and return of eating-disorder symptoms 91–92; role of parents/carers 13, 79, 90–91, 115; role of pediatricians 88–90; *see also* Attachment-Based Family Therapy (ABFT); Multi-Family Group Therapy (MFGT)
family DBT-skills 109–110; *see also* Dialectical Behavior Therapy (DBT)
Fan, X. 131
fashion models, weight of 124
fat prejudice 100
fat talk, and body dissatisfaction 9–11, 150–151
FBT *see* Family Based Treatment (FBT)
F.E.A.S.T. (Families Empowered and Supporting Treatment of Eating Disorders) 43, 88, 136
fear of missing out (FOMO) 32
feeding styles (of parents) 154–155
feelings *see* emotions
Female Athlete Triad (American College of Sports Medicine) 22
fluoxetine (Prozac) 18, 112
FOMO (fear of missing out) 32
freshman weight gain (Freshman 15) 32, 35; how to avoid 45–46

gastroparesis 16, 18
gender: and body dissatisfaction 126–127; and eating disorders 59–60, 132–133, 170
genes, and eating disorders 148, 150, 161–162
Gerke, C. K. 154
Goldschmidt, A. B. 174
Grilo, C. M. 137
group therapy: and danger of contagious behavior 66–67; and feeling of embarrassment 67–68; *see also* Multi-Family Group Therapy (MFGT)

Haggerty, R. J. 171
Haltom, C. 39–40, 177–178
He, J. 131
Healthy Weight programs 177–179
Hibbs, R. 18, 115
Hoiles, K. J. 150
Hollesen, A. 68
Hopf, R. B. 92
Hoste, R. R. 92

idealization *see* muscle idealization; thin idealization
inpatient care treatment: vs. outpatient treatment 14, 15; resistance to hospitalization 15–17
Internet: cyber-addiction 37, 40; and pro-thin/pro-dieting culture 32, 99, 107, 149, 151, 152, 175; *see also* media literacy programs
Interpersonal Psychotherapy (IPT) viii, 39, 41, 134; IPT-BN (m) for bulimic spectrum disorders 41–43
intimate partner abuse/violence (or abusive dating relationships) x, 97, 98, 113, 114
isolation: and eating disorders 162; and starvation 7

Johnson, W. G. 137
Jowett, S. 24
Julie: case study overview vii–viii; characteristics of Julie's story 1–3; cognitive-interpersonal maintenance model 18; continuum of care 15, 17; diagnosis Anorexia Nervosa, Restricting type 11–12; emotions and alexithymia 7–8, 20–21; Family Based Treatment (FBT) 13, 15; gastroparesis 16, 18; inpatient vs. outpatient care 14, 15; parents' reaction and role 5, 11, 12–16, 17, 18–21; perfectionism and anorexia 3–5; question and answer 1: sports practice and risk of eating disorder 21–22; question and answer 2: sports participation, bulimia nervosa and stable health diagnosis 22–23; question and answer 3: coach-athlete conflict and eating disorders 24;

recovery 18, 20–21; refeeding syndrome 13; relationship with coach 5–6, 7, 8–9, 11; resistance to hospitalization 15–17; resistance to recovery 12–15, 17–18; running, healthy eating and body dissatisfaction 9–11; safety behaviors 6–7; starvation and isolation 7; vegetarianism and eating disorders 6

Kaiser, E. 39–40, 177–178
Katzman, D. K. 14, 84, 88–89
Kaye, W. H. 4, 78, 112, 155
Kessler, R. C. 137
Kirk, A. A. 137
Kittel, R. 139
Klabunde, M. 4, 78

laboratory tests, stable health indicators and eating disorders 22–23
Larson, N. I. 174
Latimer, L. A. 139
laxatives: abuse of and bulimia nervosa 32, 33, 37, 41–43, 44, 73–74; stimulant laxatives 76, 78
Le, L. K. D. 171, 172, 174, 177, 179
Le Grange, D. 14, 15, 84, 91
Leppanen, J. 115
Leverington, C. T. 151
Levine, M. P. 179
Levy, S. 92
Limburg, K. 150
Litster, R. 92
Lock, J. 14, 15, 84, 91, 110, 163
LoTempio, E. 91
Loth, K. 174
Lourenco, P. M. 130

MacKenzie, K. 176
McLean, S. A 172
McManus, J. D. 137
Maeve: case study overview x–xi; characteristics of Maeve's story 146–147; diagnosis Other Specified Feeding or Eating Disorder (OSFED) 156–157; diagnosis Social Anxiety Disorder 159; eating disorders and anxiety 149–150; environmental factors and eating disorders 150; fat talk and body dissatisfaction 150–151; genes and eating disorders 148, 150, 161–162; mother's own eating disorder 147–149, 152–156, 163; mother's role in daughter's treatment 157–161; mothers/parents' feeding styles 154–155; nutrition misconceptions and cognitive behavioral therapy 159, 160; perfectionism and anxiety 148–150; question and answer 1: sharing family eating-disorder history with children 161–162; question and answer 2: revealing one's eating disorder to partners and children 162–164; question and answer 3: communication strategies for mothers and daughters in separate eating-disorder recovery programs 164–165; social anxiety and cognitive behavior therapy (CBT) 159; sports and body dissatisfaction 152; therapy and Family Based Treatment 158–159
Major Depressive Disorder, Moderate viii, 34, 37, 39
Major Depressive Disorder, Single Episode, Moderate With Anxious Distress x, 106
Mankovski, E. 163
Maor, M. 164
Marti, C. N. 46, 171
Marzola, E. 68
Masheb, R. M. 137
Maudsley Model 115
Maudsley Parents website 88
May: case study overview ix–x; characteristics of May's story 95–97; Cognitive Behavior Therapy (CBT-A for adolescents with bulimia) 110–111, 113; diagnosis Acute Stress Disorder 106; diagnosis Bulimia Nervosa, Moderate 105; diagnosis Major Depressive Disorder, Single Episode, Moderate With Anxious Distress 106; diagnosis Posttraumatic Stress Disorder 106; Dialectical Behavior Therapy 109–110; eating disorders, causes and functions of 100; idealized model of beauty and body dissatisfaction 98–100, 103; parents' reaction and role 97–98, 100–101, 103–104, 106–107, 108–113; partner abuse/relationship with boyfriend 97–98, 102, 103, 104, 106, 110, 112–113; perfectionism 107–108; psychotherapy 103–104, 106–107; question and answer 1: relationship between intimate partner abuse and eating disorders 114; question and

answer 2: need for parents not to express anger/frustrations 114–116; question and answer 3: child's refusal to receive treatment 116–117; SCOFF and EDI-3 104–105; self-cutting 102–103, 113; self-harm behaviors 97, 106; social anxiety 101; success of recovery 113–114; Treasure's animal metaphors for carers 108–109
Mazzeo, S. E. 154
media literacy programs 171–174, 179; *see also* The Body Project
MediaSmart 171
Meyer, C. 24
MFGT (Multi-Family Group Therapy) ix, 50, 55, 58–59, 60–66, 67–68, 115
Miller, R. M. 137
Mind, Body and Sport: Understanding and Supporting Student-Athlete Mental Wellness (National Collegiate) 11
mindfulness 21, 109, 136
Mitchell, K. S. 154
Miyake, Y. 8
mood disorders: co-morbidity with eating disorders vii; *see also* depression
mood regulation, and binge eating 128–129
Morgan, C. M. 137
mothers: communication strategies for mothers and daughters in separate eating-disorder recovery programs 164–165; eating disorders of and impact on children 147–149, 152–156; feeding styles of 154–155; programs for mothers with eating disorders 163; *see also* caregiver skills; parents
Motivational Interviewing viii, 36, 39, 41
Mrazek, P. J. 171
multidisciplinary care 15
Multi-Family Group Therapy (MFGT) ix, 50, 55, 58–59, 60–66, 67–68, 115
Murray, J. 98, 113
muscle idealization 60, 173, 174

National Collegiate Athletic Association (NCAA), *Mind, Body and Sport: Understanding and Supporting Student-Athlete Mental Wellness* 11
National Eating Disorders Association (NEDA): *Coach & Athletic Trainer Toolkit* 11; media-literacy resources 174; statistics re. girls and body dissatisfaction 172; website 43
National Youth Risk Behavior Survey (2013), abusive dating relationships 97
negative urgency 129
Neumark-Sztainer, D. 127–128, 139, 174
Nick: case study overview viii–ix; characteristics of Nick's story 50–56; cognitive functioning and anorexia 65; diagnosis Anorexia Nervosa: Binge Eating/Purging Type 56; diagnosis Avoidant/Restrictive Food Intake Disorder (ARFID) 56; diagnosis Obsessive Compulsive Disorder 53, 56, 57, 58; friends' reaction and role 52; gender and eating disorders 59–60; Multi-Family Group Therapy (MFGT) 50, 55, 58–59, 60–66, 67–68; outpatient program and psychotherapy 66; parents' reaction and role 50–51, 53, 54–56, 58, 60, 61–63, 64; partial hospital program 57–59, 64; question and answer 1: dislike of groups and MFGT therapy 66; question and answer 2: danger of contagious behavior in group therapy 66–67; question and answer 3: feeling of embarrassment and group therapy 67–68
Nonsuicidal Self-Injury Disorder (NSSID) 102–103

obesity: and binge eating disorder 138; blind spot of public efforts against 128; societal stigmatization of 75, 124, 152
Obsessive Compulsive Disorder 53, 56, 57, 58
Ogle, J. P. 9
online activity *see* Internet
Osgood, L. 39–40, 177–178
Other Specified Feeding or Eating Disorder (OSFED) xi, 156–157
outpatient treatment: vs. inpatient treatment 14, 15; recovery rates 17

Parent-Based Prevention (PBP) program 163
parents: anxiety felt by 19; and coach-athlete conflict 24; feeding styles of 154–155; revealing one's eating disorder to partners and children 162–164; role of in eating-disorder prevention programs 175–176; sharing family eating-disorder history with children

161–162; *see also* caregiver skills; Family Based Treatment (FBT); mothers; Multi-Family Group Therapy (MFGT)
Pariseau, C. 92
partial syndrome eating disorders, risk of and sports practice 21
Paxton, S. J. 172
Pearson, C. M. 128
pediatricians, role of in Family Based Treatment 88–90
Peebles, R. 14, 84
perfectionism: and anorexia nervosa 3–5, 108; and anxiety 148–149; and body dissatisfaction 74–75, 107–108; and bulimia nervosa 3; as heritable characteristic 107; practicing being imperfect 87–88
Pinheiro, A. P. 148
Pope, L. 139
Posttraumatic Stress Disorder 106
preventing eating disorders: chapter overview xi; eating-disorder statistics 170; evidence-based prevention programs 170–171; girls and body dissatisfaction 172; indicated prevention 171, 179; media literacy programs and body dissatisfaction 171–174; selective prevention 171, 176, 177; selective prevention and dissonance-based interventions (DBI) 176–177, 179; selective prevention and Healthy Weight programs 177–179; universal prevention 171–172; weight-control behaviors/ dieting and CBT-informed prevention strategies 174–176
Project EAT 123
Prozac (fluoxetine) 18, 112
psychoeducation 41, 61, 115, 178
Puhl, R. M. 139

refeeding syndrome 13, 80–81
relational-cultural theory 62
Reynolds Adolescent Depression Inventory-2 (RADS-2) 106
Rhind, C. 115
Rohan, K. J. 137
Rohde, P. 46, 177
Rokkedal, K. 68
Rudd Center for Food Policy and Obesity (University of Connecticut) 139
Runfola, C. D. 172
Russon, J. 92

safety behaviors 6–7
Savage, J. S. 125
Sawyer, S. M. 14, 84
Schaefer, J. 107–108
Schmidt, U. 18, 162–163
SCOFF questionnaire 35–36, 104–105
Sedah-Sharvit, S. 163
Segrin, C. 164
self-harm behaviors 97, 106; self-cutting 102–103, 113
self-induced vomiting: and Binge Eating Disorder (BED) 133; gastrointestinal and cardiovascular consequences 73–74; temporary relief from 105–106
Senokot 76, 78
Shanmugam, V. 24
Shaw, H. 171, 177
Sheldon, A. M. 151
Slof-Op't Landt, M. C. 126
Smith, G. T. 128
Smith, P. M. 9
Smolak, L. 98
social anxiety 101, 149
Social Anxiety Disorder 159
social media *see* Internet
Someday Melissa (documentary film, Judy Avrin) 73
sports: and anxiety management 152; and body dissatisfaction 152; and bulimia nervosa/stable health diagnosis 22–23; and risk of eating disorder 21–22; *see also* coaches
starvation: and anxiety 4, 16; and blunted emotions 7–8; and isolation 7
Steiner, E. 163
Stewart, T. 176
Stice, E. 46, 131, 137, 171, 172, 176, 177
stress: Acute Stress Disorder 106; and cyber-addiction 37; and emotional eating 138–140
StudentBodies™ program 177
suicidality: co-morbidity with eating disorders vii; *see also* Nonsuicidal Self-Injury Disorder (NSSID)
Swanson, S. A. 137, 138

Tanofsky-Kraff, M. 137
Tantillo, M. 60
Tavolacci, M. P. 37
television: and body images 99, 149, 151; *see also* media literacy programs
thin idealization x, 150, 151–152, 173, 174, 175, 176–177

thinspirational images 40, 99
Treasure, J. 18, 19, 61, 108, 115, 162–163
treatment: continuum of care 15, 17; multidisciplinary care 15; outpatient vs. inpatient care 14, 15; recovery rates of outpatient treatment 17; resistance to hospitalization 15–17; resistance to treatment/recovery 12–15, 17–18, 78–79, 116–117; *see also* caregiver skills; preventing eating disorders

University of Connecticut, Rudd Center for Food Policy and Obesity 139

vegetarianism 6
violence *see* intimate partner abuse/ violence (or abusive dating relationships)
vomiting *see* self-induced vomiting

Wagner, I. 92
Wall, M. 174
Wansink, B. 139
Watson, H. J. 150, 171, 176, 177, 179
weight: blind weights 37; freshman weight gain (Freshman 15) 32, 35, 45–46; weight bias/stigma 122–123, 124, 127–128, 130–131; weight cycling and dieting 125–126; weight teasing 122–123, 127, 130, 175; *see also* body dissatisfaction; thin idealization; thinspirational images; weight-management behaviors
weight-management behaviors: and body comparisons to others 99, 100, 152; and CBT-informed prevention strategies 174–176; dieting and eating disorders 125–126, 128, 131–132; and emotion-numbing 43; Healthy Weight programs 177–179; and overweight children 123; as predictor of eating disorders 174; and secrecy/ covering up 33–34, 51; and self-harm 97
Wertheim, E. H. 172
Whight, D. J. 41
White, M. A. 137
WHO, World Mental Health Surveys 137
Wilfley, D. E. 138
Wisniewski, L. 92
Wong, S. P. Y. 114

Yokum, S. 176

Zapolski, T. C. B. 128
Zubery, E. 163
Zucker, N. L. 154